GRAFTING OLD ROOTSTOCK

INTERNATIONAL MUSEUM OF CULTURES

Publication 14

William R. Merrifield
Museum Director

Jacqueline E. Bernhardt
Academic Publications Coordinator

Carol V. McKinney
Volume Editor

GRAFTING OLD ROOTSTOCK

Studies in Culture and Religion of the Chamba, Duru, Fula, and Gbaya of Cameroun

Edited by

Philip A. Noss

INTERNATIONAL MUSEUM OF CULTURES
Dallas, Texas
1982

Copyright 1982 by the Summer Institute of Linguistics, Inc.

Library of Congress Catalog Card Number: 81-51153
ISBN: 0-88312-165-4
ISSN: 0197-3746

Cover design by Jack C. Huddle

This title available at
        International Museum of Cultures
        7500 W. Camp Wisdom Road
        Dallas, Texas 75236

Contents

Preface Philip Noss	vii
Acknowledgments	ix
Map	x
Introduction Wendell Frerichs	xi

Culture and Society

Poem: The Stranger Philip Noss	2
Introduction	3
1. The Stranger among the Chamba Bouba Bernard	5
2. Gbaya Proverbs and Hospitality Dala Marcel	9
3. The Danger of Courtesy Philip Noss	17
4. Reflections on the Life of the European Bouba Bernard	27
5. Gbaya Marriage Alice Eastwold	33
6. The Gbaya Dance of Diang Philip Noss	43
7. Ordinary and Extraordinary People Kombo Samuel	49

8. Sickness, Medicine, and Sorcery in Duru Society   55
      Kadia Matthiew, Lee Bohnhoff
9. Sickness, Misfortune, and Healing among the Gbaya   65
      Cecilia Noss
10. Tradition and Modernism on Horseback   99
      Badoma André

Faith and Belief

Poem: Everything Tries   110
      Haldor Jon Noss

Introduction   111

11. The Gbaya and the Sudan Mission: 1924 to the Present 115
      Philip Burnham
12. An Interpretation of Gbaya Religious Practice   131
      Philip Noss
13. Social Pressure for Religious Conformity
      in the Fulani Community   153
      Ronald Nelson
14. Is God Vənɛb or Yaama?   161
      Bouba Bernard
15. The Chamba Rite of Vɔɔma   165
      Bouba Bernard
16. LaBi: A Gbaya Initiation Rite   173
      Thomas Christensen
17. Rites of Reconciliation in Traditional Gbaya Society 197
      Thomas Christensen
18. Wanto and Crocodile: The Story of Joseph   213
      Philip Noss
19. A Meeting of Biblical Wisdom with Gbaya Wisdom   221
      Thomas Christensen
20. Karnu: Witchdoctor or Prophet?   233
      Thomas Christensen

Contributors   247

Preface

During the early days of the Christian church in Africa, the church tended to look forward, turning away from the past and rejecting the ways of the fathers. Recently, however, as the young nations of Africa have begun to develop their own political philosophies and have sought to establish national identities through their own social systems, it has become apparent that the new mat must be woven over the old mat. In building the new, there must be partnership with the old. For the church, as for the nation, the new must be built upon the old; the new must relate to old questions and needs; the new must be experienced through symbols and forms that are known and that are meaningful; the new must fulfill the old.

This book is an attempt on the part of expatriates and Africans alike to ask questions, to learn, and to interpret in the light of the gospel of Jesus Christ what is important in the lives and traditions of African societies. A number of the essays presented here were originally papers prepared for conferences and workshops held by missionaries of the Sudan Mission in Cameroun. Several contributions are studies that were done by Camerounian students who have worked during their summer vacations at the Gbaya translation center. One chapter was written by a university professor who has conducted anthropological and sociological research in Cameroun. The introduction is by an Old Testament scholar and seminary professor who assisted the Gbaya translation team in Old Testament translation work.

The essays relate primarily to four ethnic groups of central and northern Cameroun: the Gbaya, Duru, Chamba, and Fulani. The Gbaya were traditionally a hunting and farming people who extend as a linguistic and social group from central Cameroun through the central African Republic into northern Zaire. The Duru and Chamba are peoples of the north, the former living on the plains of Adamawa, the latter living along the Alantika Mountains. The Fulani were conquerors who brought Islam to northern Cameroun during the eighteenth and nineteenth centuries and established emirates that are still important political structures today. Each of these peoples has come in contact with the Christian faith, the first three widely accepting it, the latter almost completely rejecting it.

Although these essays are presented within the framework of missiology, they have a wider application than the missiological and anthropological alone, for they treat subjects in which there has been increasing interest in recent years in Western theology and in Western thinking as a whole: hospitality, marriage and family, the healing process and treatment of the entire man, storytelling, myth, and symbol. In this book one can see a picture of the traditional African hospitality that never fails to overwhelm the visitor. One can see the necessity for maintaining good human relationships and the danger of creating bad ones. In societies where such understandings are given ritual expression, one learns about rites of reconciliation and purification. In proverbs and folktales from a culture that is still much more oral than literate, one can see the role that oral tradition plays in articulating and transmitting the wisdom of its people.

American churches speak about "partnership in mission," but except for an occasional Third World visitor to a local congregation, there are few channels for the average Western Christian to be on the receiving end of this partnership. Exposure to the spiritual blessings of traditional societies provides a means for increased partnership. In some cases, the West can gain helpful insights from cultures where basic understandings of life are relatively untouched by the complexities of a scientific culture and the monuments of man's technological skills. In other cases, the West and Africa may find that they must share the struggle, especially as Africa hastens to imitate the intruder it often resents.

Philip A. Noss

Acknowledgments

I should like to express appreciation to *Afrique et Parole*, *Ba Shiru*, *International Review of Mission*, *Missiology*, and *Practical Anthropology* for permission to republish a poem and articles previously published in those journals. Translations of texts originally written in French are mine.

P.N.

Map of Cameroun

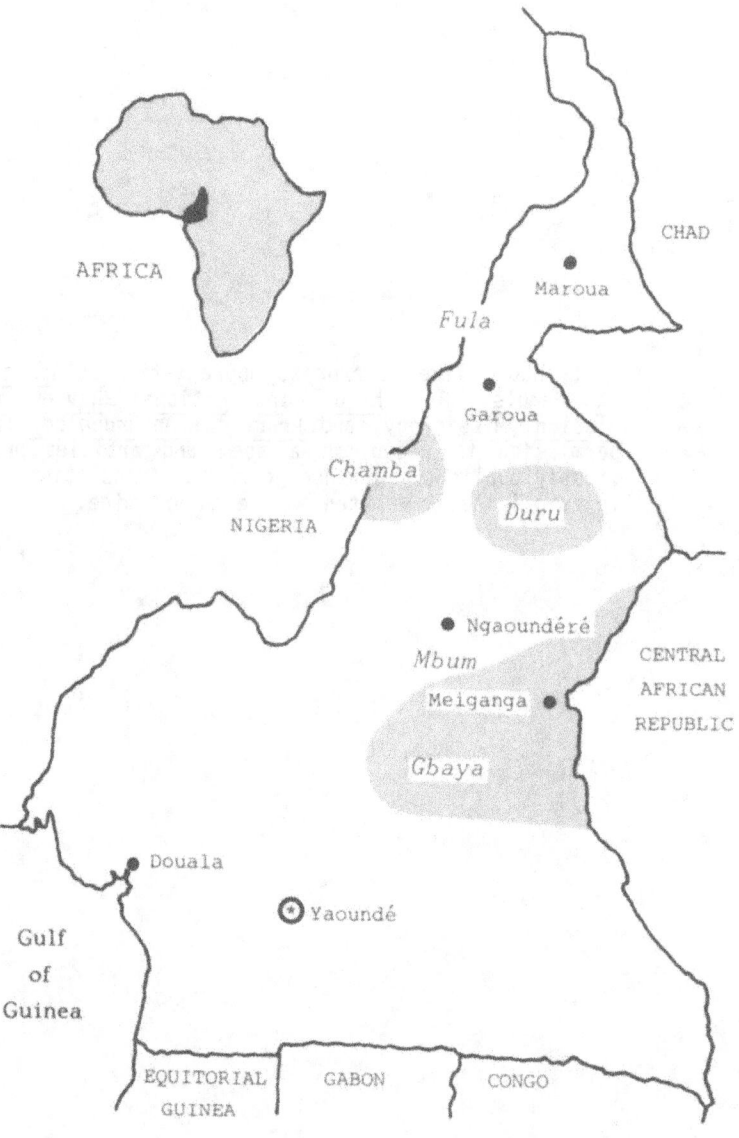

Introduction

by Wendell Frerichs

The chapters contained in this volume encompass but a sampling of a vast panorama of African traditions and the way they meet Christianity. But they represent a significant cross section of these traditions, especially since major institutions and key events in human life are explored here. In addition to the breadth of coverage, each writer represents a point of view, proposes an interpretive rationale, and practices a methodology which, while here applied to but one tradition or aspect of it, may be adapted for use in examining others.

The author of this brief introduction has assembled essays of others more expert than he. Their understandings of African culture are based on much longer exposure to it; his is rooted in but eight months of work at the Gbaya translation center in Meiganga, Cameroun. Under such circumstances his observations are made from a limited perspective and are tentative or premature. But one does observe for oneself, at least, and tries out some of one's observations on persons with broader, deeper, and longer experience. Sometimes a new observer may experience some aspects of a culture more startlingly than one who has grown accustomed to them over a period of years. So this writer has dared to venture into print on a subject in which he finds himself yet so amateur.

One thing seems clear: there is currently a resurgence of vitality and interest in genuinely African traditions. This interest is taking place at the very time when some of these traditions are in danger of being forgotten or no longer understood. Changes in nearly every aspect of life have come swiftly everywhere in the world in recent years, not least in

Africa. Even from the air one can see the expanded cities or the glare of aluminum roofs replacing thatch out in the bush. Initially, in a too easy acceptance of new values, new customs, and new gadgets of the Western world, much that was time tested was called into question and even discarded. It soon ran the risk of being forgotten. At best some customs have been retained in only a superficial way.

Why then a revival of interest in indigenous traditions just now, and to whom has it come? First, let us look at the second part of the question. Note the names in the table of contents of this volume. Mostly they are the names of relatively young people. The list includes not only Africans but, perhaps unexpectedly, also Western missionaries, the very people usually assumed to be actively engaged in stamping out indigenous, "harmful" practices and traditions.

Now let us try to discover why the revival of interest has come about. Have the Africans among the writers of this volume already rejected the gospel their parents so recently accepted? Have the younger missionaries lost their way or their sense of mission? Neither of these alternatives is to be ruled out as impossible. There are children of first and second generation African Christians who are calling into question the whole missionary enterprise, including the need for the gospel. And there are representatives of Western churches who no longer consider gospel proclamation even an auxiliary task either for themselves or for the church. They have come to Africa, for example, to help in economic development or to alleviate human misery. But the authors of this volume are people whose commitment to an evangelical understanding of the gospel is firm. They are also aware that old traditions should not necessarily go away when something new is introduced, even something so all-encompassing as the Christian faith. Our writers keenly appreciate the values of many of the older African traditions. These values and the meaning they give to key events in life may explain their resiliency just now. Old traditions meet people's needs; lest by neglect or disuse they fail to meet those needs, they are being revived, reintroduced, and reinterpreted.

Our authors are also aware that much of Western tradition, even that which was brought to Africa by Christian people, was not necessarily Christian. At least it was not the only possible Christian practice in a given sphere of life. Thus, for example, wearing Bermuda shorts may be just fine for Western men who are also Christians, but it does not represent the only practice possible for African Christian men.

Introduction

An example of something controversial and theologically substantive is circumcision. If it was practiced before any Christians or Jews entered the area and is still practiced today as a rite of passage from infancy into childhood, should it be discouraged by missionaries? Is there not some way to incorporate its traditional meaning and value into the life of the church? Can a current practice be baptized and become a Christian tradition? If there are objectionable features in the mode of observance, the church might seek to work for their removal. Meaningful aspects can be highlighted and even incorporated into the church's rituals and theology.

As a professor of Old Testament, I am reminded at this point of ancient Israel's retaining of pre-Yahwistic traditions and incorporating them into their newly adopted Mosaic faith. Yahweh, Yahweh's acts, and Yahweh's sovereignty in every area of life were central affirmations. But much that was older than Yahwism was retained with a needed reshaping to bring it into conformity with the central aspects of the new faith. Even traditions brought by new arrivals into the community of worshipers of Yahweh could be remolded, retained, and ultimately adopted by the whole community as if they had always belonged there. This was possible because of a strong sense of what was central coupled with remarkable flexibility.

A similar process could prove viable to the African Christian community. Now, precisely now, when African Christian churches are developing their own leadership and have declared themselves autonomous, it can be done. It needs to be done while those are still living who remember their pre-Christian past. To decide what is of the essence and heart of the gospel of Christ and to seek to express it in African terms, cultural as well as religious--this could be done in our day much as the Mosaic era defined Yahwism in Israelite terms. Vestiges of colonialism or Western civilization that have taken a place near the center of church life should be seen for what they are: foreign importations, distracting, perhaps even harmful, nonessentials. An example might be the strong pastoral model that the early missionaries somehow bequeathed to African churches. It probably was the model current in America or Europe at the time when the missions were begun. Unfortunately, it tends to continue a noncollegial "Herr Pastor" fashion into the present era. To this short-term observer, this appears detrimental to full participation in church life by all the faithful: the pastor, in African terms, conducts his ministry in a chief's role rather than that of a servant. Is there not a more collegial model for pastors in African society than that of chief?

Neither Western nor biblical models of church life necessarily transplant, take root, and flourish. They may indeed become institutionalized. They may remain, but as anachronisms, and to the detriment of the church. At one time we might have been less willing than today to admit that our Western church institutions are really not simply outgrowths of New Testament ones. But, aware as we are of the long period of their development, we should be less insistent upon transplanting them where they really do not fit culturally.

The African churches should be encouraged to evaluate, and then to retain or reject for church life, structures from pre-Christian African life. This evaluating, of course, needs to be done in relation to the center of the good news of God's saving work in Christ. The resulting church organization and Christian life can then become distinctively African as opposed to Western. But then, we of the West live with the developed forms of our pre-Christian cultural institutions too. State church buildings of Norway and colonial-style New England houses of worship bear little resemblance to the catacombs of Rome or to Peter's house church in Capernaum. The resulting structures, institutions, and worship forms that emerge from the various regional churches' evaluating their cultural heritage in the light of the gospel may bear little resemblance to our own. But what matters is that the faith become indigenized. Then it can finally mature and bear its own distinctive fruit to the enrichment of world Christendom. Until that happens, we are all impoverished.

I think it is true to say that early missionaries tended to call into question most pre-Christian traditions. This is quite understandable, though lamentable when carried to extremes. Those who had come out of "heathendom" into Christianity were expected to shed their traditions like an old suit of clothes and to put on the new suit of Christian traditions. Pagan culture, practices, and traditions were symbolically to be put on the bonfire and burned, together with fetishes, charms, and witch doctors' paraphernalia. The new Christian's break with the past was to be complete and irrevocable. The faith and gods of heathendom stood in utter discontinuity with the new faith and the triune God, even though the names for God and for Christian theological concepts had to be expressed in words from the old faith and the original cultural and religious context. Whether the ancestral faith and customs were in the past looked upon in any sense as a preparation for Christ is not known to me. Some Christians view it so now. The discontinuity with the religion of the past is not emphasized now so much as is the belief in a creator God in both Christianity and traditional Gbaya religions. But though the God worshiped by Christians may be identified with this remote, inaccessible deity of the past, he is now seen as more completely revealed in the Bible and in Jesus Christ.

How much of an attempt early missionaries made to understand African culture or religion or to appreciate their values, I do not know. It would be safest not to generalize about that in any event. What one does see, and the essays in this volume are an example of it, is a current attempt to understand the pre-Christian traditions for their own sake. Only in this way can their importance be properly assessed as they are reshaped by the new Christian context.

These essays are important not only for their authors who must live continually with the realities they express, but also for us in the West who are far more in need of such materials. Preconceived notions about Africans and our Christian missions among them either never were correct or at least are no longer true. To learn what African traditions really were, what their purposes and meanings were, rather than simply to lump them all together among the skeletons in the closet of "darkest Africa," would really help the church of the West in becoming coworkers with the church of Africa. Then perhaps their differences would no longer be seen as impediments that challenge removal through missionizing. Instead, they may be welcomed as complementary expressions of one faith.

If the past danger was to cut off new African Christians so completely from their traditions as to leave them rootless and struggling for meaning, the new risk may be to attempt to salvage too much from their pre-Christian past. It may seem less difficult, and certainly it requires less soul searching, to take over en masse the whole of the baggage from the past. Again, if we may view ancient Israel as a model, the result of Israel's keeping too much of the past resulted in little more than the old fertility cult being put into the service of Yahweh. At least they worshiped in the new name of God. In this modern African instance, even the name for God may remain the same, the only addition being that he has revealed himself through his son Jesus. Israel had to learn that the content of faith, especially the person of God, was to be understood in a radically different way. The uniqueness of the Mosaic faith was Yahweh himself. So, the gospel in an African context must not be just reciting pre-Christian liturgies in a new building with a cross above the entrance. It may mean that Jesus has a black face, but he must be the Jesus of the Gospels, not some local hero or legendary figure or spirit of the past. When old traditions are recited in a new house of faith, they cannot escape necessary reshaping. A custom or a ceremony put in service of the God of the Bible will rarely remain the same. When a traditional melody or rhythm is introduced into Christian worship, it receives new words, and it is used in a new context.

The Western observer who witnesses the African church at worship, in study, while reciting its confession, or while dramatizing sacred history needs to be aware that things that appear to be the same as his own may not be the same. For example, because eating together does not have the same meaning for them as for us, the Lord's Supper may convey overtones in Africa that it will not possess in the West. Baptism, as an initiatory sacrament, because of the presence of other initiatory rites in Africa, may convey meanings of which the Western observer is unaware. Even though the liturgy prescribed for a given rite has been faithfully translated into the African language from a Western tongue, it does not guarantee that the understanding of the participants will be the same as ours. Attempts to Africanize liturgies may unwittingly bring in unwanted associations when a melody or a rhythm from some secular or religious context is used. Only with the passage of time will the former associations fall away. This has been true for the Western church also when a folk tune has been used to provide melody for a new hymn.

It is hoped that this book will assist Western Christians in appreciating the cultural wealth that Africans bring with them into the church. Rather than erase the past and begin the African chapter of the church on a clean slate, the mood at the present time seems to be to try to remember the pre-Christian past appreciatively and to incorporate whatever is appropriate of its values into modern Christian life. We should welcome this, cooperate in it, and help a truly African expression of Christianity to emerge.

Part I

Culture and Society

            the stranger*

        a dusty path
        a burning sun
        an open gate
        a bidding door

        a gentle word
        a woven mat
        a brimming cup
        a broken kola

                    speech
                    myth
                    faith
                    vision

        a glimpse
        a taste
        a breath
        a dream

        the wood is consumed
        the fireplace remains

                        p.a. noss

* Previously published in Ba Shiru 7:2.

Introduction

> When I look at the heavens, the work of thy fingers, the moon and the stars which thou hast established; what is man that thou art mindful of him, and the son of man that thou dost care for him? Yet thou hast made him little less than God, and dost crown him with glory and honor.
>
> Psalm 8:3-5

All men are created by God, but all have a way of life that in different times and in different places varies and changes according to the demands placed upon it. From one people to another there are similarities and there are differences; misunderstanding of the differences frequently leads to conflict as one culture meets another.

The missionary who has worked in Africa has often enjoyed the hospitality described in chapters 1 and 2, but he may not often have understood the intricacies of the guest-host relationship, which is one of the most important themes in traditional African life. Such misunderstanding is common, even on the part of other ethnic groups living in close proximity, as illustrated in chapter 3, "The Danger of Courtesy." When the cultures are as divergent as traditional African culture and Western technological life, the probability of misunderstanding is heightened dramatically, not only on the part of Europeans and Americans toward Africans, but of Africans toward Europeans and Americans as well. Western readers, including many who have lived and worked in Africa, may be surprised by chapter 4, "Reflections on the Life of the European," in which Bouba Bernard, a university-educated Chamba, relates some of the misconceptions held by rural Africans about Europeans.

Every society is structured to provide a social system for self-preservation: a family structure for raising children, institutions for educating the young, and means of treating questions of good and evil and of coping with illness and natural catastrophes. Chapter 5, "Gbaya Marriage," emphasizes submission as a dominant theme in Gbaya social structure. The next chapter describes the earliest formal system of educating the young and of preparing them to be disciplined members of society. But society is always threatened by forces within itself and without. How these forces are perceived and some of the means by which they can be influenced is described in the following three chapters.

African societies have never been static, and the Gbaya have been as adept as anyone at adapting and adopting what they felt might be of practical value to them. However, when cultures meet, feelings of superiority and inferiority frequently arise through lack of understanding and through a desire for cultural self-preservation. Badomo André, a Gbaya comedian and artist, in chapter 10, "Tradition and Modernism on Horseback," and in his concluding poem, expresses openly the resentment, often felt but seldom voiced, that African culture is the one judged inferior. Not only did the European colonizer and the missionary judge African culture to be inferior, but also, as gently suggested by Bouba Bernard, many Africans themselves judged their own culture to be the inferior. In a word of caution, Bernard observes that the superiority of a people should be measured not on the basis of its material possessions alone, but that one should "place the emphasis on the spiritual possessions and the morality of a people in judging the perfection of its civilization." Badomo's contribution and those in the second section of this book demonstrate that African culture is rich in wisdom and understanding as well as in spiritual possessions.

1. The Stranger among the Chamba*

by Bouba Bernard

The English word "stranger" is the translation of the Chamba word **sɛɛna**, which is applied to several types of persons: 1) any person who is traveling or who is on a short visit to a neighboring village; 2) any person who for one reason or another comes to hide in your home; 3) your lover or your mistress when he or she is in your home; 4) any person who is in need of your help, for instance, a person who comes to exchange millet for some meat or who comes to borrow money; 5) any person from your own village who comes to share a meal that your wife has prepared. With the exception of the person who is traveling through your village or who comes from another village for a short visit, "strangers" are in fact neighbors and even friends who are much more your own people than they are strangers. They are strangers only in the sense that they are in need of something, and once their need has been satisfied, they are no longer called **sɛɛna**. What we will say in the following paragraphs relates to the first type of person whose status as a stranger cannot be disputed.

The stranger is dependent on his host for everything. **Sɛɛn gab gurə zɔŋ ga** is an expression that means, "The stranger does not know where the bathroom is." That is, he is unfamiliar with his new surroundings and needs to be shown where to go, how to cross the village, and how to look up acquaintances. The stranger must be willing to humbly accept whatever his host offers him. The stranger eats slowly and does not finish all the food that is set before him. He

* Translation of "L'étranger chez les Tchamba du Cameroun." Afrique et Parole 50.

avoids doing anything that would make him appear to be a glutton. In the midst of the people of the village, he acts as though he were timid; but he is very brave when his host is in danger, for example, if the house catches on fire. A stranger who is a woman helps with the housework, pounding millet, drawing water, washing dishes, sweeping the compound, and going with her hostess to gather wood in the bush. The stranger visits all his relatives who live in the village where he is staying. He avoids causing trouble lest it create difficulties for his host. He is free to decide to leave or to extend his visit as he wishes. He may even choose to remain in the village, building his **saare**, his house and his compound, getting married, and making his home there.

Providing food for the stranger is something in which the Chamba is never remiss. One of the reasons why the Chamba place great emphasis on work is **bɔb teed kə seemnu** "that you may remove shame from before the stranger." That is, one should never be lacking for something to give to the stranger. As soon as he arrives, he is offered cool water. During his visit, a chicken may be butchered for him or perhaps a goat, depending on how dear he is to you. One does everything one can to ensure that the stranger always has meat to eat. It is also important **sɛɛn oo kum kə wəl suud si** "that the stranger not be thirsty." After giving him cool water to refresh him from the burning heat of the sun after his journey, millet beer must be found for him. If possible, one offers him an entire pot, or at least a calabash, of the beer that is so greatly appreciated by all. The host also leads the guest to the relatives or friends that he should visit. The host cares for the stranger, assuring him protection and security in every way. When it is time to leave, the host says goodbye to him by giving him several measures of millet for his family. This is an obligation especially when it is the host's brother, aunt, sister, nephew, or other member of the family who has come to visit. Occasionally it happens that the host gives nothing to the stranger. In this case it is said that he **zig gə see** "he did not say good-bye."

We speak of integration into Chamba society when the stranger is Chamba himself. Chamba society is divided into clans--Lam-kuna, Saal-kuna, Deng-kuna--that are found everywhere. A stranger who is Chamba belongs to one of these clans, and in the new village he finds aunts, uncles, nephews, brothers and sisters, and brothers-in-law and sisters-in-law with whom he can attend clan reunions. However, he is

not allowed to attend gatherings called by the chief of the
village. A married woman is also considered to be a stranger
and is not allowed to participate in family gatherings held
by her in-laws. In the same way, a stranger from another
ethnic group who has no clan relationships in the village,
who has only friendship as a link, remains a sɛɛna even if he
chooses to move to the village with his family and make his
home there. That is to say, a stranger may remain a stranger
all his life if he was born in a village other than where he
lives. Nevertheless, when one has lived many years in a
village, one acquires the same rights as the inhabitants and
the same responsibilities. When this happens, the term
"stranger" is no longer used except in a joking manner.

2. Gbaya Proverbs and Hospitality*

by Dala Marcel

In general, we Gbaya attach great importance to the hospitality that we extend to a stranger. There are certain proverbs that reveal our opinions and attitudes toward hospitality. The guiding principle is summarized by the expression, "One never knows." This suggests that everything one does for a stranger, whether good or bad, may be returned by a similar act to one's son or grandson. Therefore, one is obliged to treat the stranger with care because one does not know what may occur in the future. It is for the sake of one's children and grandchildren, for example, their marriage, that one does everything he can for a stranger who, having been well treated by his host, will not refuse to give his daughter in marriage to the son of his host, should the occasion arise.

Attitudes toward the stranger

Among all Gbaya, the customs and attitudes toward strangers are similar. There are, nevertheless, people who behave in their own particular way. Thus we say:

"One beats the tomtom without participating in its rhythm."

This proverb means that when we beat the drum, that is, when we receive a stranger, we should not imitate others. We should give the stranger the best possible welcome, but that welcome must be in proportion to our own means. A poor person

* Translation of "Proverbes sur la notion d'hospitalité" in <u>Afrique et Parole</u> 50.

will not extend the same kind of welcome that a rich person will.

> "One does not prepare prunes at the foot of the plum tree."

It is not because of the stranger's reputation that he must be given a particular welcome. Whether he is poor or wealthy, he must be given the same treatment because

> "The drummer doesn't hear the sound of the drum."

That is to say, the host himself does not mention the good or bad that he does for the stranger; the guest will not mention it in his host's presence, but elsewhere.

> "A man's leg isn't a tree trunk."

We must also recognize that we are not fixed in one place like tree trunks, as this proverb reminds us. One day we will be the guest of others.

As among the majority of the people of Cameroun and in other countries as well, the stranger is a person who is sacred and who is respected. The host very much desires to win the respect of his guest, not simply fearing a bad reputation as a "bad receiver," but even wishing to have a good reputation as a host. We say that the stranger is sacred because he brings joy to the family that receives him.

> "The lion's share belongs to the guest."

We notice here that it is to the guest that one offers what is presentable, what is good, and what is to be admired. At the same time, the stranger is considered a symbol of good fortune, especially to the children; for it is when there is a guest in the home that they enjoy themselves the most. Special treats that had been hidden in storage pots are brought out. Therefore,

> "Bedbugs grow fat on the blood of the guest."

The stranger is a person who brings festivity or whose arrival necessitates festivity at which the parasites of the family enjoy themselves.

> "The iguana is salted, thanks to the cane rat."

Cane rat meat is a favorite with the women, whereas the meat of the iguana is not. Women therefore prepare the cane rat very carefully, and only when it is well done will they use a few of the remaining spices for the iguana. The same thing happens when a guest arrives. The family parasites wait until the point during a feast when the guest arrives; then they come to enjoy the rest of the feast. As soon as he is gone, they leave also.

But in spite of the great respect accorded the stranger while he is in our midst, we also fear him because he represents a certain risk. We fear that something may befall him. It may even be that some trouble may follow the stranger from where he come since

"A stranger is an unfired pot."

Obligations toward the stranger

The welcome extended to the stranger is something very serious and very important. Among the Gbaya, the reception given the guest is generally good because a guest is one who should receive a warm welcome. Sometimes the high rank of the guest makes the hosts ill at ease or shy, but the purpose of the impressive welcome is, as we have already said, the fear of a bad reputation. The welcome and the hospitality are a means of showing one's good sense and one's capacity for doing good.

"The guest's story is told on the road."

Whether the guest has received a good welcome or a poor one, he will not speak of it immediately. He will be hesitant to speak of it before his hosts. However, on the way home and in his own home, he will recount everything that happened to him.

When the guest arrives, before he enters the village or the compound to which he is going, his hosts go to meet him, they take his load to let him rest from the burden, and they greet him warmly to make him feel welcome.

"Running to meet a stranger makes him happy."

When he has arrived and has been escorted to the house, his hosts make him feel as comfortable as possible, taking care that there shall be no disorder that would trouble him. The house must be clean and neat. He is then offered a drink of water, which is considered to be a symbol of peace. This is done so that even if he wants to continue his journey immediately, he will be able to say that he was given a drink of water even though the meal was not ready.

"The guest does not inherit the house."

The guest should be taken good care of, since he is there for only a short time. The meal served to the guest is chosen with care by the host and hostess; the food must be satisfactory. After having been given warm water for a bath, the guest is called to the meal. In some rather modern families, he is invited to a table which has been covered with a beautiful tablecloth. Then he is served, because it is thought that he might be hesitant to serve himself. A light entertaining conversation is also carried on to give him a good appetite. In the case of a family that is less modern, they have to be satisfied with providing clean dishes and the invitation to eat without being embarrassed. But there are always exceptions. When the guest is related by marriage, the meal is served to him alone, and the meat sauce is prepared from special meats, not from birds or fish, above all not from bullheads.

As to lodging, the guest is given a room alone that has been especially prepared by his host. Sometimes the host will even give him his own bed, but,

"One gives one's own bed to a guest whom one knows."

One does not give one's bed to just any stranger, since people are not all the same, but only to someone in whom one has complete confidence.

In order not to be troubled during the stay of the stranger, the host must avoid doing anything that would create a bad impression. He must also know how to be circumspect.

"Don't speak blindly lest the stranger learn
your secrets."

"My hunger is my wife's hunger."

A serious conversation reveals many things, both good and bad. It is important to know how to converse with one's guest because conversation may unmask a person of his innocent appearance. If the guest is from the wife's side of the family, it means that he also belongs to the husband; and, if they have some particular feeling about him, they must do what is called,

"Family for the eyes."

This means that they must not force their guest to leave before he had planned to do so. He should be smothered with good deeds and thoughts so that he will forget that he is not in his own home.

Gbaya Proverbs and Hospitality   13

> "What happens to the short arm happens to the
> long arm."

If you compel your guest to leave before planned, you will be considered mean and selfish. And we know that one of these days the same thing will happen to you.

> "The stranger's complaint signals his departure."

If the stranger is not at ease, if he begins to complain, it means that he already wants to go home because he has undoubtedly realized that his hosts are not happy with him. Nevertheless,

> "The tadpole is happy eating soaking cassava."

If the host and his family are happy with their guest, he also will be happy and will have the courage to extend his visit. But if this is not the case, he will want to leave before he had planned.

When he leaves, the host should not accompany him very far to see him on his way, because to do so is to delay the traveler so that he may not arrive at his destination on time. He will then hesitate to come visiting again for fear of being detained longer than the previous time.

> "When you see a stranger on his way, not returning
> quickly causes him not to come visiting again."

> "Sit-down doesn't know a long road."

One who sees a visitor off is not aware of the distance his guest must travel.

Obligations of the stranger

Discretion is something that is highly valued among the Gbaya. It aids both the stranger and the host so that neither will find himself in a difficult position.

> "The inside of the calabash doesn't escape the notice
> of the guest."

The calabash is a utensil that is used for meals and that does not dry out very quickly after being washed. Therefore, if the stranger has been out for a walk, he will know on his return whether food has been prepared in his absence by observing the inside of the kitchen utensils. At the same time, he ought not to spy in the kitchen.

Recommendations for the guest fall into the same basket as discretion, for they enable the guest to maintain his conduct in equilibrium. He must not be hasty, or at least he must be calm and not act as though he were in his own home. He must not go walking too much and must avoid talking too much. As a guest, he must weigh his words determining which to speak and which to restrain. With regard to his host, his conversation should be restricted.

> "The voice of the guest is greater than the voice of the host."
>
> "The converse of the guest is with his food."
>
> "One who has come doesn't beat the drums of another city."
>
> "The guest doesn't find the new moon."

These four proverbs tell us that the guest does not talk much except with food. His voice should be heard little, and his activities should be limited.

Among the Gbaya it is very shameful and improper for a guest to complain about his reception, making the host feel that his preparation for his guest is inadequate.

> "If the guest's fingernail is hard, he will scratch his host too."

Instead of complaining, he should help his host if he is able. If that is not possible, he must simply put up with the situation.

He has certain obligations toward his host. However,

> "The stranger doesn't sit on the pestle."

This means that he will know that they want to prepare him a meal when they come looking for the pestle. He will be embarrassed when they take the pestle he is using for a chair. Because of his embarrassment he will refuse to eat the meal that they offer him. Still, a guest must never refuse a meal that is offered to him. He must taste a little of everything set before him even if he does not care for it. When one is a guest,

> "Everything caught in a fishtrap is a fish."

He must accordingly eat of everything that is offered to him without any ill feeling.

At the end of his visit, the guest must know how to leave. He must not depart secretly like a thief or like a spy.

"The chicken was in a hurry and got no teeth."

If he leaves without leaving an address, he will not receive what his host intended for him as a gift, because he was in too much of a hurry. So the guest should warn his host before he leaves.

- - - -

The Gbaya world generally considers the stranger that it receives to be good luck. Depending on his conduct, he may indeed be a misfortune. However, whatever his character, he is given a fitting reception according to traditional custom.

With the advent of Western civilization, the traditional manner of welcoming a guest into one's home tends to disappear in families that view the old way as archaic. Even so, the stranger should accept what his host offers him; it is not required to offer the guest what he is accustomed to eating in his own home.

The guest, unless he is ill, participates in his host's work. It is his wish to do this. The guest is considered to be an active member of the family in the measure that he participates in all the activities that take place in the home where he is received. It is therefore necessary to treat one's guest well, as though he were a member of the family, even if he is not a relative. He is a very important person because of the help that he brings.

3. The Danger of Courtesy*

by Philip Noss

Every man lives according to rules. From earliest childhood he is taught what he should do and what he should not do. He is taught what is accepted within the home and in the community, how he may act toward his own family, and how he must treat a guest. He is taught table manners and playground rules. But upon arriving among a foreign people, the stranger is faced with an unfamiliar situation. His own code of behavior is not the accepted system. He cannot depend on his own set of rules which differs from and conflicts with the rules of the new land. Several alternatives are open to him. He may try to ignore the new code completely; he may try to learn the basic tenets, at least within certain contexts; he may try to adopt the new code completely.

The first alternative is generally unacceptable because it suggests a reluctance to accept the new custom as valid, which further implies a rejection of the people to whom the system is meaningful. The third alternative is equally unacceptable because the countryman who recognizes the validity of his own customs will be suspicious of the stranger who appears to totally reject his own. He comes to conclude either that the way of life from which the stranger comes is without values and mores or that the foreigner is without self-respect and self-identity. Not surprisingly, these conclusions are the same ones often drawn by the visitor about the meaningless new code by which he finds himself surrounded.

---

* Previously published in <u>Practical Anthropology</u> 17:253-60 (1970).

The second of the above alternatives is the only acceptable possibility. It requires the recognition that every man possesses a valid way of life, that every people has its own values and mores. This alternative compels him to accept new ways at least to the point of recognizing what they mean so that he can knowingly respond to them in the way that they were intended. This alternative further requires that he retain his own self-respect and identity.

"Anybody home?"

The differences between the codes of two peoples are perhaps most easily seen at the point of meeting. The Gbaya approaches the residence of the foreigner with uncertainty. Normally a door is meant to be open except when it is cold, dark, or rainy, but the European prefers closed doors. The Gbaya hesitates knowing that one should not call into the house of the foreigner. He stands instead outside the door, occasionally shuffling his feet, clearing his throat, or coughing. To the European this behavior appears indirect and crude. He fails to understand that the simple knock on the door is unacceptable to the Gbaya because it signals the intruder. Only a visitor who wished to remain anonymous would knock. The friend would call out a greeting, inquiring whether anyone was home. The sound of his voice would both announce his arrival and identify him as a friend.

The conflict between the Gbaya and the European approach can most easily be overcome by leaving the outside door open. The visitor then knows that he is welcome and does not hesitate to make his presence known in the most appropriate manner. If the door cannot be left open, the frustrations to both the master of the house and the visitor are not easily overcome.

I lived for some months with my family in the home of an African friend in an isolated village in Cameroun. The house was his own, just completed, and he moved out of it so that we could live in it as long as we were in the village. When the door was open we found that the neighbor, the friend, or interested passerby felt free to pause for a moment to call a greeting or to stop in for a short conversation. When the front door was closed, the visitor assumed that we were resting, eating, or otherwise busy, and he left us undisturbed. Only if he needed to see us did he come around to see whether the back door might be open. If he found the back door also closed and desperately needed something, he would go to our

The Danger of Courtesy 19

host in the next house who would then summon us. This was the code that seemed natural--the code that must have been very close to that surrounding the house before we moved in, and we found it very acceptable. It provided privacy when we needed it, even for an afternoon siesta, but also assured the community that it was welcome in our house.

Upon entering a house, tradition ordains that the guest shall be invited to sit down. One evening I went outside briefly to where my host was sitting in front of his house visiting with a companion. I approached to ask a question and intended to return directly to my house, but the conversation was interesting and I tarried. A few minutes later my two-year-old boy came and, being in tune with the prevailing code, looked all around and led me across in front of the two men to a rock where I should sit down. My host was immediately embarrassed and apologized for the breach in courtesy, and the next day the story circulated through town about the lesson in courtesy taught by the two-year-old child.

The cattle people, the Mbororo, had another code, which neither we nor our hosts understood. They came to the house at any time; they called in or rattled tin cans whether the doors were open or closed. If the Gbaya approached to find us eating, they would discreetly withdraw until later, but the Mbororo without hesitation would enter the house and sniff the food in the frying pan or on the table to determine whether it smelled inviting. At this the Gbaya would recoil in complete disapproval. But the Mbororo code did restrain them from tasting the food. The cattle women would never request a taste of food and would rarely accept it if offered.

The differences between the manners of Gbaya and Mbororo caused friction and scorn. The Gbaya admired the nomads for their physical strength and endurance, but despised them for their lack of manners. A Mbororo might appear to be your best friend, they said, but suddenly without a word of farewell he would be gone. Some time after receiving this explanation we were able to observe the Mbororo code.

The Mbororo moved with their cattle according to the season. They were in the vicinity of our home for several months, and while there they brought fresh milk and butter for sale each day. One woman was particularly conscientious, never missing a day. As the Islamic Feast of the Ram approached, she informed us that she would not be able to make the long walk from the cattle camp to our village, but that if we would send someone she would bring the milk to the nearest point along the road. When we arrived, she was already there. She said that the following day, the day of the religious observance, she would not leave camp, but that we should send someone to her so that our children would not be without milk. The messenger returned late in the afternoon bearing the milk given that day free of charge together with a gift of choice mutton. The following day it was business as usual, but in this brief interlude we were permitted to observe something of the Mbororo code of friendship.

Several weeks later the cattle woman informed us that her people would soon be leaving to return north with their herds. Should she not arrive on the following day it was because they had already left. We wondered why she could not tell us the specific day chosen for travel, but she explained that this decision rested with the leader of the camp and he would not decide until the day before departure. For several days she continued to bring milk, and then one day she did not come, and we assumed that her people had moved. A few days later when traveling through a neighboring village an acquaintance stopped me to say that my friend the milk lady had left word that she and her people had moved. She asked him to bid us farewell for her and to greet us ten times. Once again the Mbororo code was evident and the reason for the sudden departure together with the method of coping with it became clear. In that light, the cattle woman's farewell took on special meaning.

Thus, each society has its own way of welcoming and bidding farewell. Understood within their respective frameworks, each courtesy is meaningful, but frequently when interpreted within the light of one's own code, they lead to misunderstanding and suspicion.

"The guest does not take the house"

The experiences with the Gbaya and Mbororo demonstrate the deep significance attached to the guest-host relationship within traditional society.

As we prepared to go to Africa we hoped to be able to live in a village. Long before our arrival a friend heard of our plans and invited us to live in his new house. His family had lived in it no more than several months, but when we arrived they gave it to us for as long as we would need it. Our host, his wife, and two sons moved into the older house that belonged to his brother. And his brother lived with his family

The Danger of Courtesy

in a shack out in the country by the gardens. They were the hosts, we were the guests, and as the Ancients said, "The guest does not take the house." The house will be there after the guest leaves and only the memory will remain. The visitor must be treated well, and our host assumed full responsibility for our well-being as long as we lived with him.

Living across the road from us was a Hausa merchant. He was of a different ethnic group; his way of life was different. He was there when we arrived and stayed on after we left. When I inquired about his status I was told that he was a guest of the village. When he had first arrived, he had been given two houses for himself and his family. They would be his as long as he needed them. I questioned this kind of generosity to an outsider who had come expressly to make money off the community, but they assured me that he was their guest. Furthermore, through his connections with an outside world he provided them with outlets for their products. He also assisted them by selling the bananas, peanuts, and other produce which they left in his care while they went to the gardens to work. In addition, he was Moslem, and he assumed the role of teacher for the elders who were of that faith. Thus focused on the foreign merchant, two codes could be seen harmoniously functioning on the basis of mutual respect and need.

The guest-host relationship is symbolized most clearly in the breaking of bread. To invite a guest into one's home and to serve him is the greatest demonstration of respect and acceptance possible within the code of daily life. At Christmas my family and another family were invited to the home of the chief. He invited everyone, children included. Since traditionally women and children eat apart from men, we wondered how things would be arranged. We knew also that the chief was Islamic and Christmas came that year during the Moslem fast. When we arrived we were greeted by our host and the elders. They ushered us inside to where tables were set. The chief's brother was in charge of the dinner, and once we were seated, the chief himself withdrew. We were served a beautiful dinner after which we were again together with our host. Thus as our host welcomed us into his home and provided for us according to custom without violating his own fast.

A similar situation occurred when a Mbororo family arrived at a Gbaya home. There were obviously differences in eating habits and foods. The Gbaya therefore welcomed their guests and provided them with food, which they were permitted to eat according to their own tradition.

Custom does recognize the differences that separate people. It also provides ways of bridging those differences without violation of either tradition.

To spoil a hunt

Special examples of different codes can be isolated and discussed, but no element of social order functions in isolation. Each is related to another in a complex web. Something of this multidimensional network became apparent to us within the realm of the hunt.

I had gone hunting with an African hunter once before. The animals were to be found across the river, and we asked the owner of the dugout tied at the crossing place if we could use his boat. Reluctantly, he consented. On our return the African hunter, who had shot several antelope, cut off a small piece of meat and bone as a gift for the owner of the boat. His home lay off the regular path, and the hunter went alone to deliver it. When I questioned him about the size of the gift he said that it was big enough, we had done the rowing, not the boat owner.

Two days later a friend told me that the boat owner was very angry with me. The hunter had given him the small piece of meat and bone telling him that I had killed two antelope, but there was no gift from me. My friend cautioned him against coming to complain to me because I had in fact shot nothing.

Several weeks later a missionary friend came to visit, and I wanted to take him hunting. I was told that the boat owner was in town, and I went to find him and ask if we could use his boat. He was at a drinking party and refused to come out until I personally beckoned him from the doorway.

When he had greeted me, I said that I had come because I wanted to go hunting. He replied that it was not for him to deny me the right to go hunting. I explained that I wanted to beg him to let me use his boat to take my friend across the river. His refusal was immediate. He accused me of having used his boat before, of killing two antelope, and then giving him no meat, and he began to walk away. Other villagers came to my aid and begged him to listen. I had killed nothing on the hunt, they said, and the one who had accompanied us in whose care the boatman had entrusted the boat assured him that I had not even fired my gun.

The Danger of Courtesy

He was unconvinced and began to talk. It was the villagers he was angry with, he explained, because traditional custom directs villagers to help the boatman drag his new dugout from the woods where he has felled the tree and hollowed it into a boat down to the river. In return the villagers are to be able to use the boat when they need to cross the river, but no one had been willing to help him. Four times he and his family had had to drag his boats; what they had done was not right.

Finally, the boatman had had his say and turned to inform me that I could take my friend across and that I could use the boat whenever I wished, except if I brought along another African hunter from the city.

With that I began to turn away and noticed another elder beckoning me to come. With apologies he rebuked me. I, a foreign guest, should never have done what I did. I had given a person who was disliked by the village and considered with contempt the opportunity of refusing me and attacking me as a liar in the midst of men who had been drinking and women and children. I apologized for my error and asked what I should have done.

I should have gone to the village chief with my friend. I should have told him that I wanted to take my friend hunting and that I needed a boat to cross the river. The chief would have called the boatman and directed him to take us safely across the river and safely back again. The chief would thereby have assumed responsibility for our safety, and the boatman would have been personally responsible since it was he who knew and could protect against the forces of the water. But I had gone to the drunk boat owner personally; I had been willing to talk with him and had given him a chance to abuse me in public, and now no one in the village was responsible for our safety. All in all I had done something quite wrong.

I wondered why they had chosen to scold me and not the boatman. The answer was that he had merely done what everyone would have expected of the drunk, selfish, and irritable person they knew him to be. It was I who had stepped outside myself by lowering myself to his level and allowing him to insult me. The boatman had shamed the villagers who knew what was right, and they were unhappy that I should have given him the opportunity. But even more so, they scolded the two men who had taken me to the boatman. Maybe I did not know what was right, but they were villagers and it was they who were really to blame.

My friend and I returned to prepare for the hunt. A short while later one of our guides came and asked us to bring out the guns. Unless the boatman gave his blessing, the hunt would not be successful after the unhappiness that had preceded our departure. When the boatman came he took a blade of grass, tied it into a knot, and spit on it. He directed us to hold it over the bow of the boat and untie it. Our hunt would be successful. If we wanted hippos, we would kill them. The guide explained that we were hunting antelope, but he said he had no power over land animals.

Armed with the knotted blade of grass we left the village. When we came to the crossing, we found that the boat was moored near the opposite shore below swift rapids. For two hours we tried to cross the water, but it was impossible. The hunt seemed doomed, but the guides said the boatman had another boat downriver. We walked down and found his other boat and went downriver to where we were going to hunt. That evening we hunted and all the next morning. We found nothing except cattle.

On the way home we stopped by the boatman's home to show him that we had shot nothing. When he saw that our hunt had been "spoiled" he was distressed, and said that when he had planted his crops he would personally take us hunting where he knew there were animals.

Upon arrival at home as the story of our hunt became known, the Christian leader came and told us if he had known of the difficulties of the day before he would not have allowed us to go hunting, and certainly not to use the boat. As far as he was concerned, and as a Christian he partially apologized, the boatman's words had ruined our hunt. If there are hard words before a hunt it will be unsuccessful. Our experience was evidence again of the old truth.

I asked about future hunting trips when we might want to use the boat again. His immediate response was that we must never use the man's boats unless the owner personally came and asked to take us hunting.

A short while after the ill-fated hunt I arranged to go hunting with a young man from the village. In addition to the gun I had, we borrowed one from a village elder. As he reached to hand it to me, he laid it on the ground, and I picked it up. Tradition forbade the handing of a weapon from

The Danger of Courtesy   25

one man directly to another before an expedition. When the gun was in my house, the owner came and performed a small sacrifice to ensure success. The departure itself was timed for early in the morning before anyone arose because a hunting expedition should never set out in public. We did everything correctly, following the dictates of a tradition which meant little to me. The result, or at least what happened, was a very successful hunt. Perhaps there was no relationship, but the words of the elders had proven correct. One did not go hunting following hard words. One did not take the hunt lightly. One did not violate tradition before a hunt. With a good supply of fresh meat, I was hardly in a position to refute their conclusions.

Above all, the two expeditions underlined for me the significance to a people of its tradition and custom. They also showed how at certain points I was expected to obey that code, if not for my own well-being, at least so that within their own standards they not be shamed.

Conclusion

Courtesy is the most obvious expression of the values and mores of a people. A people's code expresses the relationship that exists among persons within the society and toward outsiders. Because it is learned from earliest childhood, it becomes a part of each person, and as his expression of courtesy is misinterpreted or when he sees his code violated, he tends to withdraw and to condemn. What was intended to build a relationship leads instead toward resentment and suspicion. Living for a long time among strange codes without any appreciation for them is disastrous for the establishment of any personal relationship.

Ultimately, the code is merely an indication of respect. To ignore a people's code is to indicate a lack of respect for them. To reject one's own code is equally dangerous because it suggests a lack of self-respect. The answer must be found somewhere between the two extremes. It lies perhaps in the guest-host relationship. Only as we permitted ourselves to be guests could our host play his role. Only as we came to depend on him and need him could the relationship be fulfilled. Part of our need was for him to explain actions and words which were part of the code that we failed to understand. As we asked, he was never unwilling to explain. He was eager to suggest what our response should be, how we should respond to his code without rejecting our own. As we learned to understand and appreciate new ways, we came increasingly to respect the people among whom we lived, and at the same time they could respect us. Perhaps error can never be totally avoided, but with the establishment of mutual respect, there is room for an occasional blunder which may even further strengthen a relationship already begun.

4. Reflections on the Life of the European

by Bouba Bernard

Lifestyles of people differ depending on race and nationality, time, and place. Coming in contact with a new race or a different nationality, we find certain aspects of their life appealing and others distasteful. Thus, it is not every aspect of European life that appeals to the African, just as it is not every aspect of African life that appeals to the European.

Europeans have lived among us a long time; we see them and we feel their presence every day. Can we, because of that, pretend that we understand their actions and that they also have penetrated our customs? I am not yet an anthropologist or a sociologist, although my hope is to become one in the future, but as an amateur I will try to treat this question on the basis of a few examples.

The white skin of the European continues to be a mystery for the African who still believes that it is the blood that gives the European his white color. According to the African, if one merely presses on the skin of a European, he will begin to bleed. Therefore, the European is considered to be a fragile being who is incapable of putting forth any effort. He is unable to work and indeed does not work, it is believed, it is because of that that God has given him machines to help him in his work as well as in his traveling. A European never walks long distances on foot; in fact, for the African it is a curiosity to see the European walking at all. When an African sees a European walking, he interprets this action as an attempt to learn to walk and to teach his family to walk, occasionally even to walk barefoot like the African.

Although walking is a normal activity, for the European walking seems unwise. The African also believes that the European does not die.

Regarding himself, the African does not believe that God takes much notice or pays much attention to him. That is why God gave him skin that is black and tough in order to be able to withstand the hardships that confront him each day, for his life differs little from that of the animals. Thus, when the husband goes hunting for some days, his wife is not worried if it is the season when wild fruits are ripe. She knows that he will live on fruit.

Someone who has received an advanced education is pejoratively called a "white-black." This term is used especially for authorities such as prefects, subprefects, mayors, and above all, presidents and government ministers. Secretaries, office workers, and teachers are called "clerks." These words imply a conversion to a European way of life. At the same time, these terms do not suggest that the African is taken to be a European. The European always retains his superior position. It is rather a case of the disciple who "is not greater than his master." In his efforts toward development, the African seeks to surpass his brother who has the same skin instead of the European whose status he takes as an ideal. We have many indications of this cultural superiority.

Only an educated person is capable of seeing that the difference between the European and the African is not one of intelligence. He knows that there are minds that mature later than others but that have all the qualities necessary for catching up with the others. Such is the case among Africans. Therefore, the educated person considers himself the equal of the European in principle, but when he compares his way of life with that of the European, he sees its inferiority. For some people of timid spirit, this practical difference creates feelings that quickly develop into hate against the white who in turn soon comes to ridicule the African. Today we are aware of the sad and unfortunate consequences that arise if one measures the superiority of a people on the basis of its material possessions alone. That is why it is important to place the emphasis on the spiritual possessions and the morality of a people in judging its civilization. But let us return to our subject: what does the black think of the actions of the European?

In the first place, it is thought that the European was created to eat nothing but sweet foods like cakes, cookies, candy, slices of bread with butter and jam, and macaroni, which are called "the food of the whites," as well as lots of meat, especially canned meat. The African eats primarily foods in a natural state; the European's meals are usually composed of processed foods. The **couscous** of the African, for instance, would be poison to the European, since it is solid; his food is always soft, tender, and light. Although the European eats lots of meat, he thinks meat prepared by the African tastes different; often he think it tastes bad. It is because of a feeling of inferiority that Africans today do not dare invite Europeans to eat--"What will they think of our food?" And if they do invite a European to their table, for that day they try to prepare everything in a completely European style.

That the European should refuse to eat what the African offers is considered quite normal and not a sign of arrogance since what he is used to eating is different from what the African eats. At the same time, the African does not think it odd when he sees a European adapt to the African setting as though it were his own. This is taken as evidence not only of his humility but also of his openness and sincerity in his relations with blacks. Such a one is always welcome. If a certain European is spoken of warmly, do not go far looking for the reason. It is because his simplicity has enabled him to appear to detach himself easily from the European life-style to adopt that of the African.

Another thing is that the European takes too much time for a meal, from an hour to two hours at the table. The African would never accept that. Is it because the African's meal is not large that he takes so little time to eat it? Not at all! The men eat quickly without sitting down. It is only the women who can sit down and eat quietly. (At least they are advised to do so.) The reason is that the men are called upon to protect the family and the village against any danger that might threaten. They must always be on the alert, because they never know when they will be needed to protect some family or some village against attack. And before being called, they must have eaten so that they will not fall from hunger during the combat. The women and children, who are unable to do much, have no need to be ready. For this reason the man never wants to eat from the same bowl as his wife and his children less than ten years old. It is a scandal to be found by another African around a table with your whole family eating. Today we live in a time of peace. There is no war, there are no disorders, no slave trade; everywhere one hears talk of peace, entente, and the signing of treaties among nations. But the African does not trust what he hears. He is still suspicious of the future, and it is with reservations that he adheres to the idea of peace in the world. Occasionally, one does find Africans eating at a table with their family, but they are aware that is is not proper. It is a practice that is very difficult to fit into the African lifestyle. The proof is that if you ask them how they eat, they will answer, "We eat like the whites."

To the African, eating from separate dishes is a sign of disunity. Only those who have had an argument eat from separate dishes. Just as an Englishman sends a bouquet of flowers to someone he has hurt, so the African invites the person to eat with him from the same bowl. To set individual dual dishes is a sign of disharmony, selfishness, and arrogance, not to say unkindness. For example, cowives always eat together, but when they have had an argument with each other, they show it by refusing to share the same bowl.

An African child would have great difficulty living in a European family where all actions take on particular meaning. In an African family, any food that has been prepared is available for anyone who is hungry. Therefore children, both legitimate and illegitimate, are free to help themselves when they are hungry without first asking their mother, except when the food has not yet been prepared. But a child does not go to the homes of neighbors looking for something to eat. If he does, he is considered a thief unless the neighbor is an uncle or aunt or other relative of the child. If the child goes to other members of his family for things he wants, this is proper, and his coming is even thought to be a blessing of God. But as he grows up, he must learn to contribute to the smooth running of the family by bringing the fruit of his work. When he is grown up, if he continues to live at the expense of his family, he is considered a thief and a burden, not only for his family, but for society as a whole. Therefore, certain Africans still refuse to send their children to school because they think school teaches the child to be lazy when it comes to working in the fields.

In contrast, the European even at an early age must learn to ask for things before taking them. Should it happen that he takes something without first asking his parents or guardians, they will scold him to let him know that he is a thief. It is good to teach a child not to steal, but if he must ask for what he needs to eat and what belongs to him, when his parents are away whom will he ask for food to satisfy his hunger? If he dies of hunger, whose fault will it be? If a little African were treated this way he would feel like a stranger. It would show that his roots were not in the family. He would feel rejected; he would be like an orphan. The freedom to help himself to what he needs is what a child expects both of his own parents and of his adopted parents. A person's actions toward an adopted child are a demonstration of his character: whether unkind and selfish or a good person useful to all of society. A family that has no children and has adopted none is considered to be cursed by God for unkindness and selfishness.

In matters of food, Americans are considered much more unkind than Frenchmen, who are generous when it comes to taking care of their African kitchen help. One would wish that the Americans would be like the French and be less attached to food. It has been observed that in an American home, what remains on the table, no matter what amount, is carefully kept in the refrigerator to await the next mealtime. However, in a French home, everything left over goes to the cook, who eats it or takes it home if he wants. In that regard, the Frenchman is like the African in the way he gives. For the African, since food is needed by everyone, everyone must have some, especially when it has already been prepared and is ready to eat. Therefore, he sets it out for whoever comes to his house, even if a meal was not the reason for the visit. In generosity a person loses nothing because he is fulfilling God's will and God will grant his grace in recompense.

Some Europeans become angry or are critical of Africans who often ask them for money. I do not know whether these Europeans have tried to learn why they are asked for money. There is no smoke without a fire and, as a matter of fact, these Africans think that the European manufactures money whenever he needs it, whereas the black is not able to mint new money for lack of equipment. That is why he must ask the European. But the European thinks that it is laziness that pushes him to ask for money. If he were to follow the man, he would find that he works a large farm. But since life today is based entirely on money, the African believes that the person who is nearest to the European and who conducts business with the European is the most successful, because he will have the means to gain an education. One is forced to recognize the truth of this belief when one sees how many students are supported by Europeans, but of course there are also those who have failed under the same conditions.

In conclusion, in the African mind, the time in which we live is the time of the white. The Fula says it is **duniyaaru nasara** and the Chamba says **nasara yɛba,** which means "the world of the white." The white introduced machines to Africa, as well as money, school, clothing, and many other values. Likewise, Christianity is a religion of the white and is accepted by the African as an ideal religion, because everything that comes from the white is thought to be good. That is why many African values have been abandoned in favor of those brought by the white man.

5. Gbaya Marriage

by Alice Eastwold

There is a tendency in the Western world to think that all marriages follow more or less the same pattern. However, every culture has its own unique pattern of marriage which includes the preparation period preceding marriage, the marriage ceremony, and the way problems and difficulties are taken care of during marriage.

When a Gbaya girl has reached sexual maturity, usually between the ages of twelve and sixteen years, she is ready for marriage, and young men marry when around eighteen years of age. However, this is changing with the young people who attend schools of higher education. If boys go beyond the **brevet** (tenth grade), they may be in their early twenties when they take a wife; and girls will be in their late teens when they marry if they go to school beyond the primary grades.

When a boy has picked out a girl he wants to marry, he will bring a gift to her parents showing his intention to marry their daughter. Preferably, this gift will be a chicken, but it may also be liver or fish. If they agree that this boy can marry their daughter, the gift will be prepared and the mother and father will eat it; but, according to custom, the boy is not able to eat with them. If they decide that the boy may not marry their daughter, they give the gift back to him and he must try for some other girl. When it has been agreed that the boy may marry their daughter and the food gift has been eaten, they will tell him that he can start giving the brideprice. He usually starts with six thousand francs (about thirty dollars) and then will add to this amount from time to time. He will also give large pans, ten to twelve pieces of cloth, goats, and other things such as hoes, machetes, and spears. Some things will go to the mother and some to the father. The hoes and machetes are to show that he will be a good worker in the fields and a good provider, and the spears are to show that he will be a good hunter and provider of meat.

The boy may choose a girl who is not yet mature and who is several years younger than he is. He will still come with his gifts of intention and will pay toward the brideprice until she reaches maturity. When the girl is ready for marriage, the boy will start his **kɔfɛ** "brideservice." This is the time when he works for his future in-laws. He is called a **wi-kɔfɛ** "a man who asks for a wife." He will work in their fields, bring them wood, help them in various ways, go hunting with the father, and visit the family. He will do this for a month or two to show that he will make a good husband for their daughter. If he lives near the girl's village, he will go back and forth each day; but if the girl's village is farther away, he will stay and live with the family while he works out his brideservice. While he is doing these various tasks, the girl's parents will decide whether he will make a good husband for their daughter, whether he is a strong and good worker. This will indicate that he will take good care of their daughter. During his brideservice, he and the girl will visit together, she will prepare his food, and they will eat together. Meanwhile, her parents will observe his kindness and love for their daughter.

If the young man does not do all this and does not spend time with the family, the girl's parents will begin to question his potential as a good husband for their daughter. They will have doubts that the marriage will last or that he will take very good care of their daughter, and they will refuse to give her to him. They will then have to give back the brideprice that he has started to pay.

A girl may have several suitors at the same time. They will all be giving things to the girl's parents for her brideprice. When the girl has decided which man she wants and her parents have also agreed, the father will give back the brideprice the others have started to pay. The one who is chosen will continue paying the brideprice and will then start his brideservice. If the choice the girl makes is not acceptable to her parents, she will have to give him up and choose another suitor. Nowadays, however, this is changing so that the girl has more say about whom she wishes to marry than she formerly did. There is beginning to be a certain amount of women's liberation in Gbaya society.

When the young man begins paying the brideprice money, he receives help from his father or from other relatives. When an amount has been agreed upon, the young man will make his payment in several installments which can take up to two or three years. The total amount will usually be between ten thousand and thirty thousand francs (fifty to one hundred and fifty dollars). In some instances, the brideprice can be less, and in cases of girls with an education, the amount asked is quite a bit higher. In each case, the amount required depends on the father of the girl. If he has a "hard liver," he will ask for a higher brideprice, while a father with a "soft liver" will ask less. The brideprice agreed upon is written in a book. This record is kept by the father of the girl and a duplicate is kept by the young man who is paying, so that if any question arises as to how much has been given or how much is left to be given, they can refer to the record. This also serves as a checklist when the brideprice is being paid back after a divorce. Everything is listed in the book including both the money and the various gifts that are given.

The girl will also spend time with her future in-laws. She will live with them for several weeks, helping with work around the house, pounding cassava, preparing meals, carrying water, and sweeping the yard. This is to show that she will take good care of her husband. She has learned to do all these tasks from childhood in preparation for the time of marriage.

While the boy is working out his brideservice, he will also be building himself a house. He will also prepare and plant a cassava garden. While the house is being built, the girl lives with the boy's family, eating and sleeping there. When the house is finished, a feast will be prepared and everyone who has been invited will share in the meal except the girl who cannot eat of this meal herself. After the feast the young man and woman will go to their own house, which shows that they are married. There is no special public marriage ceremony in Gbaya tradition. Some couples, however, may have a civil marriage, which is required in order for the marriage to be legally recognized; but this can be done any time, even months and years after they are actually married.

During the marriage feast and when the couple is newly married, it does not seem like a happy time for the new bride. Rather than smiling, she will have an unhappy look, and she may even cry because she has left her parents and has gone to a strange place to live. Her sorrow may continue for some time after marriage, but she will eventually get over it. Her husband understands her situation and knows that her sorrow will be short-lived and that it does not mean that she will leave him.

It is after marriage that the couple will learn to know each other. Before marriage they are not together enough to know what the other is like or to know what the other is thinking. The important thing during the time before marriage is that the parents are pleased. Everything that is done is to try to please the in-laws and to prove that the young man will be a good husband and the young woman a good wife. After marriage they learn to work well together, their love grows, and they learn each other's thoughts. That is what is known as **mboo-zu** "molding one's head; submission." The wife must submit to her husband, but this does not mean only that she must do what he tells her to do. It means that she is to be patient, happy, kind, and helpful, and that she is to feed her family well. In other words, it means to be a good wife. In the same way, the husband is to submit to his wife. When there is harmony in the family, when husband and wife are patient with each other and when things are going well, then there is **mboo-zu**.

One Gbaya explained **mboo-zu** by saying, "The man is superior to the woman and the woman is superior to the man." They are both people; however, the responsibility of the man is somewhat greater than that of the woman. Therefore, he is the head of the house. But this does not mean that he is superior to her in everything, for she has her place of importance, and she is respected for her thinking and for what she does. When there is respect for each other, there is **mboo-zu** in the home. If something comes up between them, such as a quarrel, and the husband knows he has done something wrong or said something to make his wife angry, he does not want this to stand between them. When they talk it over and it becomes right again, there is **mboo-zu**. If he does not apologize and they do not make things right again, there is no **mboo-zu** and the wife may go back to her parents for a while. However, her parents will most likely encourage her to return to her husband; and if she does, this will restore their **mboo-zu**.

Mboo-zu also involves the children. It means more than the children obeying their parents when they are told to do something. It refers to the attitude of the whole family living together, working happily together, the children getting along well together, obeying their parents, being helpful, and doing all those things that create harmony. When there are problems with the children, when they are disobedient and do things they should not do, there is no **mboo-zu.** Both the mother and the father are involved in disciplining their young children, but it falls more on the mother than on the father since they are with her more than they are with him. The children learn to work when they are young, especially the girls. They do things on a small scale when they are very small and gradually get more advanced, preparing for the time when they will be married.

In a Gbaya family there are certain types of work the father does and others that the mother does. The husband helps prepare the gardens by clearing the land, cutting down the trees, digging up the ground, and getting it ready for planting. The wife does the planting of the cassava and the weeding, although the husband may help her. The wife's main work is her garden and preparing the food for the family. She will work in the garden all day and then in late afternoon will return home and prepare the evening meal, which is the main meal of the day. The husband may stay out and work longer, and the mother and children will eat first, saving food for him to eat later. In the Gbaya family, the husband and wife may eat together while the children are very small; but when they are old enough to eat by themselves, the father and boys will eat together and the mother and girls together. Sometimes friends will eat together, men in one place, women in another.

Divorce is common among the Gbaya. Most often it takes place in the first years of married life when the husband and wife are learning to know each other. It is a result of problems caused by the actions of either the husband or the wife. A special name is given to each type of divorce, depending on whether the wife has been sent away by her husband or the wife has left her husband.

One of the types of divorce is called **gbia koo,** when the wife leaves her husband. If a husband shows interest in another woman or commits adultery, his wife will leave him and go back to her parents. Her father will call the husband and the husband's parents, and they will go to the chief of the village for a hearing. When the hearing is finished, if the husband has decided that he will change his ways and be faithful to his wife, she will go back to him and they will try again to live happily together. If he is not willing to change, the wife will leave him and go back to her parents. In this case, the husband will not be able to get his brideprice back.

If the husband has a drinking problem, is frequently away from home, does not provide for his family, quarrels, and is cruel, his wife will get tired and leave him and go back to her family.

Another reason a wife leaves her husband is his taking a second wife. Jealousy ensues and the two wives do not get along. Some first wives are determined to stay and make life so miserable for the second wife that it is she who leaves. This does not always happen, for there are families where two wives do get along. It is particularly difficult when there are three wives, for often two can get along, but not three.

When a wife leaves her husband, he is usually entitled to get the brideprice back, but not the amount equivalent to the brideservice he gave before their marriage. In cases of adultery, however, he will not get the brideprice back. In each case, the matter is taken to the chief of the village, a hearing takes place, and the chief, who is the judge, decides whether the brideprice should be paid back or not. Sometimes, however, when the father of the girl is consulted, he refuses to give the brideprice back in order to force the girl to go back to her husband. In the case of a woman who has become interested in another man and decides to marry him, she will leave her first husband. The new husband will have to go through the same brideservice and pay a brideprice as though he were her first husband. The original brideprice has to be paid back to the first husband; and if the father does not have the money to pay it back, he will wait until the second has paid his brideprice.

A second type of divorce is **ndaka koo** "chasing one's wife," when the husband sends his wife away. Adultery on the part of the wife is a frequent reason for sending her away. This also occurs when a wife is interested in other men, when she flirts with them and, because of this other interest, does not care for her husband and children. He will talk to her and scold her; but if she continues to disobey, he will become exasperated and send her away.

Another reason for sending a wife away is stubbornness and quarreling, when she does not take proper care of her family and refuses to fix her husband's food (this may be a form of revenge against him). In these situations, there has been no **mboo-zu** on the part of the wife. As far as the brideprice is

Gbaya Marriage

concerned, sometimes the father of the woman will give it back, but sometimes the husband is so exasperated that he tells his wife to go and keep the money too. Other times he will want the money back, but it will be refused. This will then be brought to the chief who will decide whether it should be paid back or not. If he decides it is the fault of the woman that the divorce has taken place, he will tell the father to pay the brideprice back. The father often tries to get his daughter to go back to her husband, which she may do, and the husband will take her back. If she continues as before and is sent away again, it is unlikely that her husband will accept her back again.

Another common reason for the husband to divorce his wife is failure to bear him any children. Having children is very important to the Gbaya, for it is the children who will care for them in their old age. It is the duty of the boys in the family, especially the oldest boy, to care for their aged parents. This is not the duty of the girls, because, when they are married, girls are released from some of their obligations to their parents. They now have the responsibility of helping care for their husband's parents when they are old. If there are only girls in the family, the parents will be taken care of by other male relatives. If the wife has no children after three to five years, it is very likely that the husband will send her back to her parents and will marry someone else. The woman's parents will find another husband for their daughter, but she may remain single since the word will get around that she cannot have children.

Although it is usually children that stabilize a marriage, there are some couples who will stay together even if they do not have children. They will usually have relatives' children living with them whom they care for and raise. These children then have a stabilizing effect on the marriage. Adopting children is rare. When asked why this is seldom done, the answer is usually, "I don't know. It is not good."

After becoming a Christian, a man with two wives may decide to send the second wife back to her family. In this case he is not entitled to get his brideprice back. Furthermore, he has to pay three thousand francs in addition to the original brideprice. If he has three wives and sends two away, he has to give three thousand francs to the father of each of the wives.

A third type of divorce is called **yua koo** "fleeing one's wife." This occurs when a husband leaves his wife who is chronically ill or who has an incurable disease. Wives will leave their husbands for the same reason. A mother brought her baby to the Well Baby Clinic at the hospital at Garoua Boulai. When asked the name of her husband, she said that she did not have one. When questioned further, she said that she had had a husband and two other children, but that while she was pregnant this time, her husband, thinking that she would die during childbirth, left for the Central African Republic, taking the two older children with him. She now planned to follow her husband and expected to be received back into the family. If she had still been ill, her husband would not have taken her back. However, when a wife has been left because of a long illness, even though she recovers, she still may not be taken back by her husband, who has probably married someone else by this time.

If a wife leaves her husband, there is the possibility that she can return to her husband and start over again; but if a husband sends his wife away, the marriage is ended and there is no chance for her to come back.

In all these cases, the question arises as to whether the marriage is ended or is just a temporary separation. It seems that the marriage is not actually terminated until the woman or the man marries again. The divorce is finalized when the brideprice has been paid back to the husband. When the couple is divorced, the children stay with the father since it is he who paid the brideprice. If the mother has a small baby, she will keep it until it is three or four years old. Then she will send it back to the father.

There are several occasions when the wife will go to stay with her family for an extended period, but there is no thought of leaving her husband in these cases. Sometimes she will just go for a visit to her parents, and it is not unusual for her to stay several days or weeks if they live some distance away. She leaves happily and returns happily. There are also times when the wife gets peeved over something that has happened in the household and goes to her parents for a while. In one family, the wife got tired of doing all the household work, while the sister-in-law who was living with them did nothing to help. The wife walked out and went to visit relatives for two weeks. She came back, apparently happily, and was well received. But the sister-in-law stayed on, since she was a widow with no children. She had no home but that of her brother.

When a baby is born, the grandmother will often come to stay for a while to help care for the baby and mother. When the baby is strong enough to travel, the mother will want to visit her parents with the baby. She may stay up to six months with her parents at this time. The husband is apparently agreeable to this, and the two make an agreement between themselves as to how long she can stay.

After the birth of a baby, the father will send a gift to his parents-in-law as a token of appreciation that their daughter has given him a child. There are many occasions when the husband has to give gifts to his wife's parents. Even if the agreed-upon brideprice has been fully paid, he is still obligated to give gifts from time to time. Sending a gift to the in-laws after the birth of each baby is one of these occasions.

These are a few aspects of Gbaya marriage which help one realize that each culture has its own unique practices. However, in every culture it is important and necessary to have harmony with submission and reconciliation in the family to make a happy and lasting marriage.

A Gbaya woman, showing facial scarification

6. The Gbaya Dance of Diang*

by Philip Noss

The "mission" church has frequently condemned all dance as unacceptable in Christian life. The Gbaya dance of **diang** is a celebration of the creation of social order and life and is comparable, not with Western ballroom dancing, but with the Old Testament dances of joy and salvation (Ex. 15:20-21; I Sam. 18:6; Ps. 149:1-3). Dance, like song and speech, is a form of human expression that may be used to praise the Creator who gives not only life on earth but hereafter.

The Gbaya of Cameroun and Central African Republic were traditionally hunters and farmers. Their meat was the game they killed; their staple foods, the crops they planted. Theirs was a life of mobility necessitated by the movement of game and the search for new and fertile farmlands. The institutions developed by the Gbaya were those that could move with them. The most mobile art forms are the verbal arts, the freest institutions are those of dance, and it was these that the Gbaya developed. There were dances for hunting expeditions, for harvest celebrations, for drinking parties, and for nighttime games. There were dance festivals to mark each major event in life, birth, initiation, marriage, and death.

The greatest Gbaya festival was called **laBi**, a rite of initiation in which a young man died to return to life as an adult. In **laBi** he learned a language forbidden to women and the uninitiated, and he learned the values and mores of his people. At its conclusion he returned to his home dancing the songs of Gbaya tradition.

* Previously published in <u>Practical</u> <u>Anthropology</u> 18:264-68 (1971).

A second Gbaya festival was **to**, an initiation rite said to be older than **laBi** but not as rigorous. It also had its own language and was restricted to men who could be initiated into it in addition to **laBi**.

A third Gbaya festival was **diang**, the first of all Gbaya dance festivals.[1] Its function was to provide a young boy with his first formal introduction to discipline and endurance.

Diang was celebrated as a one-day festival for boys six to eight years of age. It was normally performed at the beginning of the rainy season before the children and their families moved from the village to the gardens. The initiates were called together in the village square and were asked to kneel or bow over to be hit with slender sticks. The switching was meant to sting, not to injure, and those who stoically refrained from crying were said to have been initiated into **diang**. An alternate procedure was to lead the boys to a nearby river where their elders would rub itchy reeds on their bare bottoms. Those who bore the itching without crying had fulfilled the demands of **diang**. The successful completion of the initiation was then celebrated in the village square with dancing and games.

Diang never attained the status of **laBi** or **to**. It did not have its own language; it was not secret; it does not seem to have been part of a religious rite. It has not been practiced for some decades. Yet, within Gbaya history and thought, **diang** occupies a most important position. Mr. Kombo Banda, about fifty-five years of age and a ranking elder in the town of Bouli in central Cameroun, gives the following account of **diang** and its origin.[2]

> The great festival of the Ancients of long ago was like a dance. And what I'm going to tell you today is about the first dance festival of the Ancients. What was the first dance? The first dance was **diang**. The elders performed **diang**.
>
> Now **diang** isn't anything more than this. The child-

---

[1] Gbaya women had their own dance festivals. The girls' equivalent of **diang** was called **naayeng**. It was for girls ages six to ten and consisted mostly of dancing taught by older girls and a final dance competition.

[2] The narration was recorded in February 1967, in the home of Mr André Abari, a merchant and catechist in Bouli. The translation given here was made from the transcription of the original recording.

ren didn't recognize the authority of their elders. They wandered here and there, so the parents prepared a great feast of cassava and big sesame balls. They set the food out and called the children to come to eat, "Let's have fun! Naangazigoro!" **Naangazigoro**--what is that? **Naangazigoro** is the children, **diang** is the food prepared from cassava.³

    Oh honeycomb, diang kpol-e,
      Kpol! Kpol!
    Oh honeycomb, diang kpol-e,
      Kpol! Kpol!
    Oh honeycomb, diang kpol-e,
      Kpol! Kpol!
    Look at what the children do with themselves,
      Kpol! Kpol!
    Oh honeycomb, diang kpol-e,
      Kpol! Kpol!
    Oh honeycomb, diang kpol-e,
      Kpol! Kpol!
    Oh honeycomb, diang kpol-e,
      Kpol! Kpol!
    Oh honeycomb, diang kpol-e,
      Kpor! Kpor!

Then they said, "Hey! Hey! Hey!" and that one ended. That's the first part of the dance. That was the elders! That was the very first dance among all the Gbaya. When the earth began, the first dance that the Gbaya originated was **diang**.

Then they began another one.

      Frogs' eyes-e!
    Oh honeycomb, diang kpol-e,
      Frogs' eyes-e!
    Oh honeycomb, diang kpol-e,
      Kpol! Kpol!
    Oh honeycomb, diang kpol-e,
      Kpol! Kpol!
    Look at what the children do with themselves,
      Kpol! Kpol!
    Oh honeycomb, diang kpol-e,

---

3 The staple food of the Gbaya is cassava. From the raw root a flour is made, then mixed into a dough and served as a main dish. It is usually served with a meat side dish; but when meat is lacking, certain vegetables may be prepared as a sauce.

> Kpol! Kpol!
> Oh honeycomb, diang kpol-e,
> Kpol! Kpol!
> Oh honeycomb, diang kpol-e,
> Kpol! Kpol!

And that's the first part too. Aha! That's the **diang**, the first dance of the Gbaya.

Then, aha! They began another song, the main song of the dance. Then he (the dance leader) would come and sing:

> Yaa! Bamboo-sprout meat!
>   Gezengere, don't come up empty,
>   We do ours in the Mbal.
> Diang-e, bamboo-sprout meat!
>   Gezengere, don't come up empty,
>   We do ours in the Mbal.
> Diang-ee!
>   Gezengere, don't come up empty,
>   We do ours in the Mbal.
> Ee-diang, the bamboo-sprout meat ones!
>   Gezengere, don't come up empty,
>   We do ours in the Mbal.
> Diang-ee, bamboo-sprout meat!
>   Gezengere, don't come up empty,
>   We do ours in the Mbal.
> Oh mother, diang-ee, bamboo-sprout meat!

Hey! Friend! Let's go, hoo! What's the matter?

> Diang, the bamboo-sprout meat ones!
>   Gezengere, don't come up empty,
>   We do ours in the Mbal.
> Diang, the bamboo-sprout meat ones!
>   Gezengere, don't come up empty,
>   We do ours in the Mbal.
> Un! Deux! Jus'!

I say that now, but that came after the white man arrived. We used to end with "Hey! Hey! Wanto!"

The preceding account of **diang** was given as a performance in which the song, accompanied by the rhythmic beating of sticks, was sung by narrator and audience. It was sung in three parts, two introductory stanzas calling the participants to dance, and the main stanza which was the dance itself. It was traditionally sung to children who were called **naangazigoro**, a praise name meaning "honeycomb" and referring to the young bees. The children were active and clever, and a frequent nickname for such a child is **Zigoro** "Honey bee." The song tells of the children's plight. They have nothing to do with themselves but go around from house to house in search of food. In their quest, they are compared to the darting eye of the frog. The refrain of **Kpol! Kpol!** and its variant **Kpor! Kpor!** is an ideophone describing the young people as they cluster around the food that has been prepared and set out for them.

The third stanza reflects a time when the Gbaya were without meat and had to eat their cassava with a sauce made from bamboo sprouts, a practice still followed when meat is scarce. Those who eat the bamboo sprouts are called "bamboo-sprout meat ones." **Gezengere** is an ideophone describing the line formed by the children as they dance. The refrain continues with the children's boast that they do not come up from the river empty-handed. They have been successful, they have proven themselves to be brave, and the scene of their triumph was the Mbal River. Throughout the song, the leader shouts encouragement to the dancers, "What's the matter? Come on!" and the lead lines and refrain are repeated as long as the participants wish to dance.

The signal at the end where the narrator counts in French, "One! Two! Jus'!" represents the contrast between the past and the present. Traditionally the song would have ended with an invocation of Wanto, but now it ends with the numbers of the colonial education that have displaced the traditional systems of education such as the dance festivals. The final word **Jus'** is short for **juste** "Stop just there!" Wanto is the hero of ancient tradition. He is a comic fictitious character whose most frequent activity is the search for wife, food, and dance. Any unusual sound that he might hear becomes the rhythm of song and dance. Occasionally, he turns the power of dance against someone else who, overcome by the spell of the rhythm, invariably falls victim to Wanto's selfish whims.

Mr. Banda in his account and subsequent explanation of **diang** made very clear the integral part played by the dance in the structuring of Gbaya society. There was no unity among young and old, no interdependence between generations, no society until the elders called the children together to share a meal of cassava and bamboo sprouts. After eating, they taught the children songs and urged them to dance, and this was the origin of the festival of **diang**--a celebration of the creation of Gbaya community and society.

The narrator in his discussion of the festival extended its significance to the realm of contemporary political power. He cited the position of the District ruler who is accompanied on his travels by drummers beating songs in his honor, one of which begins, "All the people receive their food from the ruler." Through the ruler's ability to care for his people he is able to attract more subjects. As his subjects increase in number, his power and influence become greater. The beginnings of this relationship are found in **diang**.

From the narration, the songs, and the explanation of **diang** given by Mr. Kombo Banda, it becomes apparent why Wanto cannot resist a dance. It becomes clear why every occurrence in life may evoke dance. Dance is, after all, the celebration of life itself. And **diang** represents the beginning of Society without which Gbaya tradition repeatedly affirms there can be no life.

7. Ordinary and Extraordinary People

by Kombo Samuel

The Gbaya word **bii** means "person, human being." A person possesses **ɔmi** "breath," **dan-tɛ** "soul," and **giyɔ-tɛ** "shadow." When a Gbaya is alive, he possesses these three elements which together comprise life and form the whole of the body (**kii-tɛ**).

The Gbaya consider breath to be a vital aspect of life. Traditionally certain illnesses were identified with reference to breathing. If a person made a hoarse raucous sound when he breathed, he was thought to have tuberculosis; and when he breathed with a rattle in his throat, it was malaria. Breath characterizes one's state of health, whether one is in good health or in poor health. When a person dies, it is said that "the breath is finished." The Gbaya were not aware that even though breath had ceased, a person could be revived by artificial respiration. That is why it used to happen that people who appeared to have drowned or to have been asphyxiated were sometimes buried alive.

Dan-tɛ means literally "friend-body" and refers to the soul. It takes precedence over the breath and does not leave the body before the person dies. At death it is said of a person that "his soul departed."

"Sleep is the elder of death," the Gbaya say. When a man dies, he enters into a sleep from which he will never awaken. While a man is sleeping, it is believed that his soul is wandering somewhere and that it will come back at a particular time. To awaken a sleeping person suddenly may unintentionally cause something terrible to happen, because his soul is not in him.

A wandering soul indicates a man's departure from among his people and is called "the image of the person." If one encounters a straying soul, it is necessary to make it return to the sleeping person. This is done by taking a mimosa branch and then returning to the village, going to the home of the person who is asleep, and whipping him with the branch to make his soul come back. This is not a matter of sorcery. The pain caused in the body by the whipping will make his soul come back.

The shadow of a person is also very important, for the Gbaya say that without a shadow, there is no existence. One must never play with the shadow of another person. If one takes a machete and slashes the shadow of someone, it means that one has killed that person. Tradition refers to this in a tale about Wanto, the hero of Gbaya folktales. Wanto's uncle had an instrument that destroyed the shadow of everything. Before leaving on a trip one day, Wanto's uncle called him and warned him not to use the instrument without his knowledge. But as soon as his uncle left, Wanto ran into the granary and took the instrument. He destroyed many things; but when he noticed his own shadow, he stopped. Everywhere he went, his shadow accompanied him. Guided by his instinct, he wanted to free himself of his shadow. He stabbed it with the instrument and immediately fell dead. The shadow, according to this tale, is considered to be the person himself.

When a person dies, the first thing one hears is the announcement, "He is already dead," or, "The breath is finished." If it is a baby or a very old person, people say, "He went home." The Gbaya believe that there is a hereafter where the dead sojourn. This is a little like the Hades of the Christian faith. When a widow mourns her husband's death, she says, "You go ahead; I will come and join you." At death the soul changes aspect. The "friend of the body" becomes a "god-body" (sɔ́-tɛ). This soul belongs to God, the Creator God, who is the supreme God of the Gbaya. Since all the dead were believed to belong to the Creator God and serve as intermediaries between man and God, they were traditionally venerated under the name sɔ́-daa "god-fathers" or "spirit-fathers."

The Gbaya say that all the dead are among us. We do not see them, but they see us. Tradition tells us that once a certain man died, and everyone came for the mourning. Seized by a certain power, one mourner saw something strange--the dead had also come to be at the mourning. He also recognized some of the members of his family who had died earlier. The

Ordinary and Extraordinary People

dead came each in turn to wash their faces with the ritual libation to make themselves invisible before going among the crowd. The man went and moved the libation pot, placing it elsewhere; then he seized a whip and began whipping the dead. Everyone thought he was mad because he appeared to be whipping empty spaces. When the dead ran to where the libation had been, they saw nothing. They looked everywhere until they found it. Then they disappeared, and the man did not see them anymore. A few days later he died. According to the story, the dead are not far from us, and that is why the Gbaya traditionally buried their dead near their homes.

There are two types of people, the "pure-stomach people" and the "sorcery people." The first are ordinary people who possess breath, soul, and shadow. The second are extraordinary people who possess four elements; the fourth element is what distinguishes them from ordinary people. In addition to breath, soul, and shadow, they have **dua,** the power of sorcery.[1]

Several words are related to the word **dua.** The word for goat means literally "great-sorcery." Goats are often black, and the Gbaya say that all domesticated animals that are black in color are sorcerers and belong to sorcerers and can render services to sorcerers. Another term means literally "intestine-sorcery" and refers to brothers and sisters who inherit the power of sorcery through their mother. If the mother is a sorcerer, all her children will be sorcerers, and all her daughters will have children who are sorcerers. The power of sorcery is something that one receives at birth. As soon as the child sees the light of day, his mother gives the power of sorcery to him through his navel. However, he may

---

1 As shown in chapter nine, E. E. Evans-Pritchard's classic distinction between witchcraft and sorcery is not entirely accurate for the Gbaya and for neighboring peoples. The terms "sorcery" and "sorcerer" have therefore been retained from the French **sorcellerie** and **sorcier** used by the authors of this and the following chapter.

Editor's note: Though the author has not distinguished witchcraft from sorcery, traditionally in British and American anthropology these are distinguished as follows. Witchcraft refers to the permanent capacity or tendency to do evil which results from having a witchcraft substance within one's body. Sorcery refers to magical rites and practices performed for malevolent purposes. Sorcery is a subset of magic while witchcraft is not. This article has subsumed witchcraft and sorcery under one term, **sorcery.**

CM.

refuse to accept it, in which case his mother may either kill him or maim him for having dishonored her. The child is then free from sorcery. But the expression "intestine-sorcery" is used specifically in reference to brothers and sisters through the same mother, and not in reference to sorcery.

Sorcerers can also be divided into two categories, "the killer sorcerer" and "the seer." The killer sorcerer is one who acts against the ordinary person. Moving under the impulse of sorcery, his tendency is to destroy. He kills by eating the liver of his victims. He is dominated by the spirit of sorcery, which always directs him toward evil. This spirit often affects his character, making him lazy, jealous, gluttonous, garrulous, or teasing.

Sorcery has many methods of destroying a person. Sɔlɔk is a word of Mbum origin that is a method of using sorcery to kill a person by wringing his neck. If a sorcerer wants to use sɔlɔk to kill a person, he goes into the bush and mixes certain magical materials together. This substance he holds in his hand and wraps in the leaf of a mimosa tree. He then becomes invisible and goes and stands along the path where his intended victim often passes. When the victim appears, he strikes him in a magical way. The victim feels nothing at the time, but in the evening the spell becomes a high fever, and he vomits and dies.

Another method is to use a lightning bolt to kill a person. If someone wants to kill with lightning, he goes to a partner who also makes lightning. The two work together, since one man alone cannot make lightning. One is responsible for the lightning and the other for the thunderbolt. The two of them wait for a time when it is going to rain. The one who makes the thunderbolt turns himself into a little animal, goes into the victim's house, and either twists his neck or enters through his anus and comes out his head. What is very strange about this is that one accused of having killed by a lightning bolt does not deny it.

Sukang is also a word of Mbum origin, referring to sorcery that kills a person with needles, fragments of broken bottles, or tiny pieces of metal. The sorcerer gathers these things together, heats them with certain magical materials, and then looks for his enemy. Standing near his enemy, he injects these things into him unawares. In the evening the victim becomes very ill and dies, unless a healer is successful in removing them.

"Spearing the soul" is a procedure whereby one kills someone's soul in revenge for a crime committed. If a man, a woman, or a child dies in a village and it is discovered that it was a sorcerer who caused the death, the relatives of the dead person go to someone who spears souls. This person places a fish trap before the family of the dead person, saying, "If it was you who killed my brother, come out for me to see." If the accused did indeed kill the family's relative, he will appear in the trap. The person responsible for spearing souls then gives a needle to a member of the family, who thrusts it into the trap. When he withdraws it, it is covered with blood, affirming that vengeance has been carried out. After a few days, the criminal will die.

The opposite of spearing the soul is "calling the soul." This is the practice of calling the soul of a person to bring him back to life again. This is done by none other than a seer. When a man or woman is about to die, a seer may be called to bring his soul back, thereby bringing the dying person back to life.

The seer is the second type of sorcerer. He is one who has refused to do evil. Having greater power than the killer sorcerers, he keeps separate from them so that he may guide the village. He stands beside the chief and denounces all the arrogant sorcerers to him. That is why the other sorcerers try to take away his power. If they succeed, they kill him. The seer is the protector of ordinary people. He gives them charms, which are worn around the neck, the hips, or the wrist, to protect them against the destructive sorcerers. He can also prepare potions which are to be drunk or given in injections. The charms and the potions are, in a certain sense, antibodies that fight against **sɔlɔk,** lightning, **sukang,** and sorcerers that eat people.

The term for seer means literally "the master of the Gbana." The Gbana is a dance to denounce a sorcerer so that he will no longer perpetuate evil. It may also "cover sorcery," that is, recognize the power of sorcery in someone and thereby prevent evil. No one but a seer can denounce another person as being a sorcerer. If an ordinary person is accused of being a sorcerer, he must perserve the honor of his family by committing suicide. He pulls a knife and plunges it into his stomach to make his intestines come out, proving to everyone that there is no spirit of sorcery in his stomach. After his death, an old woman in the family will sprinkle the accusers with water, placing a curse on them. From then on, a plague will be upon the family until the old woman who holds the village libations intervenes. These libations are what calms the plagues that can ravage a village. She takes a branch of a tree of the **annonacée** family, dips it in the libation, and sprinkles it in all directions. Only then will the calamity cease.

If the liver of a person has been eaten by a sorcerer, either a seer or a sorcerer may put it back. If it is a seer who has been called to heal the sick person, he kills a black goat and takes its liver. He then heats a machete until it becomes bright red; he withdraws it from the fire, lays the goat liver on the sick person's side, and presses the machete over it. In this way a transplant is accomplished.

A sorcerer too can heal a person. If he has been accused of eating the liver of a sick person and is himself convinced that he did, and if he is threatened by the sick person's family (who may even bring the sick person and lay him in front of his door), he may feel in danger and will be obliged to put back the liver.

Why is the liver of a goat used? The goat is an animal that is well known to man, but it is not just any goat whose liver may be used. It must be a black goat--or a black cat or dog. Black is a color that is not favored by the Gbaya who say that all black domesticated animals are sorcerers. There is a close relationship between the seer, the killer sorcerer, and domestic animals. There is also a relationship between the ordinary man and these animals, for the liver of these animals can replace the liver of an ordinary man. The liver of wild animals cannot be used.

In death, the difference between the ordinary man and the extraordinary man again becomes apparent. When an ordinary person dies, his breath ends, his shadow disappears, and his soul changes from a friend of the body to a spirit, and nothing remains but the corpse. When a sorcerer dies, the spirit of sorcery comes out and flees in the form of an animal; and when this animal dies or is killed, that is the end of that spirit of sorcery.

8. Sickness, Medicine, and Sorcery in Duru Society

by Kadia Matthieu and Lee Bohnhoff*

The subjects of sorcery and illness are intertwined in Duru society to an extent that makes it difficult to treat the one without at least touching on the other. Many illnesses are said to be caused by sorcerers, and their cures must be sought not in medicines, but in some ritual to counter the effect of the sorcery. Part I below concentrates on the various types of illness and which kinds of medicine must be sought in each case. Part II examines the topic of sorcery.

I

Although the Duru do not have separate words for natural illness as over against mental or spiritual illness, it is abundantly clear that the Duru do distinguish between separate types of illness according to their origin and the treatment they require.

1) There are illnesses caused by food; for example, green mangoes or spoiled meat.
2) There are illnesses caused by the ancestral spirits or by certain bush spirits.
3) There are illnesses caused by failure to observe a taboo.
4) There are illnesses caused by sorcerers.
5) It seems that there are other illnesses that come from no known cause; for example, syphilis and measles.

* In the original version of this paper, Bohnhoff discussed sickness and medicine, and Kadia treated sorcery.

It cannot be said, therefore, that all illnesses are caused by some evil spirit or by sorcerers. Some are due to human negligence or excess, such as having eaten too many green mangoes, while others arise from having broken a taboo. In the following paragraphs, attention is concentrated especially on those illnesses caused by ancestral spirits and those due to broken taboos.

Ancestral spirits

Ancestral spirits (**nyoob**) may return from the village of the dead and make people sick, if the villagers forget to give them food. They may cause headaches, stomachaches, backaches, pain in the eyes, fever, itches and skin eruptions, or abortions. They often send snakes to bite people, and sometimes they "stop up a person's neck" so that he cannot talk for several days, but his hearing is unimpaired.

Two other spirits (**hen hog** 'bush thing', and **yigid bɪd** 'evil spirit') can possess people or cause insanity.

Two dwarf spirits may be considered together. The **ngbaa** live at the foot of certain trees and large rocks; the **taye waa vʋ** 'small gods' live in the forest. Both kinds of dwarfs are about two feet tall. If someone offends them by throwing stones or by stepping on the eyes of the **ngbaa** children, or if someone forgets to offer them the first fruits at harvest time, they can cause headaches, stomachaches, fevers, or itches and skin eruptions. The **ngbaa** can also twist a person's head ninety degrees from its natural position and leave it there, and the **taye wa vʋ** can give a sore foot to anyone who throws stones or who steps on their eyes while walking in the bush.

Broken taboos

Taboos among the Duru are passed on in each family, or more specifically, a person's taboos are those observed in the village where his ancestors were born. The following is an illustrative list of taboo animals or objects and the consequences of eating them or of breaking the taboo:

animal or object	consequence
chicken	blindness
goat; grey duiker	blindness
hippopotamus	leprosy, skin eruptions, or swellings and pox

Duru Sorcery 57

animal or object	consequence
wild pig	constipation
burning wood from the **zam dıgı** tree (English name unknown)	blindness

It is possible to break a taboo without knowing it. For example, if a friend invites someone to eat, it is impolite to ask what food it is; one simply eats it. Only later, if the guest falls ill, does he begin asking questions about what his host served him!

Ways and means of healing

How can the cause of a lingering and otherwise inexplicable illness be found? One must visit the diviner (**gan**) and he will explain which spirit or ancestor is offended and also what needs to be done or what sacrifice will satisfy the spirit. Naturally he requests pay for his services.

One may also seek help from someone who knows how to "hold the chicken against the chest." The questioner must give him a chicken, and he will perform one of several possible rites, but the central element is to examine the internal organs of the chicken. He will then announce the cause of the illness, either that it was the sorcerer **sey,** or that an ancestor spirit has been offended, or some other cause. It is also possible that the questioner may have to visit still another person in search of the remedy to be prescribed, because a single person cannot always provide both the diagnosis and the prescription.

Before turning to the cures for illnesses mentioned above, a word must be said concerning the meaning of **gam,** the word usually translated 'medicine' in English and French. There are at least four meanings for this word: a) medicine or medicinal herbs; b) remedy in a very general sense; c) an object kept by a sorcerer and used to perform his magic, or an object which gives him his power, or even an object used to expose and fight against sorcerers; and d) a sorcerer's power itself.

But the means of healing are more extended than this, because there are also rites and sacrifices to satisfy offended spirits or to make them leave the sick person. In short, there are several ways and means of treating the sick:

1) medicinal herbs, roots, and other folk medicines;
2) sacrifices of food or rites prescribed by the diviner, or other person who knows how to do this, in order to chase away a certain spirit;
3) special medicines used to heal an illness caused by breaking a taboo;
4) the medicines, actions, objects, or means used to foil three types of sorcerer: **sey, mbʊgʊ,** or **sukăŋ**.

Herbs and roots

Almost everyone knows some of these plants, but some people know a lot more of them than others. A sick person or a relative can go to these people and pay them to receive medicine for specific illnesses.

Sacrifices and rites for the spirits

It is not difficult to prevent or combat illnesses caused by the ancestral spirits. The food sacrifices due them at all times must not be forgotten. If these offerings do not bring the desired result, a person can curse and insult the spirits, ordering them to leave him in peace. Offerings to them are left at places where two paths cross, or at the family offering altar. Since it is not difficult to chase away these spirits, anyone can do it.

It is very difficult, however, to exorcise the spirit **hẽn hõg** 'bush thing' which causes mental illness. The perfume or incense **zʊgʊ** must be used, and only those who know how to do so can chase away the spirit successfully. The other spirit causing loss of one's mind, **yigid bɩd** 'evil spirit', is also very difficult to exorcise. Some meat and bones must be burned inside the house, then placed on a piece of bark, carried out, and left in the road. The ancestors must also be invoked. When the spirit smells the burned meat and bones, it flees and the sick person gets well.

Food sacrifices are required to cure illnesses caused by **ngbaa** spirits, and the person sacrificing must pronounce the words **ngbaa liilii** (meaning unknown). He must then place some ashes and leaves on a piece of bark, carry them out of the house, and leave them in the road. For the other dwarf spirits, the **tay waa vʊ**, the exorcist must also place ashes on a piece of bark, carry them outside the village, and say, "Leave us in peace." Since it is not difficult to chase off these spirits either, virtually anyone can perform the rite successfully.

Cures for broken taboos

There are medicines to cure certain of the illnesses caused by broken taboos, but not all. Blindness, for example, is impossible to cure. But there is a remedy for skin eruptions and itches that can be mixed with the victim's bath water.

Protection against sorcerers

Illnesses caused by sorcerers and the means used to secure healing will be treated in detail in Part II below.

There are also certain preventive medicines used to avoid illness or to foil the attacks of sorcerers. Anyone living in Cameroun even a short time soon learns about several of these. Certain tree seeds, amulets, or rites involving certain roots and herbs are supposed to protect against certain illnesses or attacks. A more detailed discussion of these measures will not be undertaken in this paper.

II

In Duru culture there are five kinds of sorcerers and sorcery:
1) **soog,** murderers
2) **mbυgυ,** a) eaters of children, b) murderers of adults, and c) protectors of the village and the chief
3) **sey,** the art of stealing "souls"
4) **sukăŋ,** poisoned needles
5) **ngbatii,** "playful" sorcery

Soog

Soog are men, not women, but one **soog** alone cannot kill anyone. There must be a group of three, four, or five before they have power. For example, if someone does something to another person that he does not like, he just goes to a **soog** and asks him to kill the offender. But the **soog** will not do it for nothing, of course. The person requesting his services must kill a chicken, make some couscous and two or three pots of wine, and provide some flour. He takes all this to the **soog**, who will then call his friends together to make their medicine against the man's enemy. In addition, a **soog** must have certain objects; for example, he may use the sexual organs of persons, obtained by digging up graves, to make his medicine.

This power of **soog** can be bought, since it is the knowledge of how to kill people. It is not inherited. If a man wants to get this power, he must pay a lot of money in order to learn the secrets. Once he has bought this knowledge and the medicine is his, he still does not have everything necessary. The man from whom he buys this knowledge will ask him for a person, perhaps his mother, his sister, his older brother or his father. It is always someone he loves very much. When he hands over his relative, the **soog** gathers his friends and they kill the man or woman who was handed over to them. The man wanting to become a **soog** has now fully paid for his medicine and has become a **soog**.

A man may become a **soog** against his will. The **soog** eat their couscous at noon especially, with a chicken or fresh fish sauce. Their medicine is mixed with the sauce. A man may come upon two or three people eating, and they ask him to share their meal. If he is hungry, he eats. After two or three days, they perform their rites in order to kill someone. This person falls sick, in his field, for example, and does not know who has done this to him. But the man who ate the **soog's** medicine with them is irresistibly drawn by their medicine to the scene of the crime, even if far away. They tell him, "The other day you ate our couscous, so now get yourself out of this as best as you can." And they abandon him standing before the victim.

The man's only hope is to wash the face of the sick person, who is already half dead. But when the man has washed the victim's face, he returns to consciousness and recognizes him. The victim returns home, falls ill again, and when questioned, tells how he saw this man doing certain strange things to him in his field. Immediately, the elders know that the man is a **soog**. They arrest him and "tie him up."

How can a **soog** be "tied up"? There are several ways, one of which is the following. A small bamboo may be split and slipped over the **soog's** head above his ears, then tied tightly in front and back. When they tap on the end tied to the forehead, the **soog** confesses everything that he has done. The man who was tricked into becoming a **soog** tells how he found these three people eating, how he ate with them, then how they tried to kill their victim, and how he himself arrived on the scene of the crime. The persons he names are arrested, taken off into the bush, and made to stand trial by poison. Since they are guilty, they die from the potion given them. A **soog** may be exposed and killed in this manner. If a person is innocent, he vomits up the potion without dying.

Mbʊgʊ

There are three types of **mbʊgʊ**: one "eats" children, another kills adults, and the third type protects the chief and the village from foreign **mbʊgʊ**. All mbʊgʊ are adults. Young people have their own types of sorcery, as will be seen below. Some **mbʊgʊ** are born with this power; others buy it, but it is only the third type of **mbʊgʊ** that can buy power.

The first type of **mbʊgʊ** seeks to kill the children of people who treat him badly. After his enemy's wife has given birth and the baby is two or three months old, he gathers four or five of his **mbʊgʊ** friends and they go to the enemy's house and steal his child. Not physically, but by their knowledge and magic, they steal his soul, cook and eat it with a meat sauce. In two or three days the child dies. Exactly how this is done is known only to the **mbʊgʊ**.

Like the **soog**, some **mbʊgʊ** are pressured into handing over a member of their family to be eaten, although they may like this person very much. This can happen because when one **mbʊgʊ** eats a child provided by another **mbʊgʊ**, he is indebted and must provide a member of his own family when it is his turn. After each member of the group has provided one person to be eaten, the group may disband.

To illustrate the second type of **mbʊgʊ**, let us take an example. I love a certain woman and keep going to her house, but she refuses to stay with me. If she sends me away two or three times and tells me she does not want to see me in her house, I might go to my fellow **mbʊgʊ** and say, "There is that woman over there; I have tried everything to make her stay with me," or, "I want to marry her, but she has refused. We must kill her." We then perform our rites and kill her easily.

The third type of **mbʊgʊ** are older people who buy a certain object, **zʊg kii**, which is a type of plant. They keep it hidden, but it gives them power to protect the village and the chief. If a **mbʊgʊ** from another village comes close to them, they can spot him and denounce him so he can be driven away.

There are also some **mbʊgʊ** that kill themselves. If one of them is shocked or depressed about something, he can go alone to the edge of a marsh and perform his rites. No one knows what he does exactly (this is what the elders say). When he has performed his rites, he returns to his house and dies two or three days later.

It is also possible to investigate the **sooɡ** and **mbʊgʊ** through autopsies. When a person dies, was he a sorcerer? Who killed him? Was it a **sooɡ** that killed him? Or was it his fellow **mbʊgʊ** who killed him? The elders perform an autopsy. If he killed himself, they find his heart full of wounds and blood. Or they may find his lungs full of holes. They remove these organs, show the relatives, and tell them, "Here is what your child did. It is he who killed himself, not someone else that killed him." There is therefore no trial, because he has committed suicide.

Sey

Persons who know **sey** are found also among the Fulani, the Mbum, and other ethnic groups. It is a kind of knowledge or magic difficult to explain. It can be bought. It consists in knowing how to steal the shadow, or soul, of a person.

For example, if a man knows **sey**, he looks for an opportunity to talk to someone, and while talking he touches him lightly. It is now all finished as far as his soul is concerned, because it has been stolen. But the man does not kill it; he keeps it under a tree, in his house, or in his field, and makes it work every day. It does not sleep at all, but works continually in his garden, digging and weeding. His field is always clean. Meanwhile, the body of the person whose soul has been stolen is at home and gets thinner and thinner. Finally, someone will ask the chief, "Why does this person get thinner and thinner like that?" He answers that perhaps someone has stolen his soul. The chief sends out a message for everyone in the village each to bring some water and give it to the sick person. All this water will be poured together, and the victim will bathe in it two or three days in succession. He will regain his health, because the person who stole his soul was necessarily among those who brought water, and with the water, the sorcerer automatically brings back his victim's soul. In this case, no one ever finds out who actually stole the soul.

As a deterrent to sorcery, persons who practice **sey** may be beaten. If they are punished severely enough, they abandon their sorcery.

Sukãng

Everyone in northern Cameroun knows the poisoned needles called **sukãng**. It is especially the Mbum who used them. The Gbaya and Duru did not use them before, but they bought this knowledge from the Mbum. The Mana and the Goom also practiced this. **Sukãng** is a very, very thin type of metal wire. A person can make lots of these wires, throwing them like shot from a shell toward a victim. No one knows exactly how they throw them, however.

A person who knows how to throw **sukãng** takes some needles, coats them with poison, and throws them at someone. They enter the body and cause a lot of pain. If a person feels intense hostility, he aims his needles into his victim's eyes, or into his ears so he becomes deaf, or into his lungs to cause pain there.

Certain persons have preventive medicine against these needles. They have power to catch these needles in midair. While someone is throwing needles, such a person catches them. After several minutes, the one who caught the needles goes up to the thrower and shows him the needles in his hand and says, "Here is what you did. Is it good to do that? What did this person do to you? Did he lure your wife away? Did he steal something? Or did he refuse to give you food? What you are doing here is not good; you must stop it." After the scolding, the one who threw the needles says, "Okay, I won't do it anymore." It is almost a kind of game by then.

There are also certain people who know how to remove these needles from a person's body, although they do not know how to throw them. They earn money by removing them from the bodies of victims.

It is rare to throw more than three, four, or five needles into a person. If five or six are thrown, the person dies on the spot. The person who knows how to withdraw these needles usually prepares a large quantity of them at home and hides them on his person before he goes to remove needles from a victim. Once he has removed the needles from the person in pain he mixes a lot of his own with them and shows them to everyone. "Here is what I found in this person." He may display fifty or sixty needles, but it is not true. He only took out one or two, then added all the rest himself so he could collect a big fee.

Ngbatii

Ngbatii is also widely known in northern Cameroun. It is especially the young people who encourage their peers to do this. It is not, however, a skill one can buy.

If, for example, someone is walking along with a young man who possesses this power (he may be hunting or just walking), his companion may shoot an arrow at a bird in a tree. When the arrow lodges in the tree, the shooter will ask his friend to climb up and get it for him. As soon as he climbs the tree, the sorcerer tricks him and does something so that when he looks down at the ground, he sees that he is surrounded by a lake full of hippopotamuses and crocodiles. He does not dare climb down! There was no water there before, nor hippopotamuses, nor crocodiles. He must promise to give the sorcerer one of his relatives, his mother, for example, if he wants to be saved. Once the sorcerer agrees, the victim looks at the ground again and sees no more water, no more hippopotamuses, no more crocodiles. He climbs down, but the sorcerer has already gone off and killed the person given to him.

Another **ngbatii** trick is to keep one's mother, or another woman, from preparing food. From morning until night she can keep her cooking pot on the fire, but the water will refuse to heat up. The young person thinks that if he allows the woman to fix the food early while he is away, perhaps he will not get any of it. Then when he returns, he makes medicine to cause the water to boil normally, and the woman begins to prepare the food. He stands alongside just waiting for his share. Once he has eaten, he says thanks and leaves.

9. Sickness, Misfortune and Healing among the Gbaya

by Cecilia Noss

A note on method

This study is based on a total of seven and a half years of residence among the Gbaya, never as a full-time researcher or medical worker, but with a variety of experiences from running a front-door medical dispensary in the bush, to having our own children in the local schools, to discussing medical beliefs and practices with women's classes. I would write down experiences that were told to me concerning sickness, misfortune, and healing, or which I observed directly. As language competence grew, I began also to record people's comments and interpretations, given spontaneously or in response to my questions. Those questioned included men, women, and children, Gbaya traditional medical practitioners, Gbayas trained in the practice of Western medicine, and Western medical practitioners working in the area. My contacts with Gbaya traditional medical practitioners have been relatively limited, and though friendly, not especially fruitful. Other Gbaya have explained to me that traditional practitioners fear blame if something goes wrong. They fear the disapproval of "certified" practitioners, even though the Western-trained Gbaya medical practitioners are well aware of the traditional medicine being practiced. The Gbaya traditional practitioners are even said to fear being put in jail, although I have not heard of a single case of this happening and some traditional local authorities will accept a diviner's assessment of guilt in legal cases.

I am indebted to many individuals who considered my questions sincere, though sometimes naive, and patiently tried to answer and explain. I am most particularly indebted to three individuals with whom I had frequent and extended discussions over a period of several years, concerning points that often must have seemed to them repetitive.

There is, first of all, Daniel Sodea. He was raised as heir to an uncle who was a Gbaya chief, Moslem teacher, and herbalist. Daniel himself served with De Gaulle's army in Europe, where he was converted to Christianity. Upon his return from the army, he was trained by missionaries as catechist, or lay teacher. After serving as catechist and evangelist, part of that time for a hospital of the Evangelical Lutheran Church of Cameroun, he retired.

Secondly, I am indebted to his wife, Madame Pauline,[1] who spent many years of her childhood working with and learning from her grandfather, an herbalist who also assisted at difficult childbirths and knew medicine to counteract witchcraft and sorcery. Madame Pauline has had a number of other traditional practitioners in her family, both herbalists and diviners, but has never practiced medicine herself, because, her husband says, "When one practices medicine, people are always coming, and she (with ten children and field work) did not have the time."

The third person to whom I am indebted is Paul Tenmbar, a young family man who has completed French school through roughly the fourth grade. His father was a trainer in boys' initiation, and several members of the family are skilled in the use of herbs. He was employed as our cook, but became a personal friend and one of our instructors in Gbaya culture.

Most of the generalizations which these three individuals and other Gbaya make grow out of their own life experiences. Having known each of them over a period of several years, I have sometimes learned of experiences in their lives that explain general statements they had made much earlier. They have given me the Gbaya viewpoint to the best of their knowledge, but it may differ at some points from that of Gbaya with different experiences. Thus, even though stated as generalizations, much of the material is subjective. As they were quick to point out, they obviously could not say exactly how a sorcerer used medicine to kill, but would report "what some people say" or "what the old people say." All three have had extended exposure to Western missionary ideas, which may

---

1 Madame is a given name. White people arrived in her village the day that she was born, and that is why she was named Madame. Pauline is her baptismal name.

have been incorporated at some points in their opinions. What is notable is that, despite the exposure, traditional views are still strong. Church members are at least as likely as any other segment of the population to be victims of witchcraft.

Health, medicine, and disease from a Gbaya perspective

A delightful description of the relation between health and the dance was given me, not in the discussion of health, but in the discussion of the importance of dance.

> The things that gives happiness to us Gbaya more than anything is dance. When people dance, they find health/quickness of body. In the days of our grandfathers, when you came to a village and there was no dancing, there was hunger. Dancing and the happiness of children, these are things of health, and there is food as well.[2]

The Gbaya word **yina** can be translated "medicine." Medicine can have a broad or narrow meaning even in English, but the range is even wider in Gbaya. **Yina** can refer to a living plant with medicinal uses or to an infusion made from parts of that plant. "Doing medicine" can refer to the treatment which, depending on the nature of the illness and the healer, can include acts such as ceremonially bathing the patient, or removing needles from his body which have been thrown there by a sorcerer. "Remedy" might be a good translation for **yina** used in this sense, and it may also include injunctions against greeting a person with a handshake or eating certain foods. Food restrictions in the absence of sickness are also included in **yina,** and are referred to as "simple medicine," formerly taught to young girls undergoing initiation. There are protective medicines such as a medicine to protect one's hunting dogs from being struck by a snake, or one's fields from theft. The blacksmith specializes in the latter, and has other medicines for one who has stolen from a protected field, or sworn untruthfully on the blacksmith's iron.

There are medicines to help a student do well in his examinations or to help a soccer team win a game. In certain cases, a diviner may use medicine to find the person responsible for a death by witchcraft; now that it is forbidden to kill accused witches, or to subject them to a trial by poison, he may bury **yina** on the grave of the victim. In due time the witch or witches responsible will become ill and

---
2 From an interview with Daniel Sodea, March 4, 1978.

die. Vengeance medicine is also used when lightning has struck a person or his dwelling. (Lightning striking in this way never "just happens," but is always caused by someone with the special power to do so, using lightning in order to kill.) A specialist who knows the vengeance medicine to use in this case can rub medicine mixed with oil on the foreheads of all the residents of the village (or of the neighborhood, if it is in a town). Again, the person or persons responsible will become ill and die. Lastly, there is **yina** which can cause sickness, depression, misfortune, or death to an enemy, i.e., "sorcery."

A European may be tempted to divide the various categories of Gbaya medicine into those that do or are supposed to have a physical effect, i.e., herbs, and those that work through mystical or magical means, but it must be remembered that to the Gbaya, all medicine, if strong enough, is expected to have the desired physical effect.

When a person is ill, he lies on a mat in the yard, or on a bed or mat by the fire in the kitchen or in the house. Concern is expressed by family and friends who come to greet and sit with him. Failure to visit a sick relative or friend is a serious matter and more than a breach of etiquette.

The concern the Gbaya have about an illness depends on how serious they think it is. They use herbs as initial treatment or, where available, they go to a dispensary or hospital outpatient clinic. An adult who is not gravely ill may seek treatment on his own, and school children often go to a dispensary unattended. Once I saw a schoolboy bring a younger brother, gravely ill with pneumonia, to a dispensary.

If the patient does not respond quickly or decisively enough to initial treatment, or if the sickness is severe or perceived as strange from the beginning, much discussion ensues among those surrounding the patient about what the disease is and who has medicine to treat it. When there is disagreement about where to take a sick child, the father will usually make the decision. He may threaten other family members, "If you take him off in the bush and he dies, you will pay." Due to the deference given to age, a particularly strong paternal grandfather or grandmother may override the father. If the treatment does not give results satisfactory to all members of the family, another faction may win out; they may bring in a diviner to treat a family member who is a patient in a hospital or dispensary, or may remove him and take him to a diviner. In other instances, patients not responding satisfactorily to treatment by one or more traditional practitioners, will be brought to a hospital or dispensary. Village elders become involved if the patient or victim is an important person or the circumstances particularly frightening. There is fear of blame, either for being thought responsible in some way for the sickness, or for not acting responsibly when treatment is sought. Naturally, the goal is to find a treatment that will cure, and one option after another will be tried until the patient is either cured or dead. One Gbaya commented that in the beginning it does not matter much where treatment is sought; the fact that the family is trying is what matters. By the act of seeking treatment, wherever it is sought, the people surrounding the patient show their good faith and concern, which is an important support to him.

The question of where to go for treatment was simpler in former days when one merely had to find out who in the extended family or local community or nearby Gbaya communities had the correct medicine or knew of a traditional medical specialist. If they failed to find a cure in one locale, they would look for treatment in communities farther away. Now, with the movement of Gbaya into larger, multiethnic communities, and with the introduction of Western medicine, there are numerous options for treatment.

Western medicine is represented by dispensaries and hospitals administered by church or government and staffed by trained Gbaya personnel, by Camerounians of other ethnic groups, and by expatriates, usually missionaries. Despite grossly overburdened resources and facilities and the strangeness of Western concepts and methods, they have been popular simply because treatment in them often has the desired effect. In certain situations, there is an advantage since the Cameroun government encourages the use of Western facilities. Employees covered by social security receive payment if their babies are born in a hospital, and additional payment if the mother of the child had prenatal examinations there.

Nigerian patent medicines make fleeting appearances in the marketplace and are beginning to be used by Gbaya who have become accustomed to pills and cough syrup from Western dispensaries and hospitals. Injectable penicillin and other Western drugs are occasionally available in the market, partly due to inadequate control of dispensary stocks. Indiscriminate use of the drugs often results, not always to cure an illness, but as a protection against getting sick.

In many Gbaya communities where Fulani also live, one sees Fulani merchants displaying plant and animal-product medicines for sale in the market place. Gbaya say they mistrust these because they have their own products with which they are more familiar. They also mistrust them because the Fulani medicine is being sold "in commerce," although the same could be said for the Nigerian patent medicines. Gbaya say they prefer that an herbalist or other practitioner see the patient in order to make a diagnosis.

Fulani Moslems have medical practitioners who are consulted by the families of Gbaya patients. The Fulani practitioner is called **mallum** 'teacher', but he may also be an herbalist, or a diviner, or know medicines made from their holy book, the Koran. Having "the Word of God," theology written in a book, assumes great importance for Gbaya followers of both Christianity and Islam. But, whereas Christians will read or quote from Scripture in times of sickness, the **mallum** can provide medicines made from passages of the Koran sewn into leather amulets, or medicine made from ink washed off slates on which passages from the Koran had been written. **Mallum** are believed by Gbaya to have special powers in matters of witchcraft and sorcery. Like Gbaya diviners they can cause the death of another person, and some will do this for a client upon payment of a sufficient fee. Unlike Gbaya diviners, a **mallum** may shut himself up in his room for a period of seven days and nights for this purpose. Christian Gbaya say the **mallum** often agree to kill for a fee, whereas Gbaya diviners rarely do so.

With the influx of Hausa into the area, one of their practices has gained popularity with the Gbaya. There are Hausa practitioners who cut out the uvula of persons diagnosed as having an uvula that is too long, with the resulting symptoms of sore throat and coughing. Gbaya patronize these practitioners even though this operation is frequently fatal.

There are two aspects to the Gbaya diagnosis of a disease, recognizing it and finding the cause. If the family is able to recognize the disease, they will look for a healer who is reputed to have a cure for that disease. If the patient is taken for diagnosis to a healer who can recognize the disease, it may help the patient if the appropriate medicine is chosen and administered. Even though the disease is recognized by a lay person or a specialist, if it is life-threatening, persistent or fatal, underlying causes to explain why this disease struck at this particular time are sought. There

Healing among the Gbaya

may be only speculation, or the answer may be seriously sought through divination.

In talking about concepts of specific diseases, it is important to remember that Gbaya lay people have no popular medical guide, nor do Gbaya traditional healers have written medical texts. The concept each individual Gbaya has about a particular disease is based on his personal experience with that disease, or what others relate to him about their personal experiences. The grandmothers and the traditional professional healers have had the most experience and are more likely to recognize a disease and know what to expect of it. Gbaya, both lay and professional, have had more experience in observing the natural course of a disease, unaltered by drugs, than have their Western counterparts.

Certain diseases common enough or distinctive enough to be widely known have names that are borrowed from other languages in the area, although the way in which the name is applied by the Gbaya may not be exactly the way in which it is applied in the neighboring ethnic group. Among such diseases are measles (**ndukusu**) and whooping cough (**kalambako** or **kalamboko**) each of which follows a distinctive pattern. Others are smallpox (**gazindang**), gonorrhea (**hɔrsɔ**), and syphilis (**ngabila**).

Other terms given as disease names refer to what in English would be regarded as symptoms:

Ta nin bem (literally "stone teeth child") is convulsions.

Mbɔrɔ is a mucous discharge from the nose and throat. When **mbɔrɔ** "does" a person he has a mild cold or feels a cold coming on; when it "takes" a person, he has a severe cold. The Gbaya **mbɔrɔ** can also kill.

Fere is a disease in which breathing is labored. It could be pneumonia, asthma, or sometimes tuberculosis.

Hääte is literally "swelling body" and is named as one of the diseases that kill children.

Zar pi nu is a verb which may refer to unconsciousness, and is sometimes named as a disease.

Other diseases are named by their location in the body: "that in the head," "that in the chest," "that in the stomach." Often symptoms are described: "he has diarrhea," "he has a cough," or "I have a splitting headache." Other descriptions are: "my chest aches," "my whole body aches," "I have no strength" or "his body is all soft."

People are often said to die of a stopped-up throat or a broken neck, even when examination does not show this to be the case. This may be due to the relation the Gbaya perceive between breath, spirit, and life, so that any disease affecting the neck or throat is considered to be very grave and probably due to sorcery. The belief may also come from the fact that the most obvious signs to an observer of death are that the person first ceases to talk, and then he stops breathing.

Intestinal worms, which can sometimes be seen in the feces, are known to be a cause of sickness and discomfort even when they are not seen. Worms in the teeth are thought to be the cause of toothache. The Gbaya name for malaria, "worm sickness" is said to have preceded Western teaching that malaria is caused by parasites. If a child has a fever and vomits, "worm sickness" is a likely diagnosis.

Gbaya today know about the existence of other parasitic diseases such as schistosomiasis and ancylostomiasis (hookworm disease) because they have been diagnosed in a hospital or dispensary laboratory, but I have not known a Gbaya lay person to suggest these as possibilities from symptoms presented. Very low hemoglobin is extremely prevalent in Gbaya women and is common in Gbaya children. The Gbaya know of this condition and describe it as "not enough blood," perhaps because that is how it has been described to them, but I have not known of a Gbaya other than professionals trained in Western medicine to look for or recognize the symptoms which are easy to check, namely a pale inner cheek or inner eyelid.

In the case of less commonly seen diseases, especially those that differ from patient to patient in severity and manifestation, the variations are not recognized as the same disease. An example is poliomyelitis which is relative common and usually mild and is not recognized to be the same disease as crippling or fatal forms.

Diseases that are recognized are somewhat less likely to be considered the result of sorcery or witchcraft, even when they are fatal, than are unfamiliar and unrecognized combinations of symptoms. On the other hand, diseases affecting the throat or neck such as meningitis or diphtheria, recognized as sɔlɔp,[3] are believed to be caused by sorcery.

3 Or **solok**.

If a child dies from a disease that is recognized, such as measles, the explanation that "measles killed the child" may be accepted without much further speculation. But even in such a case speculation may become complex. Not one, but several causes working together may be suggested.[4] "Measles killed the child. But before the child got measles it was not well. There was some sickness in the head since shortly after birth. The child was thin. The mother did not have enough milk because her husband had left her and she did not have enough food herself to eat." Beyond that it comes out that the woman's husband had had a falling out with her brother over a joint business affair, there was a breach in the relationship, and perhaps sorcery was involved.

While the patient lives, finding the underlying cause of his illness may be crucial to his successful treatment. If a disruption of relations exists, the parties may need to be reconciled. If an enemy has caused the sickness, misfortune, or accident through witchcraft or sorcery, confronting him with the fact that the victim's family knows what he is doing may persuade him to cease his evil deeds. If he is not so easily intimidated, medicines specific against witchcraft or sorcery may be used on the victim's behalf. That is why, if disrupted social relations are obvious to observers, strong factions in the family often refuse to take the patient to a dispensary or a hospital, arguing that this is "not a thing for white man's medicine."

One would, however, be wrong in assuming that Gbaya never seek treatment at Western facilities for conditions thought to be caused by witchcraft or sorcery. When the mother of a young woman struck down but not killed by lightning was questioned about having taken her daughter to a hospital for treatment, she replied, "Well, it worked, didn't it?" Accidents are often thought to be a result of witchcraft or sorcery, but victims are usually taken first to a hospital or dispensary, if one is available. The family of the patient or victim in these cases hopes that the combined forces of the "white man's medicine" and God will be strong enough to overcome the calamity. "White man's medicine" is successful often enough to assure its place as one of the options even in cases thought to be caused by witchcraft or sorcery.

---

4 Gbaya are not the only ones to perceive a multiplicity of causes. Dr. David Morley in _Pediatric Priorities in the Developing World_ (1973) demonstrates a strong relationship between underweight children and measles fatalities.

There are three diseases about which there is often strong argument against taking the patient to a hospital or dispensary. The first is meningitis, or diseases resembling meningitis, which is thought to be caused by sɔlɔp, a form of sorcery for which there are specific countermeasures. When patients with this disease are brought to a hospital or dispensary, they often to not respond quickly enough to satisfy the frightened family and are removed before treatment can be completed.

Many Gbaya say that if a child with measles is taken to a dispensary, he will die. No doubt this comes from observing that less severe and uncomplicated cases of measles treated at home usually recover, while the children taken to the dispensary, because they are gravely ill, often do die.

It is a well-known fact that white men do not have medicine for hepatitis, whereas herbal medicines for this disease are known to every African ethnic group in the area. Gbaya observe that Europeans often suffer months from hepatitis, and even die, whereas Gbaya treated with herbal medicine usually recover much more quickly.

Traditional medicines are often employed in the treatment of colds, sores, convulsions, whooping cough, intestinal worms, and other common illnesses, because they are cheaper, more readily available if there is no dispensary in the community, but I am not aware of any reluctance to seek Western treatment for these ailments.

As long as an illness is mild or responds readily to treatment, or is not lingering or life-threatening, there is little concern to find the underlying cause. When death occurs, except in the case of an old person who had a full and good life, there is much talk and speculation about its cause. If a child dies, the father of the child may call together the important men and women close to the family and ask them what they think killed the child. As has been mentioned, they may name a disease such as measles as being solely responsible for the death. They may say that God took the child. When an older person dies, the consensus may be that God took him or simply that it was his time to die.

An older person who realizes he is dying, knowing the ugliness of accusations, may say, "No one is responsible for my death. It is my time to die," or "It is God's will."

If the family does not accept that it was a disease that "just came" which killed the person, or that it was God's will, or the person's time to die, speculation and accusations will continue. The only way to know for certain the cause of death is through divination, and even then the answer is often inconclusive.

There are methods of divination that an ordinary person may use if he knows them. One of these is to rub a taro yam hard between the palms of the hands, naming in turn various suspects or possible causes. If the root does not break up, the person named is innocent. If it does break up, he is guilty. Or a stone may be rolled with the palm of the hand back and forth on a bed of rock while suspects are named. If the stone suddenly stops when a particular person is named, he is the guilty one. Poison may be poured on a termite colony, and if the termites die, the person named is guilty. Or poison may be administered to a chicken. If the chicken vomits the poison and lives, the person named is innocent; if it dies, the person named is guilty. With any of these methods one answer is never taken as conclusive. The method is repeated several times; only if it results in the same answer every time will that answer be accepted.

Blacksmiths can also divine, using bits of metal that either do or do not fuse, or that do or do not break apart once fused.

Diviner specialists, **wan gbana,** will be discussed in greater detail later in this chapter. They do not use methods such as the above, but use inherent powers in combination with dance and objects that they study in order to "see" what is the underlying cause of illness, misfortune or death. Not just one diviner is consulted, but several, and they must agree. If they do not agree, it is, the Gbaya say, because some are real diviners, and some are lying. The ability to "see" is not questioned, and the diviner is never considered to be mistaken. The only thing that can account for the lack of consensus that sometimes exists is that one or more of the diviners are lying.

Much of the actual divination or consultation with a diviner is done quietly by the family, for there are dangers in making accusations. Now that the government has forbidden poison trials of accused witches, they are not sought out as much as formerly. Vengeance-medicine works without naming the person or persons responsible.

There is a pervasive belief among older Gbaya that there is more sickness now than formerly. At times they imply a link between certain diseases and modernization. Among them are cancer, "sugar disease" (diabetes), and "salt disease." The Western diagnosis of "salt disease" in one particular case was hypertension, and the patient was told not to eat salt. Europeans introduced sugar in place of honey and commercial salt in place of "Gbaya salt," which is made from ashes. Gbaya complain that **fere** used to be a mild diease, finished in two or three days, but now it may kill. Another complaint is that one can feel perfectly normal and yet the doctor examines the blood and says, "You do not have enough blood." A woman may have a very low hemoglobin count by Western standards, yet puts in a hard day of field work, carries home firewood on her head and her baby on her back, and prepares the family's evening meal.

There are several factors which may contribute to the Gbaya opinion that there is more sickness among them now than formerly. Like older people everywhere, elderly Gbaya tend to idealize the past, although these same individuals also remember the hardships. Some conditions that previously were not identified may be diagnosed now. With increased travel and communication, people now hear about the sickness or death of relatives living at some distance. With greater mobility there is also more exposure to communicable diseases. Living in larger communities may bring certain health advantages: increased food for those that have cash, Western medical facilities, a safe water supply (though in only a few of the largest cities in the country). But it also brings disadvantages: crowded living conditions, loss of access to fields, sewage disposal problems, and stress from changing lifestyles and values. Less hardy infants are now surviving into adulthood, and they become less hardy adults. And perhaps, although there is no way of checking this, now that there are more options available in medical treatment, some Gbaya may be inclined to seek treatment for condition such as aching muscles or tired feet, which they formerly would have accepted as natural.

Social causes of disease and misfortune

In former days when ceremonies of worshipping God through the ancestors and through the spirits of nature were faithfully and meticulously carried out, God was the source of all good things: game, health, fertility of crops, and many children. It was natural, if any of these blessings were not forthcoming, to consider whether the ceremonies had been neglected or improperly done. When sickness or misfortune began to plague a family or community, likewise one of the first questions was whether the ceremonies had been neglected or improperly done. If this was thought to be the case, they were repeated.

The Gbaya have given up their traditional religious ceremonies with amazing rapidity. Only an occasional hunter, perhaps with one other participant, today performs a token ceremony. This has all but eliminated a whole range of speculation in the case of sickness, misfortune or death.

Certain bathing rites are still performed, evidently less often than formerly. In Thomas Christensen's chapter on Gbaya rites of reconciliation (pp. 197-211) and in Philip Noss's on Gbaya religious practice (131-51), the authors describe the **simbo** rite performed after the killing of a person, a leopard, or an eland. When a man on a journey has been unfaithful to his wife, he is supposed to undergo a ritual bathing. A pregnant woman who has been unfaithful to her husband is bathed by an old woman to insure a safe delivery. Immediately after the death of a child, the parents remain in the house and do not change their clothes while in mourning. When they emerge, an old person who knows how to perform the ceremony bathes them, and they discard their clothes of mourning. These rites need to be studied in greater depth to understand the Gbaya concepts surrounding them, what they may have in common, and their relation to Gbaya concepts of sickness. **Nding** 'dirtiness' is sometimes mentioned in relation to sickness or misfortune. Various explanations are given for this, such as literal dirtiness, the dirtiness of sorrow needing to be washed away, and dirtiness of the spirit resulting from sexual license. Bathing after mourning seems also to involve a hoped-for change of fortunes.

Gbaya often speak of seeking the "way" or "path" to honor God or to do something properly. Finding the "way" assures health and good fortune. Christian Gbaya have mentioned that they are not as meticulous about the way in which they worship God in the church as they were in traditional religion, at least not as regarding attention to detail in the rites and ceremonies. Gbaya today, Christian or not, do not attribute sickness or misfortune to improper honoring of God. But in some cases they will acknowledge that the sickness or misfortune may be caused by failure to observe one of the bathing rites.

When an underlying cause for sickness or misfortune is identified by Gbaya today, in a vast majority of cases it is thought to be social. Either the person is responsible for his own misfortune, or bad social relations are responsible, or evil individuals using witchcraft or sorcery are responsible in cases where jealousy and hatred can be observed.

Occasionally a Gbaya may be held to be directly responsible for his own misfortune or death. It might be said of an older child who had been persistently mean and unruly, looking for trouble, "The evil that he did came back and landed on his head."

When an infant dies of **gbeza,** the misdeed of one of the parents strikes back at them through their child. This disease illustrates the difficulty one encounters in trying to interpret a people's explanation of the cause of a disease as "naturalistic" versus "mystical" or "supernatural." The main symptom of **gbeza** is that the infant gasps for breath. The cause, according to the Gbaya, is that one of the infant's parents has had sexual relations with someone other than the spouse. This is a "naturalistic" cause in the Gbaya mind. A Westerner might consider it to be a "mystical" or "supernatural" cause unless he considers that the disease being described may be neonatal syphilis.

A person may become sick as a result of stealing or lying, but it is not the act alone that is believed to cause the sickness. If a person steals from a protected field, it is the medicine protecting the field that causes him to become sick.

When a person is suspected of having stolen something or of having killed a child by witchcraft or sorcery, he may be accused of the crime. Then, having gone with his accuser to a blacksmith, he will take hold with him of the blacksmith's iron, and swear by the iron that he is innocent. If he is actually guilty and does not have the blacksmith bathe him, he will develop severe diarrhea within two or three months, his body will "soften" and "redden," and he will die.[5] It is said that what kills him is shame, knowing that he has lied.

Deaths are more commonly attributed to bad family relationships than to witchcraft or sorcery. When the community observes that the members of a family "have not been living together well," that one had spoken harshly to another or about him, they will be blamed if he dies. If a child's parents have "spoken harsh words at him," and he dies, they will be blamed and warned that if they have another child

---

5 "Redden" means to take on a reddish or brownish hue. Women with low hemoglobin counts have this characteristic, as opposed to a darker skin tone.

they should treat him properly. A child may be blamed for the death of a parent by having neglected him or caused him heartache. A spouse will probably be blamed for the death of the other spouse if there have been harsh words and strife between them or if the wife has left her husband against his will. When bad relations exist within a family, another family member--even a child--might say, "You had better fix up the thing that is between you, because if one of you dies, the other will be blamed."

The Gbaya belief that neglect and a bad relationship could cause the death of a family member led to the widow-beating abhorred by missionaries and colonial administrators. Not every widow was beaten, although vindictive in-laws might attack an innocent widow. Likewise, husbands who had mistreated their wives, children who had given heartache to their parents, and parents who had not loved their children were blamed and beaten. Now that beating is no longer allowed, it has been replaced by railing at the guilty family members with harsh words. In contrast, a widow who has lived well with her departed spouse is honored after his death by rubbing oil with a red extract from camwood on her shins.

Incidents also occur in which one person threatens another quite openly with death and the second person becomes ill and dies. Or a man threatens a pregnant woman and she dies in childbirth. The one who made the threat may be believed by the community to have used witchcraft or sorcery to bring about the woman's death. Nevertheless, the participants and the unfolding of events are visible to the community, and such experiences confirm the existence of witchcraft and sorcery to the Gbaya people. Two examples may be cited.

In the first case the crops of a Gbaya evangelist were eaten by the cows of a Mbororo (Cattle Fulani) herder. The case was taken to court, and the Mbororo was ordered to pay damages to the Gbaya, which he did. But the Mbororo also threatened, in the presence of witnesses, "You will never use that money." The evangelist subsequently became ill with a terrible disease that rotted his body so that it stank even while he was still living, and he died. The community assumed that the Mbororo, who could not be found, had "done medicine," i.e., used sorcery against the evangelist, for the Mbororo are reputed to be good at this. In this case, the patient was not taken to either the local government hospital or the church dispensary, because it was assumed that it was not a disease for "white man's medicine."

The second example concerns a pregnant woman who resisted the advances of a man who was not her husband. He threatened that she would die, and is said to have done the sort of sorcery known as **sukang,** throwing needles into her body which entered at her temple and traveled to her uterus where they killed the child. The baby was born dead, and the mother died soon after. It is said that Gbaya men often kill women this way at the time of childbirth.

Skeptical Westerners are inclined to suggest coincidence in such cases. Another possible explanation, in keeping with our Western tendency to look for biochemical causes, comes from speculating on a case documented in Gustav Jahoda's The Psychology of Superstition. It concerns a Canadian woman who died unexpectedly after undergoing uncomplicated minor surgery. When she was five a fortuneteller had told her that she would die at age forty-three. Her forty-third birthday was a week before the operation, and she had told her sister and a nurse that she did not expect to survive the operation. "Post-mortem examination revealed extensive hemorrhage mainly of the adrenal glands, without any other pathology that might explain it" (1969:8-9).

The same book further relates experiments in which new rats were introduced into an established rat colony. The newcomers were attacked, and although the injuries sustained were light, many of the new rats died. "Post-mortem examination indicated that one of the organs most radically affected was the adrenal gland; it may well be, therefore, that such a response to intense stress is common to various mammals" (1969:9).

Western researchers and analysts have tried in various ways to explain the emergence and persistence of beliefs in witchcraft and sorcery in societies where these beliefs are held. Though not attempting to explain the beliefs, I might point out that it is not at all illogical in a society that perceives bad personal relations as causing sickness and death, and sees threats made that result in death, to believe that certain individuals who are hateful or jealous can cause sickness, misfortune and death through covert means.

Gbaya can give their own reasons for their beliefs in witchcraft and sorcery. One reason is that persons on occasion confess to having killed someone, or having tried to kill someone with witchcraft. Sometimes the confessions are under torture or threat of torture, but sometimes not. In one case a person went privately to his intended victim. He confessed that he had planned to use lightning to kill the other man, but said he was prevented from his evil deed because a dense fog surrounded the house so that he could not find it. In another case, all the residents of a village had been rubbed with medicine to determine who had been responsible for lightning striking and killed another person in the village. A man in the village later became sick, and before he died he confessed to the crime.

Another proof in the Gbaya mind is that when trials by poison were still allowed, poison was administered to those accused of having killed victims by means of witchcraft. If the accused was innocent, he would vomit the poison and live; if guilty, he would die from the poison. Seeing accused persons die in this manner was an impressive experience and taken as proof of witchcraft by Gbaya who witnessed it. After the death of an accused witch in a trial by poison, his abdomen would be cut open and the witchcraft substance would be searched for. If it was found, that was irrefutable proof of his guilt. If the witchcraft substance was not found, poison was administered to other candidates until one died and was found to have the substance. Then the matter was closed.

I thought that this would be one of the easier proofs to challenge and asked a Gbaya whether he had ever known anyone who had drunk the poison and lived. He responded yes he himself had been put on trial. He drank the poison, vomited, and lived. Astonished, I immediately asked if he had not been afraid. Of course he was not afraid, he said, because he knew that he was innocent.

There are the innumerable stories that any Gbaya can tell of incidents that can have no other explanation than that witchcraft or sorcery was at work. Coincidence is a feeble and implausible alternative. One of the most impressive I have heard is related in Ruth Christiansen's For the Heart of Africa. In March 1954, Paul Sippison, one of the Gbaya leaders in the young church, prepared to leave on a trip to meet with some missionaries.

> Before he left, Paul's wife, Nalau, pleaded with him not to go. She told him she had dreamed that a messenger had told her that Paul had been killed by lightning. He sympathized with her, but he did not waver. "Nalau," he said, "I am in God's hands; what is to happen will happen no matter where I am."
>
> He went. At Djousami, he stopped to rest. He wished to reach Meiganga that evening, but one of the catechumens

who was taking care of the outpost and whose wife was preparing their evening meal, wanted Paul to wait and eat with them. The two were conversing in the catechumen's living quarters, when suddenly a terrific discharge of lightning threw the catechumen's wife to the floor. She was unhurt, but frightened. She called to her husband and to Paul but received no answer. She went for help. When other men came and opened the door, they found Paul Sippisson and the catechumen, both dead, lying on the floor. Their clothes were burned badly (1956:216-17).

In trying to describe Gbaya beliefs in witchcraft and sorcery in the English language, one immediately confronts problems of terminology and categories. It would be more precise to use the Gbaya terms exclusively, but this makes for difficult reading for one who does not know Gbaya. The term sorcery and, even more so, the terms witch, witchcraft, and witchdoctor have negative connotations that the sensitive researcher would like to avoid. However, some standard terminology is required in order to discuss and compare the concepts between cultures using many different languages. Most anthropologists use the terms witchcraft and sorcery following Evans-Pritchard in his classic study, Witchcraft, Oracles and Magic among the Azande.

The Azande made the following distinctions between a witch and a sorcerer:

> Azande believe that some people are witches and can injure them in virtue of an inherent quality. A witch performs no rite, utters no spell, and possesses no medicines. An act of witchcraft is a psychic act. They believe also that sorcerers may do them ill by performing magic rites with bad medicines (1937:21).

> To Azande themselves the difference between a sorcerer and a witch is that the former uses the technique of magic and derives his power from medicines, while the latter acts without rites and spells and uses hereditary psycho-psychical power to attain his ends. Both alike are enemies of men (1937:387).

Among the Gbaya there are ordinary people, and then there are people who possess a special power, called **dua**.[6] **Dua** is a power passed by a mother who possesses it to her children, male and female. Anatomically, **dua** is something that can be

---

6 See "Ordinary and Extraordinary People," by Kombo Samuel (pp. 49-54) for further discussion of **dua**.

seen in the small intestine at postmortem examination of people who possess it. Various features of the abdominal anatomy have been described or suggested by researchers working elsewhere in Africa. Gbaya say this feature is found in chickens. A Gbaya who had just butchered a chicken showed me the **dua**--a closed branch of the small intestine.[7]

Dua is a power that ordinary individuals do not possess. One form is the **dua** that is said to "eat" people, and the Gbaya verb used is the same as the verb to eat food. The result in the victim is sickness and, if unchecked, death. Evidence that the Gbaya think of this in a literal way was found in a play presented at a church conference. Two characters, playing persons with **dua**, working together to try to kill a victim, put their mouths to the chest of the character playing the sleeping victim, and made chewing motions. (For a résumé of the complete skit, see the appendix.)

Ordinary Gbaya cannot tell exactly how a person with **dua** manages to eat a victim. It is said that the person with **dua** somehow gets a piece of his victim's liver, the seat of the emotions, cooks it and eats it. If it is a female person with **dua**, she may share it with her children. Some individuals have **dua** to gain wealth, ascribed to people to whom wealth comes easily. One form of **dua** enables its possessor to cause lightning to strike a victim. When this happens, or even when it strikes nearby, **dua** power is responsible. Another form of **dua** enables the person possessing it to turn into a snake or a dangerous animal in order to kill a victim. If a buffalo that has been shot by hunters turns on them, this may be taken as a reasonable reaction of the buffalo, but if an unprovoked buffalo charges, that is someone's **dua** at work. By itself, **dua** is not destructive; a diviner has **dua** but does not wish to harm people. He uses his **dua** to help people.

Dua, being a power which is inherited and which can be shown in an autopsy as an anatomical feature, fits the general category of witchcraft, with a person with **dua** being a witch. Considering the action of **dua** as psychic only does not quite fit, for as mentioned above, a physical act is at least sometimes thought by the Gbaya to be involved. In some places researchers report that a witch can be responsible for deaths without even knowing that he or she is a witch. I have not found any Gbaya who would admit, even unwittingly through roundabout questioning, that a person with **dua** might be act-

---

7 The **dua** in chickens or other animals does not "follow," i.e., seek out to cause harm to, humans.

ing without his own knowledge. Of them it was said, "They are conscious of the evil things they do, they are conscious of their evil words." The question is not completely closed in my mind, however, for I realize that I gathered my data from individuals with more self-confidence than some in the society.

Some researchers working in other parts of Africa have found that accused witches are usually women, and that diviners, in their function as witch-finders, are usually men. Other researchers report that witchcraft can operate only between certain kinship relations and is not allowed to exist within other relationships. Among the Gbaya, both persons with **dua** and diviners can be either men or women. Witchcraft can exist in any relationship in which the persons are known to one another, and in which one of them is a person with **dua**. The first place to look when witchcraft is suspected is within the immediate family. If the guilty party is not found there, one looks at the extended family and those living nearby. In former days, the extended family constituted the neighborhood, but this is not always the case today. After ruling out the neighbors, one looks among acquaintances, perhaps a coworker. The only exclusive aspect of **dua** is that it is passed from the mother to her children, both male and female. In other details, Gbaya beliefs about **dua** correspond with certain witchcraft beliefs in other parts of Africa, and with former and sometimes persisting European beliefs: that witches go out especially at night; that they often gather and work in groups; that they can identify other witches in the community; and, when swimming, more of their bodies than is natural remains above water.

Other descriptions given by Gbaya about the negative workings of **dua** provide an interesting comment on the psychology of individuals with destructive feelings and their effect in a community. One could say that the Gbaya, through their belief in witchcraft, have a stronger and more concrete concept of the power that jealousy and hatred have than do most technological societies.

There was a seeming lack of consensus among the Gbaya I talked with, or even with the same individual at different times, about whether a person with **dua** is a willing, or an unwilling participant. Some certainly are willing, they have a hunger for victims and keep alert for potential victims. One individual gave the analogy of a person with physical hunger passing another man's fields. Hunger compels him to take some food from the fields, and he returns to the village but does not tell what he has done. Hunger compelled him, but unless his body had joined with hunger, hunger alone could not have taken the food.

Some say that a person with **dua** may not want to eat victims, but when he tries to resist his **dua** it will keep on troubling him until it causes him to become sick. Others say, "People with **dua** do not want to eat people, but they 'get lost' (an idiom now used for erring or sinning)." Another explanation: "He may not want to kill; it may be lack of strength against the force of **dua** that is his problem. But he knows what he is doing. When he hates someone or covets something belonging to another, he becomes a murderer."

Members of a family where **dua** is known to exist are not feared if it is obvious that they are living peaceably with their neighbors, though one would be foolish to incite a disagreement with one of them. If a diviner is called in to find out who is the person with **dua** responsible for a sickness or death and the diviner names a good person that everyone knows, the community will not accept his verdict; they will say the diviner is lying.

When a community accepts as true an accusation that someone has used his **dua** to eat a victim, usually his hatred or jealousy has been obvious to them, at least when they think back on situations leading up to the accusation. In every case of witchcraft explained to me, there was a pre-existing situation of jealousy or hatred, or a confrontation between the victim and the accused witch. When children are victims of **dua**, it is said that the parent of the child was the true target; adults are often too difficult to kill, whereas children die more easily. Gbaya say that a person with **dua** who is eating people is not usually found out until he has not one, but many victims. This would certainly imply a great deal of caution on the part of the community in even accepting accusations made through divination. Sometimes, however, in situations where fear was great and emotions ran high, caution was forgotten and the person accused of killing another by means of **dua** was subjected to trial by poison. If he died but yet the anatomical feature providing **dua** was not found after his stomach had been cut open, the process was continued until someone died from the poison and was found to have **dua**. Caution might also be cast aside in the case of a sick person near death, whose recovery hinged on the diviner's being able to name the person with **dua** responsible.

Some persons with **dua** admit it openly and even make threats like, "I will kill you like a chicken." Many will keep away from such as that. Others praise them. But is is said that the persons with **dua** who threaten people openly are not very dangerous. The dangerous ones are those who hide it.

A person with **dua** cannot kill a victim for no reason, though it may be only that the other person was too successful. Needing a reason may cause the community to suggest an infraction on the part of the victim: someone is trying to kill that man because he once left his family and went off to spend some time in town.

Although ordinary people do not believe their unexpressed negative feelings and dreams about another could be manifestations of **dua**--for everyone has such feelings and dreams-- ordinary people may unwittingly aid a person with **dua** to find a victim. Persons with **dua** are always around, and always looking for victims, so they may take a negative statement an ordinary person makes about another as an excuse to kill him.

Whenever an enemy uses medicine to cause the sickness, misfortune, or death of another, this fits the standard definition of sorcery. This is not the same as using **dua** against a victim, but some Gbaya say that those who do use such medicines are persons with **dua**. Others say the medicines are different, and it does not necessarily have to be a person with **dua** who uses them. The names of some of these medicines have been borrowed from surrounding languages, and the Gbaya share some of the concepts with a number of other ethnic groups.

One of these, **koro,** is a Gbaya word meaning "rain." It is not the same as the **dua** that enables one to change into lightning but is described as a medicine that causes sudden death to its victims. Deaths such as falling from a mango tree, hemorrhaging from the nose, falling dead suddenly at the side of the path, anything that comes "as suddenly as being struck by lightning" may be attributed to **koro.**

Ngbatu, a Mbum word, is a form of sorcery known for a long time to the Gbaya. This medicine can be buried in or near an enemy's house to cause him sickness, misfortune, or depression. If this is the cause, a diviner can tell the victim and locate the **ngbatu.**

Sɔlɔpor or **sɔlɔk,** also a Mbum word, is a kind of sorcery which stops up the throat of the victim. One who knows how makes this medicine, wraps it in leaves, and holds it in his left hand. He waits for an opportunity to catch his victim alone on a bush path and strikes him with the medicine. The victim cannot talk or name his enemy. He returns home and will die unless treated by someone who knows the medicine to counteract sɔlɔp. When the victim drinks this medicine, he vomits the hair and ashes which have been stopping his throat.

Sukang, also a Mbum word, are needles, small bones, or other such objects thrown into the victim by one adept at this form of sorcery. A Gbaya diviner can extract them. Sometimes the physical manifestations of **sukang** are a prickling sort of pain, but deaths such as that of the pregnant woman and child previously described are also blamed on **sukang.** One can be an accidental victim to **sukang,** as when one happens to step between the sorcerer and the intended victim. Festival days, when there are crowds of people, including people of other ethnic groups, are times of danger from sorcery.

The neighboring Fulani have introduced **ginaazi** to the Gbaya. These are little devils or evil spirits that live in the bush. They especially like to catch victims who are alone in the bush at noonday or after dark. Seeing one can cause sudden insanity. Before the Gbaya learned about **ginaazi** from the Fulani, they would not have thought about being afraid alone in the bush, for they were hunters and gatherers. One of the tangled tales of sorcery explains how a local Gbaya man became mentally unbalanced. He had been a normal adult with a responsible position in a dairy, buying milk from Mbororo (Cattle Fulani) women. One day the Mbororo women became angry because they felt they were not being fairly paid. They did medicine to cause him to see a **ginaazi,** which unbalanced his mind.

Certain patterns can be seen in Gbaya concepts of witchcraft versus Gbaya concepts of sorcery. The only cases of witchcraft that I have collected operated within the Gbaya community. One informant said there was more **dua** when people lived in small communities, i.e., extended family grouping, but that there is less in towns where one sees everything, even metal roofs (a sign of a certain affluence). Cases of sorcery very often involve other ethnic groups, which are reported by the Gbaya to practice sorcery more than the Gbaya. Gbaya seldom have the same intense personal relationships with persons of other ethnic groups that they do within their own group, but there is often an underlying mistrust and suspicion of the other groups.

Gbaya medical practitioners

Certain Gbaya ailments are so common that nearly everyone knows a treatment for them, although treatments are by no means always the same. Among these are a plaster made from termite hills for the rash of measles, various medicines for whooping cough with the object of making the child vomit and clear the phlegm from his throat, medicines to ease cold symptoms, medicines to help sores to heal, and medicines to cause intestinal worms to die and be expelled in the feces. Many people know a plant or a bark to use in preparing medicine for the treatment of hepatitis. When a particular treatment is used and the patient recovers, the treatment is thought to be the correrct one. The reputation of particular medicines and healers is spread among the Gbaya by word of mouth.

Older women are especially skilled in the use of herbs and other pharmacopoeia from the bush. In former days if one sought out one of the older women in the family, or if she volunteered to treat a disease or injury, she was not paid in goods or money for her services, but a grateful patient, when recovered, would do a favor for her such as gathering firewood or drawing water. These days, when many Gbaya complain that everyone thinks about money, many of these women expect to be paid for their services, though the payment might be minimal if the patient is a member of the family. Other older women will say, "I'm giving this medicine free."

Professional medical practitioners fall into three categories: midwives (somewhat peripheral to this study); **wan yina** "Chief or master of medicine"; and **wan gbana** "Chief or master of the Gbana," a dance used in divination. To minimize confusion to the reader, I will refer to **wan yina** as "herbalists," although their medicines include treatments and are not limited to herbs. 'Medicine men' might be another translation, but to Western readers such a term would tend to connote only magical treatments. **Wan yina** (herbalists) are described by the Gbaya as "Our doctors before the (Western trained) **dokta** came."

I will refer to **wan gbana** as diviners. They are individuals who have chosen to use their **dua** constructively, to "see" the future, or the causes of sickness and misfortune. Gbaya say, "**Wan gbana** are our wise men" and "They know the deep thoughts of people." A compliment was paid to a missionary doctor when a Gbaya said, "White people do not have much

dua. Their **dua** is medicine. Dr. Jacobson is a **wan gbana.**" Diviners also treat the victims of witchcraft and sorcery.

There is often a crossing-over between the professions. An herbalist may assist at difficult childbirths, because a midwife ordinarily does not have many resources for dealing with complicated deliveries. One such herbalist, in the role of childbirth attendant, would do episiotomies when necessary. In the case of a breech presentation, he would lift the feet of the patient above her head. The infant would slip back into the womb and reportedly turn and come out head first as is normal. The child would die, but the mother would be saved, which was often not the case when a woman was unable to deliver a child in breech presentation.

Some herbalists, though not possessing **dua,** divine in other ways, examples of which have been already given in this paper. An herbalist may know specific medicines either to protect a person or to treat a victim of witchcraft or sorcery. Even though he cannot "see" the perpetrator of the crime, he may know the vengeance-medicine to bury on the grave of the victim to cause the death of the perpetrator. Or he may know the vengeance-medicine to rub on the inhabitants of a village to find who has caused death by lightning.

A diviner is often an herbalist as well, and may be a midwife, especially in the case of a female diviner. A diviner may begin medical practice as an herbalist, and later undergo the public ceremony and dance celebration directed by practicing diviners, in which the would-be diviner's **dua** shows itself by a violent jerking in the abdomen. It may be said of such a practitioner after years of experience, "He is a great **wan yina** and a great **wan gbana.**"

The categories are further complicated in that a Gbaya diviner has the power to kill, and some may do this as a service to a client. But when they do kill, it is said that they do not use their **dua** to "eat" the victim. Rather they kill him through the use of medicines, i.e., by sorcery.

Some herbalists and diviners seem to be born with their knowledge of healing and may express it as a gift from God. Others begin as apprentices to an experienced practitioner with whom they live and assist with his or her work. This practice seems to be dying out. An apprentice diviner would not need to have shown his **dua** before beginning to learn his trade, but is is assumed that he would always be a person with **dua.** Otherwise, he would be afraid to live in such a highly-charged atmosphere.

Once an herbalist or diviner has begun his practice, he expands his knowledge by exchanging information with other healers--even with Fulani **mallum**. Herbalists and diviners may on occasion turn down a case. They may look at a patient, see that nothing is going to cure him, and tell the family that they cannot treat him. Or a diviner may see that the cause of a person's illness is not sorcery, and tell the family to take the patient to an herbalist or to the dispensary.

All of these Gbaya professionals are paid for their services, and paid well in terms of the local economy, in cloth, other goods, and increasingly in cash. A diviner can command a particularly high payment. It is therefore surprising that the traditional healers do not appear wealthy by local standards. Some, in fact, appeared more poverty-stricken than their neighbors. One Gbaya explanation is that their practice is suffering with the popularity of Western medicine. Another is that old people are often eccentric--who can tell what they do with their money?

A subjective observation that I make, on admittedly slim evidence, is that the midwife and the herbalist that I got to know best both seemed eminently qualified for their work. The midwife is buxom, quiet, and capable, the type of person who instills confidence in others. The herbalist showed an uncommon solicitude toward small animals, children, and pregnant women. She is the type of woman who, when a small child climbs upon a sifter, worries that the child will fall, whereas another woman worries about the sifter. She is also the only Gbaya I saw who would greet and carry on a one-sided conversation with a severely-retarded adult in the community, exhibiting friendly interest and absolutely no condescension.

Madame Pauline, one of the three Gbaya who provided me with ethnographic data on sickness and healing, lived and worked with her grandfather, an herbalist, as she was growing up. She remembered and showed me many of the ingredients, method of preparation, and dosages of herbal treatments. She gave the following description, which I have translated freely, of her grandfather's work:

> I stayed with my grandfather and saw the medicine he did. When a person was ill, the family came to him and said a person of theirs was sick. And Grandfather said, "Bring him quickly so I can see which sickness it is."
>
> When he saw the sickness, he would say, "Yes, I'll treat it. You'll bring payment?" They would agree to bring

Healing among the Gbaya

ten cloths when the sickness was finished. And the sick person would stay with Grandfather. Grandfather would go out and gather things, put them on the fire, pour the medicine out, put it in the mouth of the person who was hurting. In the morning he brewed medicine, put it in his mouth. When evening came he brewed medicine, put it in his mouth over again. The next day he did it new, put it on the fire, gave it to the sick person morning and evening. We did it new over again like that. If we kept it, it would turn bad.

When that medicine was completely finished, Grandfather said, "It's finished, bring me the ten cloths. Oh, I see you are a cautious person, bring me just five." They brought five and thanked him and they were friends. They went out and gave testimony to others that their person had lived.

If a person had a lump in the stomach, Grandfather would put medicine on the fire, give it to them so that they would have a bowel movement and pass the lump onto the ground. Because in those days the medicine for a lump in the stomach was to make the person have a bowel movement. It was **barbar** that they put on the fire and drank.

Worms are different. When you have worms and eat food you vomit and vomit. For that you take roots of **hɔfi** and roots of **yoyo** and **dumba**. You put it on the fire, and drink it. It's very bitter. You don't eat anything until afternoon.... The medicine did its work inside you like that along, until you passed them on the ground. Then in the afternoon you could take food.

Grandfather had hepatitis medicine.[8] When it was in the eyes, that showed it was hepatitis. They brought the person and Grandfather did hepatitis medicine because not all people did that medicine. The medicine is **borndong**. You shave the bark but you don't touch it with your hands. You hold it with another stick. You put it on a pot on the fire, not in the house, at the edge of the clearing.[9] You pour it out with a dipper. You put it in the mouth of the

8 The whites of the eyes of a hepatitis patient take on a yellowish cast.

9 On another occasion Madame Pauline explained that the reason for the care in handling the bark was regard for cleanliness. The reason the medicine was made in the yard and not on the cooking fire in the house was that it was thought that if smoke from the medicine preparation got in the eyes of another person, he or she would become ill with hepatitis as well.

sick person. He urinates on the ground and urinates the essence of the sickness on the ground too. You do that about three times and the person will be a lot better.[10]

When Madame Pauline demonstrated the preparation of herbal medicines she had learned from her grandfather, the majority were made from roots of grasses or plants, from whole small plants, or from the bark or inner bark of trees. If bark was used, it was sometimes scraped and the scrapings worked with the hand under water, then the liquid strained. More often the ingredients were put into a pot of water on the fire, singly or in combination, and were boiled vigorously for ten to fifteen minutes. The liquid was then strained and cooled.

There is a growing renewal of respect in the Western world today for many traditional herbal medicines that do have pharmacologically effective components. As with other aspects of Gbaya beliefs about disease, knowledge is based on experience. Not every patient who recovers does so because of the effect of the medicine given him, although this is a misconception not confined to the Gbaya. Nevertheless, skilled and experienced herbalists no doubt have discovered and made use of efficacious herbs.

As for a diviner, an important part of his treatment of patients is "seeing" and telling them the underlying cause of their illness. Gbaya diviners use a variety of physical objects with which to see: they may gaze into a calabash of water, they may throw porcupine quills or pieces of cane and study how they fall, they may make marks in the dust. But it is actually the diviner's **dua** that gives him the power to see, and as has been mentioned, he knows the deep thoughts of people. The diviner questions his patient about his dreams and knows where the tensions lie in the community.

Diviners sometimes announce a dance to which people can come and ask advice on matters troubling them, including sickness and misfortune. The mood on such occasions is rather lighthearted. A person may consult a diviner privately or publicly. When a person is gravely ill and close to death, and a diviner is called in, "then there is no laughter." Sometimes a dance is part of the naming process, sometimes not. The guilty person may be named or only indicated.

When someone is named as being responsible for the sickness of a client, there are several options. A diviner may counsel the client to repair the broken relationship. A

---

10 Madame Pauline, recorded in Meiganga, Cameroun, December 1976.

family member, such as the husband of a patient, may go to the family of the person suspected and discreetly suggest that if there is anything between them, they should consider it forgiven. He may mention that his wife is not feeling very well and is not sure what the problem is. If there has been a confrontation between the patient and the suspected person, the husband may mention that his wife is feeling a bit troubled about the exchange and would like to give the suspected person a small gift as a goodwill token.

Some families are more direct and will confront the person named with the fact that they know what he is doing. The patient's family threaten that if their family member dies, the guilty person or persons will have to pay or else he will be killed. The other party may be intimidated into repairing the relationship, or at least stop "eating" the victim.

Even knowing who is responsible may somewhat relieve the patient's mind; for he has suspected that someone hated him enough, or was jealous enough to want him dead, but he has not been sure who it is

Once a victim has died, there is less attempt than formerly to pursue the one responsible. Trials by poison are no longer allowed, and vengeance medicine does not require naming the person responsible.

The diviner also practices medicine to counteract witchcraft or sorcery. A Westerner might think that antiwitchcraft or antisorcery medicine practiced by a diviner is conscious manipulation on his part. A Gbaya with ambivalent feelings toward diviners says, "When they give medicine to me and I recover, they say it is the medicine they did that made me recover." Without being able to prove it, I suspect that both diviners and herbalists often do believe that it was the medicine they "did" that resulted in the recovery or change of fortunes, and that they may choose a similar pattern of therapy in the future in similar circumstances. The Gbaya talk about seeking "the way" in matters of medicine, just as they talk about seeking "the way" to properly worship God.

I knew of a team of practitioners, a female diviner married to an herbalist, who spent three days trying to work out the proper treatment for a nephew and his wife whose firstborn twins had died shortly after birth. Despite inconvenience to the family, the healers hesitated and changed their minds about the ingredients needed for the medicine, which was at first to include dirt from the twins' grave and a chicken. I was later assured by several people that the only reason for the delay would have been the healers' honest searching for the correct medicine. In the end the treatment included bathing the young couple, who were supposed to leave the clothes, shoes, and any jewelry they had been wearing at the time of the deaths at the site of the bathing. As it actually worked out, the husband's brother substituted a worn-out shirt for the shirt the husband had been wearing. The young wife was also instructed never again to greet people by the hand, the usual Gbaya manner of greeting. I was told that this injunction was common enough that other Gbaya, noting that she did not greet them by a handclasp, would know it was because of medicine. If she was fearful for the welfare of future babies, she would be careful to keep the injunction. But if she forgot and greeted someone by the hand and a baby subsequently died, her act would be thought to be the cause. This young couple later became the parents of a healthy baby, proving that the medicine was effective.

Further remarks

The Gbaya advise Westerners working among them that it is only wasted effort to try to talk them out of their beliefs in witchcraft and sorcery. Witchcraft and sorcery are things they see. And as a Gbaya remarked, "If you say you do not have a mat and I can see you have a mat, what am I to think?" Even though the government's outlawing of trials by poison for accused witches had the effect of "allowing deep water to cover the evil-doers,"[11] Christians find comfort in the fact that even witches die, and hope that in any specific instance of witchcraft God may be stronger. Christian Gbaya find some pleasure in the missionary teaching that evil people will have to pay for their deeds after death.

A fundamental question poses itself. What is the relation between the existence of tensions in interpersonal relationships and sickness or misfortune? It may be true that people who do not have biochemical explanations for disease, but are in need of some kind of explanation, find explanations in the existing interpersonal tensions. It may also be true that witchcraft claims exist because some people in the society have found that other individuals are more easily intimidated than themselves. Perhaps Western medicine needs to pay more attention to the effect of interpersonal relations on health. Gbaya say, "If the house (i.e., household) does not sit well,

---

11 The most recent trial by poison that I know about in the Meiganga area was held in the village of Meidougou in 1960.

nothing goes well." As was suggested in this study, the Gbaya, through their beliefs in witchcraft and sorcery, have a strong conceptualization of the power for destruction in situations involving jealousy and hatred. This is an insight that should not be dismissed.

There is a problem, however, for the Western practitioner who might want to try to deal with this question in the African context. I asked a Gbaya who is director of a dispensary whether he would ever suggest to a patient who exhibited a great deal of fear, that the patient should remedy any bad relations that might exist between himself and another person. The director replied that he would not make such a suggestion because of the danger of "false accusations" and that he feared that tensions would thereby be increased.

Gbaya acceptance of Western medicine as one of several medical options that they may try in case of sickness has been mentioned. Western medicine enjoys a generally good reputation as an option, because it often works. Still, it is clear that traditional practitioners often have more time for dealing personally with patients, for bathing a feverish child, or a midwife helping a new mother until she regains her strength. The traditional practitioner often deals with the tensions and fears that are troubling the patient's mind. It is very difficult to duplicate this aspect of care in the overcrowded hospitals and dispensaries serving the Gbaya. Praying with a patient before surgery in a mission hospital is one way of responding to the broader needs of the patient. Some Western practitioners are more careful than others to give their patients explanations of causes and treatments. This is the reason given by Gbaya for preferring one medical facility over another in a community where two Western facilities exist.

Even though Western treatment of sickness is accepted, Western teaching about the biochemical causes of sickness is not so easily accepted, even when presented by a respected member of their own culture. Experience disproves the logic that microbes on flies' feet carry sickness to uncovered food, which will cause the person eating the food to become ill. Gbaya know very well that they will not throw out food that a fly has landed on, and usually no one who eats it gets sick. I asked then why they do cover their food, and the answer was, "In order to keep it warm." Everyone in the community drinks the same amoeba-infested water, and yet only some people at certain times become ill--so where is the proof that amoeba cause illness? Western health workers will have to present more convincing evidence of their claim that flies bring disease.

Appendix

[Summary of a skit given on the occasion of the dedication of the church at Lokoti, Cameroun, April 2, 1978.]

There was a man who had a wife and four children. There were two persons with **dua**. There was a diviner. There was another woman. The man who had four children went hunting and killed an antelope. They came back. His wife cried, "Oh father oi! We found food." They danced the antelope dance. They butchered the antelope and put it on the fire. They prepared lots of cassava to go with it. They ate it with their children. They did not give any to the persons with **dua**. Then night fell.

The other woman (without **dua**) went to the house of the person with **dua**. She said the man had not shared the antelope meat, the person with **dua** should kill him. The other person with **dua** said to the first, "Yes, let us go. We will kill him together because he is an important man."

The persons with **dua** arrived at the man's house. Everyone was sleeping. One said, "Whom shall we kill? The wife? The children?"

The other one said, "The woman said we should kill the man."

The man was sleeping. The persons with **dua** put their mouths on the sleeping man's chest and made chewing motions. When they had finished eating, the persons with **dua** left. (A child crowed like a rooster to signal dawn.)

The man whom the persons with **dua** had eaten began to be sick. He said, "Ho, my liver is hurting. My head is splitting."

They called a diviner. They said, "Our father is sick. What is hurting our father? Look for this thing."

The diviner said, "I did not bring my things for divining here. I left my things for seeing in town." They brought his things for divining to him.

They gave money. They played the drum. He began to do the divining dance. He said, "It is the antelope that you killed and did not share. That is why someone is eating you."

The diviner said, "It was the woman who caused them to eat you."

The children said, "What shall we do so that our father may live?"

The diviner said, "I will go back. I will seek medicine that I can do for him."

Then suddenly the sick man's older brother appeared. Someone had been sent to tell him his brother was sick. The older brother scolded the wife. They called the diviner to come. But when the diviner heard that the older brother had come, he ran away. He was afraid the older brother would do something bad to him because he had lied.

After the diviner had run away, they took the sick man to the dispensary. (End of skit.)

--As related by Daniel Soldea, April 1978.

References

R. Christiansen. For the Heart of Africa. Minneapolis: Augsburg Publishing House, 1956.

E.E. Evans-Pritchard. Witchcraft, Oracles and Magic among the Azande. Oxford: The Clarendon Press, 1937.

G. Jahoda. The Psychology of Superstition. London: Allen Lane, 1969.

D. Morley. Paediatric Priorities in the Developing World. London: Butterworth, 1973.

An elderly Gbaya woman

10. Tradition and Modernism on Horseback

by Badomo André

Colonialism came and taught its modern ways to Africa, but after the passage of time, tradition has begun to reexamine its cultural heritage to draw the best aspects of custom from it. The child of Africa and the child of colonialism are human beings; and both are unable to abolish one or the other way of life, for both ways are intelligent and useful, especially in this era of materialism when everyone wants to be his own master. Therefore, in order to accommodate their march toward the future, the two have borrowed the same horse and ride together in dialog.

Totem

According to ancestral convention, Gbaya social organization was based on totems to which the Gbaya were subject and to which they continue to be subject. In spite of the times and pressures of modernism, the Gbaya have not abandoned the totem.

There are many Gbaya with different dialects and varying speech styles. There are the Gbaya Yaayuwee, the Gbaya Lai, the Gbaya Kaka, Gbaya Gãāmona, Gbaya Bangando, and the Gbaya Poro, to name only a few. But all are subject to the totem, the taboo that forbids eating a certain animal or a part of the animal. There are ten main forbidden animals, each associated with a clan:

Clan	Totem
Bugui	Hippopotamus

Clan	Totem
Bogani	Lion
Bofɔrɔ	Elephant
Botana	Tortoise
Boŋgɔya	Wild boar
Bokɛɛ	Mouse
Bogbata	Hare
Bolati	Leopard
Bonaafio	Heron

Each of these groups is a clan; but within a clan two groups are distinguished, the **nam** and the **koo-wi**. The first is the paternal relationship according to the totem of the father's clan. All those in this group have the same taboo, and the members of the various subgroups of each clan may marry each other. The second term refers to the blood relationship through the mother, which is referred to specifically as **nyak-zang-dua** meaning "the lineage of the intestinal alliance of sorcery." It is this relationship which is the more strict, both relating to supernatural things and to marriage. For example, sorcery is most powerful when it is blood relatives who act together. Likewise in marriage, members of different subgroups of a clan may marry, but members of a blood relationship may not marry even if they are members of different clans. A member of the Bugui clan may not marry someone of the Bokɛɛ clan who is related to him through birth, whereas a member of the Bugui clan may marry someone related through his father who is also a member of the Bugui clan. When two members of the same clan have married each other, a pot is placed upside down on top of their house as a symbol of their marriage within the clan.

Looking briefly at the Bible, we note God's command in Leviticus 18:6, "None of you shall approach anyone near of kin to him to uncover nakedness." The system of social order which our ancestors followed and which we continue to follow was established before the arrival of the gospel of Christ among us; yet the two are parallel.

Ethics

Ethics can be said to be the instruction that teaches the rules to follow in order to do good and to avoid doing evil. This instruction took place for the most part during one's youth in initiations divided according to sex. There was also a means of providing coeducation among adults.

Tradition and Modernism 101

LaBi was the male initiation whose purpose was moral instruction for the young men of the tribe, guiding them into a spirit of physical and intellectual work. The young men were taught that courage was indispensable for well-being. They were taught to defend themselves against attack from other peoples, to be generous toward all human beings, and to live and speak properly in their own society as well as in a strange society.

Zaabɔlɔ was the girls' initiation. Its purpose was to teach homemaking, how to avoid divorce, and to understand that a woman's relationship with society would be judged on the basis of her character. As she grew up, the girl was taught that her goal should be to have a successful home life, for that was what society was based on, since the education of a people and of a nation begins in the home. She was taught to obey all the taboos and to know the value of traditional medicines.

In the evenings beside the fire, tales, riddles, proverbs, and legends were a means of teaching values to all levels of society. The tales were created by intellectuals who were not recognized except after an event about which they created a tale. The tales, proverbs, and riddles were born out of daily events in people's lives. But since the era of forced labor and the more recent arrival of modernism, the initiations have ended and the role of tales has become less significant. The transmission of ideas through the creation of tales has virtually ceased.

Traditionally in Africa and especially among the Gbaya, ethics fell into three categories:

1) Loving one's fellows, whether they were of the clan, the tribe, the land, or were outsiders.

2) Having sympathy for one's fellow. The African in general is a person gifted with a spirit of sympathy, but this was more generally true in the past than after the arrival of the white man.

3) Helping one another. Mutual help was and remains the guiding principle in African society and especially among the Gbaya. "If you don't look after your fellow, the Creator God won't look after you," said the elders; and the Bible says, "So whatever you wish that men would do to you, do so to them; for this is the law and the prophets" (Matt. 7:12).

Marriage

Marriage is the legal union of a man and a woman. "If you don't get seeds, you'll be a beggar when the heavy rains come," said the fathers. Marriage among the Gbaya is praiseworthy when it has been properly arranged by the two young people and by their parents according to the steps outlined below.

Searching for a wife is the task performed by the relatives of the young man, his father, his mother, his father's sister, or a grandparent worthy of the name. The young man may also take part in the search, although at a slight distance. This search is primarily based on the character, the life, the social relationships, and the family background of the girl. As far as beauty is concerned, that does not hold major importance in Gbaya marriage.

Observing the girl is the second step and it is one of major importance. The adage says, "You best look at the woman, lest later you regret." This is the time when the parents take their responsibility to heart and establish contact with the girl's family, and many are the questions that are asked in the surroundings of the potential in-laws.

Throwing the **kana,** the first part of the brideprice, is the basic step in marriage and is considered to be a solemn declaration of the young man's love for the girl. This declaration must be recognized by her parents, for, as the saying goes, "Accepting the gift means accepting the suitor." The boy's request for the girl must be taken seriously, and from the time of the gift he is put to the test.

The test that the girl's parents give the young suitor takes the form of brideservice. It involves physical labor and is a time when the young man and the girl's family get to know each other. It is the time when the young man demonstrates his willingness to work by observing all the taboos and by working hard and eating little.

Following the brideservice comes the request for the girl's hand. The family of the boy asks the girl's family to kindly give them the girl. This request is made without the girl's knowledge, but the boy will be aware of it. The delegation that goes to ask for her is usually made up of three or four persons, such as the mother of the boy, an aunt, the grandmother, and sometimes an uncle. If the girl's parents refuse the request, they must return the brideprice.

Tradition and Modernism

Leading the wife away is the culmination of the scheme that the parents of the couple have woven against the girl. The girl struggles physically against her abductors in refusal to leave her own family and join another. It is a serious fight between the girl and those who accompany her. In any case, it appears to her parents as though she does not want to leave them.

The installation of the bride in her own home is the last step. It is a ceremony carried out by three people, the couple and the boy's mother. It lasts three days and includes first the nuptial meal which is vegetable sauce and couscous. During this time, the couple is forbidden to eat meat of any kind. They are closed up for three days to keep them safe from any possible harm that might cause even a drop of blood to be spilled, for that would be a violation of the prayer for fertility. Since taboos also play a part in fertility, these taboos have an effect both on the girl and on the fertility of her womb and on her family.

That was traditional marriage, but marriage today is nothing more than an episode in life that has little significance and that allows itself to be broken without great import. Marriage is merely a means for a liaison to enrich oneself. Marriage today is the symbol of selfish love in contrast with the love of traditional marriage.

Work

Work is the effort, the action, involved in doing something. It is applying oneself to fulfilling a project. According to the fathers, "Laziness doesn't find a corpse." The lazy hunter will not make a kill.

There are so many different kinds of work that it would not be possible to name them all. In general, the various aspects of work are reflected in tales, legends, dramatic poems, and love poems; for it is in them that society depicts its intellectual being, its artistic being, its ethics, and many other aspects of its life.

The tales, riddles, proverbs, and legends present the art of building a house or a bridge, the art of fishing and hunting, of discovering medicinal plants, and of communicating with wild animals. In these tales, one finds that the wife is a good potter, an excellent homemaker, and a very faithful wife to her husband, because selfish love would be destructive.

In the whole area of work there was cooperation, without specific restrictions of time, in order to defend the home, the clan, and the village against any disaster that might strike: famine, illness, or attacks by other people.

Old age

Old age is the last step of life. Among the Gbaya, a person is considered old when he is around seventy-five years of age. He is considered the depositary of much knowledge in the areas of science known by the ancestors, in social life, and in experience of every kind. "The aged is the bag of protection," we say. His relationships hold with all levels of society. Never is he insulted, because his curse may have immediate effect. Old age is happy when it has a large number of family members. For the old person, to be alone is hell. The man who never married, the old Gbaya says, is a man who has fallen short.

Ancestral teachings are a law of supreme importance for the old Gbaya. He believes in God and counsels the next generation. For the most part, the Gbaya is a good storyteller who can tell about events he has experienced; he gives birth to tales, legends, and proverbs in which instruction is never lacking. Thus, the old person communicates ethics in teaching children, who are the pillars of the future generation; and he communicates the value of good work, which is the source of happiness for society. The old person considers every thief to be an enemy.

The old person loves to live in his birthplace, in the arms of his son. The old couple have an exemplary home, they are peacemakers in family affairs. "If you listen to the advice of an old person, his cane will remain in your hand" is an ancient saying.

The death of an aged person is a festive time for everyone because he lived a long time and has now "gone home." The death celebration takes place in two stages. The first includes the three days after the death, and the second is the funeral a year or two later, depending on when the family sets the date. The mourning ceremonies reflect the life of the old person. The hunting dance, the warrior dance, initiation dances, dramatic scenes, the fire in the yard, all portray the actions and deeds of the old person who just died. As the saying goes, "Consider the death of the aged, and do the same." That is, in reviewing his life, may it be an example for you.

Religion

By definition, religion is the worship rendered in faith to a divinity. The Gbaya have two forms of worship.

Sɔ-daa is the divinity of the fathers. It is invoked by the father of the family or, in his absence, by the oldest son. The ceremony takes place behind the house at a special fireplace at a fixed time, near nightfall. The meat most often used is a fish, the bullhead. If a chicken is used, it is the mother's brother or his son who attends and performs the ceremony. When the prayer relates to life in general, a chicken is sacrificed, but if it relates to hunting, a fish may be offered. No woman, no matter what her social status or age, may participate in the ceremony.

Sɔ-kao is the celestial divinity who is worshiped to ensure the well-being of society. The ceremony is performed by all the leaders of the clans in a particular village. It is held some distance from the village at the foot of a hill, at the foot of a tall tree, or beside a rock. The reason for choosing the particular place is that **Sɔ-kao** created the hill or the tree or the rock to be greater than all the others, and this greatness is taken to be a reflection of the Creator. The prayer of the people is that

> the women will have many children in the coming year,
> the fields will yield abundantly,
> the village will be peaceful and calm,
> the population will be bathed in good health,
> and everything will progress in peace.

The **Sɔ-daa** are then the intermediaries between a family and the Creator God who is **Sɔ-daa;** and when a person dies, his soul goes to join the God who created him.

Today **Sɔ-daa** are still invoked among Gbaya who are hunters or farmers, but in general this form of worship has been abandoned. However, many who no longer know the ancient formula regret that it has been lost. The worship of **Sɔ-kao** is no longer practiced except by a few of the clan leaders who do so individually.

African culture in general, and Camerounian culture in particular, suffered from the first steps of the invader who came as a bearer of modern life with the Bible in his hand and a flexible sword under his tongue. The culture of the African prince and his entourage was savage, the invader said, and he imprisoned the culture of the people and banished it in order to implant his four seasons, autumn, winter, spring, and summer everywhere he went.

But African seasons refused to be banished, and the blood that circulates in us as much as the seasons do remained faithful to what we were. Today, the seasons and the blood continue to search for what was best in the last steps of a perishing way of life, as tradition dies under the repeated accusation that it is savage. Meanwhile, the Gospel writer would say, "Judge not, that you be not judged" (Matt. 7:1).

- - - - - -

I had lit my fire
  before my hut filled with gaiety;
Around it were seated
  sheep, leopard, lion, goat,
  all together in a domestic spirit.

A white speck burst forth from the opposite shore.
It was the arrival of a fisherman with a pole
  for a thousand hooks;
On the edge of the forest it was the arrival of a
  woodcutter with a flexible axe on his shoulder;
At the lookouts on the savannah it was the arrival
  of a hunter with an iron flyswatter.

He disembarked before my hut,
  asked me to show him my home.
I told him it was here.
Everything is savage here
  he said about all and in all and for all.

I sent everything into the water of the river
  and of the sea:
Excellent canoeman, excellent diver,
  he gathered all.
I threw everything into the trees of the forest;
Swift woodcutter, he searched everywhere.
I abandoned things in the bush;
Able hunter, he brought it all down, game for his bag,
Everything that was called savage
  by him the white cat.

Coming back with a smile under his moustache
  to tell me that I was civilized now;
Then naked without my bow and arrow
  he invited me into his noisy canoe,
far from the shore that was home to me.

Dive and come close, he said to me,
  with hands outstretched.
I cannot swim far from here, I said;
Without quiver and bow you are civilized like me;
Do not be afraid that you will drown.
I believed, I dived, I swallowed the first mouthful
  under the piercing eyes of the white cat
With the smile under his moustache: he sees me
  drowning, he continues to smile, arms half-stretched.
He sent me a canoe--with holes in it.

The tree of the chained dugout
  was the tall tree which was behind my house;
He even forced me physically to seize the tree
  through the effort of my arms.
The Romans in passage through this place
  in writing the fourteenth chapter
  in the line of verse thirteen said:
So then, let us stop judging one another.
Instead this is what you should decide:
Not to do anything that would make your brother
  stumble or fall into sin.

                                    Badomo Beloko André

Part II

Faith and Belief

Everything Tries

The plants grow up, up, up;
They try hard to reach for it
But it is too high for them.
The mountains try;
They are in the heights;
They try, it is hard,
They cannot; they stay like they are.
The birds go up, up,
But not high enough;
They get tired,
They come back down tired, unhappy.
The fish live in the depths of the waters;
They never stop looking where they can.
Even the chickens give thanks
Once the water is in their throats.
The praying mantis always prays for food.
Everything tries for
          HEAVEN!

                    Haldor Jon Noss

Introduction

> Think not that I have come to abolish the law and the prophets; I have come not to abolish them but to fulfil them.
>
> Matthew 5:17 (RSV)

Traditional African thought affirmed the existence of God, and the fathers handed down a faith that included tenets of belief and forms of worship. What is the significance of these traditional beliefs and rites for the Christian church? What is the relationship of the spiritual possessions of African cultures to the truths of gospel revelation?

In the first chapter of this section of the book, a historical survey of the Sudan Mission is presented by an anthropologist who portrays both the commitment of the early missionaries to their call and the broader social, economic, and political aspects of their work, of which they were only partially aware. The author's questions of what the Gbaya really believe and whether the church will be able to play an effective role in the future are the implicit theme of the remaining chapters of the book.

The Gbaya, being very pragmatic about their lifestyle and their religion, adopted Christianity as an alternative and as a supplement to their traditional way of life. Some of the problems faced by the young church are described in "An Interpretation of Gbaya Religious Practice." The next chapter describes Islam, a society which, unlike the Gbaya, is exclusive rather than inclusive; Ronald Nelson's "Social Pressure for Religious Conformity" shows the strength of Islam as a religious and social structure in holding the faithful together against the encroachment of other practices and religions, including Christianity.

Too often the story of Christianity in Africa has been one of encounter and conflict. Traditional religion has been seen as inimical to the gospel, and the early missionary and the early African Christian alike combatted heathen beliefs and practices with zeal and fervor. However, in his own mind, the African Christian frequently retained much of what his fathers had taught him, for it still had meaning and it was still relevant to his life. There was truth in the spiritual legacy his fathers had bequeathed to him.

The last seven chapters in the book are treatments of specific Chamba and Gbaya topics in which the writers, one a Camerounian student, one a missionary theologian, and one a missionary linguist, seek to bring together African tradition and the gospel into a partnership that is not syncretism, but fulfillment.

Bouba Bernard's argument in "The Chamba Rite of Vɔɔma" is that the Chamba concept of God may be clarified by the Christian understanding of the Trinity. He explains the significance of a traditional rite by saying that it was given by the Creator God to enable man to combat evil and to live together in harmony.

The dominant rite in Gbaya society was the boys' initiation known as **laBi**. Christensen describes the rite and underscores its significance for Christian thought as a covenant. The concept of a new birth and a covenant relationship is central to the ancient rite of initiation. The church offers a new covenant in Christ. Is it not legitimate to understand baptism as a rite of new birth and initiation into God's kingdom?

A frequent theme in folktales and in ritual is that of discord within society. What is important in daily life is man's relationship with his fellow, for how can he injure an almighty God? Traditional life included numerous rites for restoring broken relationships; and Christensen, in describing them, maintains that the Christian message and the Christian church must respond to the needs of Gbaya society. The gospel must be brought into Gbaya tradition both through its symbols and through its rites.

At the level of myth and story there are many universals. But in the account of Wanto and Crocodile, a Gbaya pastor sees an immediate correlation between Gbaya tradition and the Bible, suggesting that the Gbaya tale bears the same message and is, in fact, the Old Testament story of Joseph. Christen-

Introduction

sen, in the following chapter, demonstrates the similarity of proverbial themes in biblical and Gbaya thought.

The final chapter, "Karnu: Witchdoctor or Prophet?" by Christensen, poses an intriguing and difficult question to Western Christianity. It is a question of God's revelation to man, for in reading the two accounts of Karnu's life, the European "historical" statement and the Gbaya oral account, the question "Who was Karnu?" cannot be escaped. The question is relevant today because Karnu and the events surrounding his life and his death have become legend and myth within the Christian community. His message is considered to have been prophecy. Can the Christian church accept, as the Gbaya Christians themselves have already done, that Karnu might have been a Gbaya John the Baptist? What does Christ mean when he says that he has not come to abolish but to fulfill?

Christian layman leading Christmas service at Balkosa, Cameroun

11. The Gbaya and the Sudan Mission: 1924 to the Present

by Philip Burnham

This article is based on more than two years of anthropological field research among the Gbaya and the other peoples of Meiganga subprefecture in Cameroun, begun in 1968 and continued intermittently since then.[1] This field research brought me into touch with the approximately fifty American Protestant and French Catholic missionaries who live and work in the Meiganga region and who are virtually its only inhabitants from Western countries. These missionaries were very helpful in introducing me to the area and in aiding me with the many logistic problems that one encounters while working in such a rural African region. On a personal plane, I have made many friends in the missions, and I am much indebted to the missionaries for their friendship and hospitality.

Missionary life in Meiganga subprefecture formed a part of my research topic, for the days are long past when one might attempt to study an African people like the Gbaya as if they existed in isolation from their wider social and political surroundings. This is especially true with regard to the relations between the Gbaya and the missionaries of the Sudan Mission; for as the title of this article indicates, this

1 My initial field research in Cameroun spanned a twenty-one month period from 1968 to 1970. Since that time, I have returned for three shorter visits totalling ten months in 1973, 1974, and 1980. This research was financed by the University of California at Los Angeles, the WennerGren Foundation, the Social Science Research Council of Great Britain, and the Hayter Fund of the University of London. Thus far, the results of this research have appeared in Burnham 1972a, 1972b, 1975, 1979a, 1979b, and 1980. Other anthropological studies of the Gbaya people include Hilberth 1962 and Tessmann 1934 and 1937.

contact has lasted for more than fifty years and, in many respects, has constituted the Gbaya's most significant and enduring contact with Western culture. I have therefore counted it as a part of my job as an anthropologist to try to understand as much as possible about mission society beliefs and history in relation to the missionary effort among the Gbaya. Missionaries from both the Protestant and Catholic missions have been understanding enough to be open with me about their work and their motivations, and I in turn have tried to be as frank as possible about my approach to mission work as a topic for anthropological study. For example, in 1969 the Sudan Mission was kind enough to invite me to speak at their annual conference, and at that time I had the opportunity to discuss a number of topics I shall treat in the present paper.

I recognize that, for many missionaries, such an anthropological study is flawed from the outset by its questioning approach toward religious motivations and its unwillingness to rank Christianity as a form of belief system superior to other religious systems--Gbaya traditional beliefs or Islam, for example. Nevertheless, despite such differences in approach, I hope that those missionaries who read what follows will accept that it represents a sincere attempt on my part to analyze the encounter between the Gbaya and the Sudan Mission as I have been able to document and observe it.

Gbaya Life: Historical and Social Background

Through travelers' accounts, oral histories of the Gbaya themselves, and other sources, we are able to push our historical knowledge of the Gbaya back to about 1840.[2] During the nineteenth century, Gbaya society consisted of many small groupings of families, scattered thinly over the savanna, that were loosely organized into territorially defined units containing several hundred people. The organization of these clan territories was largely based on ties of patrilineal kinship among their inhabitants; and, although Gbaya society of this period had no real chiefs, each territory had a leader who led his warriors on raids against other groups, organized the defense of the territory, and conducted the group's other external affairs such as intergroup trading expeditions. But political organization and leadership among the Gbaya were quite fluid, and the allegiances and locations of the independent hamlets shifted frequently. The Gbaya

---

2 Burnham 1980.

The Gbaya and the Sudan Mission 117

agricultural economy of this period was oriented largely toward subsistence, with manioc serving as the main crop and hunting playing an important role.

As early as 1840, the Gbaya came into contact with the invading armies of Muslim Fulani who had penetrated northern Cameroun from Nigeria following the declaration of a Muslim holy war by Usman dan Fodio, a Fulani leader. Initial Fulani contact with the Gbaya was either in the form of slave raids by the mailed Fulani horsemen against the small Gbaya hamlets or in the form of trade between Gbaya groups and Muslim traders for such commodities as slaves, ivory, and kola nuts. Gbaya war leaders themselves soon became involved in slave raiding and slave trading and were able to increase their power among their own people by paying tribute to Fulani chiefs and receiving in return weapons, horses, cloth, and other prestige goods which they could distribute to their supporters.[3] Along with this Fulani contact came Islam, which was adopted by Gbaya leaders and a few other men but which seems not to have influenced the beliefs of the majority of the Gbaya people very deeply.

Gbaya religion of the precolonial and early colonial periods can best be described as a collection of separate rites and beliefs, including sacrifices to a man's immediate male and female ancestors, group sacrifices to a spirit specific to the locality where each Gbaya group lived, and a number of other rites oriented towards the achievement of success or good fortune in undertakings such as hunting, warfare, or relations between the sexes. Beliefs in witchcraft were prominent and provided the basis for interpretation of misfortunes such as lightning striking a village, death, sickness, and interpersonal quarrels. Several initiation ceremonies were also important in Gbaya life and served to train both men and women for later life while also marking the stages in their social and intellectual development.[4] But one of the most important facts about Gbaya religious and intellectual life was the extent to which beliefs might vary from group to group and from individual to individual. Gbaya society lacked priests or other full-time specialists to formulate religious doctrine. There were no national cults or shrines that might stabilize Gbaya religious activity and belief. And aside from the initiation groups which themselves were transitory, there

---

3 Burnham 1979b.
4 Vidal 1976 provides the most complete description of Gbaya initiation ceremonies.

were no churches or other forms of religious or educational congregation to standardize or propagate religious and other cultural beliefs. Certain individuals, due to their age or personal inclinations, acted as witchcraft diviners or organizers of sacrifices for the community on occasion, but organization and leadership in Gbaya religious practice were just as fluid and variable as the shifting hamlet groups in which the Gbaya lived.

This character of individualism has always been a marked quality of the Gbaya belief system and continues to characterize it right up to the present day. This has meant that Gbaya religion has always been able to adopt or accommodate to alien religious beliefs easily, without social trauma. Since, to a large extent, every man's beliefs are his own business, the content of Gbaya religion can change substantially. Even formal conversion to another religion can take place without producing marked conflicts or contradictions within Gbaya society and culture. A feature of the Gbaya religious scene today that never fails to amaze outside observers is the frequency with which single families may contain members of more than one religion without experiencing conflicts.

By 1924, the date when the Protestant missionaries first encountered the Gbaya in the Meiganga area, the Gbaya had been living in close relation with the Muslim Fulani for at least seventy years. Since the establishment of colonial rule in the 1890s, the Fulani had, if anything, increased their political influence over the Gbaya. Although warfare was now outlawed, the Fulani political system was used by the German colonizers and their successors, the French, as a means of administering the Gbaya, in particular for collecting taxes. No European colonial administrators were permanently present in the Meiganga region until 1929, and so the Muslim Fulani lifestyle served as a dominant model for Gbaya culture change in this early period.

The first Protestant missionaries were drawn to the Gbaya and to the Meiganga area largely because of the sociopolitical situation described above.[5] To Missionary Gunderson and his several coworkers who founded the Sudan Mission in the Meiganga area, the Gbaya appeared as a largely "heathen" people who, resenting the domination of the Muslim Fulani, would

---

5 Christiansen 1956 gives an interesting account of the early years of mission work in the Meiganga area.

The Gbaya and the Sudan Mission   119

convert willingly to Christianity as an evident salvation not only for their afterlives, but for their daily lives as well. In the main, this judgment has not proved mistaken over the years, and comprehension of this fact is a necessary element in understanding the continuing Gbaya "nationalism" displayed both by the Protestant Gbaya and the American Protestant missionaries in Meiganga even today. However, Gunderson perhaps underestimated the political force of the opposing Muslim Fulani system; and particularly in the early years of mission work, progress was slow.

Another important element in the history of the Protestant mission among the Gbaya has been the fact that the mission was a "faith mission" for more than half of its total existence. This is to say, the missionaries who worked among the Gbaya did not derive financial support from any larger mission organization at home in the United States and had to depend for their finances on contributions from individuals and congregations with whom they were in personal touch. The 1930s and 1940s were very trying decades for the mission from a financial point of view, and the early missionaries had very limited material resources at their disposal. The most important result of this financial situation was that the early missionaries lived a lifestyle that was relatively close to that of their African hosts, with much the same food, habitation, and means of transport. There was little money available for mission activities of the institutional sort, such as schools, hospitals, or economic development projects. The early mission work was mainly concerned with direct evangelism and with limited literacy work in the Gbaya language to give access to the Scriptures. Such an orientation was not solely the result of weak mission finances, of course. Evangelism was the overriding personal "call" of all the early mission workers, and their willingness to expose themselves to material hardship was seen as a form of witnessing to their missionary zeal and faith.

Given the social and political conditions in which they were working, it is not surprising that the bulk of the Protestant missionaries' early success was among the nonpowerful members of the Gbaya society--that is to say, among the women and the young. Indeed, although in the modern day approximately one-half of the total Gbaya population count themselves as Christians, most converts continue to be drawn from among these categories; and the adult Gbaya men who are practicing Christians have, for the most part, grown up in the Christian faith. From an economic or political point of view, there appear to have been very few reasons why an adult Gbaya man would have converted to Christianity in the early days of the mission effort; and although this situation has modified somewhat at present, the scales are still tilted in favor of Islam because of its close ties with centers of economic and political power within Cameroun.

Economic and political development in the Meiganga region got under way very slowly in the 1930s and 1940s. The Meiganga subprefecture with its European staff was established in 1929, thus reducing direct Fulani political influence. A few small European gold mining operations were started in the mid 1930s; they employed several hundred Gbaya. The extension of the motor road network in the 1940s and early 1950s also aided the development of the local market economy. But the Gbaya were touched only slowly by such modern influences and remained content for the most part to pursue their traditional life in this rural, out-of-the-way corner of Cameroun. Meiganga town itself, the largest in the 17,000-square-kilometer district, probably counts no more than six to seven thousand permanent inhabitants even today, and labor migration of young men to the distant larger towns and cities of Cameroun has never been an important influence in the area.

After the Second World War, a major new element was injected into the religious picture in the Meiganga area with the foundation of the French Catholic mission. From the outset, the character of the Catholic mission work was considerably different from that of the Protestants, with particular stress being placed on education at the primary, secondary, and occupational training levels. Direct evangelism received less emphasis than it did in the Sudan Mission, but it is difficult to judge whether these differences were more the result of different mission philosophies or were due to the fact that the Protestant mission was already so well entrenched among the Gbaya. The rate of Gbaya conversion to Catholicism was small at first, but today has grown substantially. Yet, the Protestant mission still continues to benefit greatly from its much longer association with the Gbaya. Despite the significance of the Catholic mission effort among the Gbaya as a comparative case, I do not have the space to consider it here; what follows relates specifically to the Sudan Mission and its work.

The pace of change quickened in the 1950s and 1960s as the Gbaya became more and more involved in the cash economy via sales of manioc and maize, their main crops. In the Protestant mission field, an important development was the link-up

The Gbaya and the Sudan Mission   121

in the 1950s between the Sudan Mission and the Evangelical Lutheran Church and later the American Lutheran Church in the United States, a move which gave the mission a firm financial base but which also ended its independent status and made it answerable ultimately to the American Lutheran Church Board of World Missions in Minneapolis. With this increase in financial backing, the Sudan Mission was able to expand its activities significantly and improve the standard of living of its missionaries. Missionaries were now paid a regular salary and vehicle allowance, and better schooling became available for their children. Many new mission buildings were built, and the quality of missionary housing was improved. During the 1950s, a hospital was built and staffed at Garoua Boulai. The system of French language schools was expanded. And in 1958, a theological seminary was founded at Meiganga to train African pastors.

Nonetheless, the mission lost little of its evangelistic orientation. Most of the missionaries in the 1950s and early 1960s shared the goals of the mission founders and viewed these new mission activities primarily in terms of their effectiveness in winning converts. Certain of the older missionaries, for example, maintained a strong opposition to the founding of French language school, considering literacy in Gbaya adequate for diffusion of the Gospel. Pressure to modify this relatively fundamentalist view of mission work has never been strong within the mission and has only emerged as a significant force in the last fifteen years, both as a result of the recruitment of younger missionaries and the economic development orientations of outside bodies such as the American Lutheran Church Mission Board and the Lutheran World Federation in Geneva, Switzerland.

Whatever the exact motivations for this significant expansion of facilities and the mission's visible physical plant, the fact remains that in the last fifteen years the Sudan Mission has become a much more bureaucratic organization. By the late 1960s, most missionaries spent their time working in offices, surrounded by small groups of educated Gbaya pastors and other African workers. The mission station in Meiganga has grown into what is virtually a small town of its own, with the spacious landscaped mission grounds surrounded by the houses of Gbaya Christians and situated on a separate hill away from the rest of the town.

A major element in these changes has been the growing pressure for an independent African church, a development that has arisen relatively recently along with secular pressures to Africanize institutions. The establishment of the Meiganga Theological Seminary was a necessary step in this development; and as Gbaya pastors have been ordained, they have replaced American missionaries in the direct evangelism work, especially in the outlying towns and villages. Also important was the establishment in 1961 of "The Evangelical Lutheran Church of Cameroun and the Central African Republic," the institutional basis for the gradual shifting of control from the mission to the Africans themselves.

Having sketched in very broad terms the major historical factors that serve as indispensable background for the understanding of the Gbaya experience of Christian mission work over the last half century, I now want to turn to the analysis of some of the main sociological and ideological factors affecting Gbaya Protestants in Meiganga today. For the sake of convenience, I have grouped these factors under four headings; although it must be emphasized that for the Gbaya themselves, all these elements are seen to be linked as a complex whole.

The mission "call" and missionary conservatism

As already noted, the missionaries who joined the Sudan Mission from its inception up until very recently have been motivated by a personal "call" to mission service that was quite narrowly and explicitly defined in terms of the evangelization of the "heathen" Gbaya. The personal nature of the "call" was accentuated by the "faith mission" character of the undertaking, since the missionaries who joined the Sudan Mission prior to its association with the American Lutheran Church were very much aware that they could not count on the support of a large organization back home and that they had to rely to a large extent on their personal determination and conviction to carry out the mission work. From the start, therefore, the Sudan Mission has been stamped with this individualistic quality. The charismatic power of the personality of Missionary Gunderson and several other early leaders counteracted these individualistic tendencies to a certain extent; but ultimately, the concept of the personal call provided an incontrovertible rationale for each missionary to engage in a very personalized form of evangelism if he so desired. In practice, the personal call to mission work often led to individual missionaries setting themselves up in a particular Gbaya locale and becoming intimately associated with the local population over a long period. In relation to the overall mission work, such missionaries became almost

The Gbaya and the Sudan Mission   123

free agents in their own districts, since they could resist any efforts by the mission to transfer them by invoking their personal call to continue working in the same district. I should emphasize that I am not calling into question the sincerity of the motivations which led many of the faith missionaries to adopt such a personalized style of mission work. I am simply attempting to show that as a logical consequence of a certain form of religious motivation, the social relations between the Protestant missionaries and the Gbaya assumed a particular form, that of the long-serving missionary controlling his own personal "flock."

For the most part, the missionaries of the Sudan Mission derive from uniform social and regional origins, that of lower middle-class rural or small-town families of Scandinavian or Germanic origins in the American Midwest, and the conservative morality of this group was transmitted to the Gbaya hand in hand with their Christianity. The dominant American missionary working within his local Gbaya parish could maintain an extremely strict surveillance of the behavior of his catechumens, and baptism was granted to adults only on the basis of exemplary records. The early missionaries took an uncompromisingly negative view of traditional Gbaya culture, as exemplified by their unwillingness up until very recently even to incorporate traditional Gbaya melodies into their church liturgy. Such a common and socially important African custom as drinking beer was combatted with prohibitionist ardor. The missionary point of view with regard to the changes that their work might produce among the Gbaya was essentially a protective one; the missionaries felt that they were attempting to introduce the Gbaya to what they judged to be the morally positive side of Western civilization while avoiding or insulating against the materialistic and morally "bad" effects of the Western contact.

The combined effects of bureaucratization of the missionaries' work and the progressive Africanization of the parish evangelism have consequently been difficult for the older faith missionaries to accept. While wishing the budding African church all possible success, the missionaries often judge the young church's teething troubles to be the result of a relaxation of moral standards rather than the substitution of one culture's moral principles with another's. Moved from parish work to office jobs in the central mission stations, the faith missionaries find themselves engaged in so much paper work, disputes among African teachers, and many other administrative problems that they have difficulty relating to their original personal mission call. One major result of this new situation is a developing restlessness among older missionaries that has translated itself into attempts to set up new evangelization efforts among ethnic groups less touched by Christianity than the Gbaya. But the main resolution of this conflict will inevitably be the progressive replacement of the aging faith missionaries by younger mission workers more in agreement with the modern nature of mission work in postcolonial Africa.

Gbaya "nationalism" and Christianity

The decision of Missionary Gunderson and his coworkers to orient their efforts chiefly toward the Gbaya, who were judged to be a "heathen" people exploited by the Muslim Fulani and therefore ripe for conversion, has fundamentally influenced the work of the Sudan Mission in Meiganga ever since. The early missionaries, for example, rapidly set to work learning the Gbaya language and translating Christian literature, judging correctly that to approach the Gbaya using their own language would symbolize the missionaries' commitment to the Gbaya people. The Gbaya understood this message; and even though political and economic realities weighed against the mass conversion of the Gbaya to Christianity, even those who remained Muslim clearly appreciated this missionary gesture as a statement of the equal worth of Gbaya culture compared with that of the Muslim Fulani.

What the missionaries have never fully come to grips with is the highly political nature of their choice to approach the Gbaya under these conditions and in this way. The Gbaya read the missionary message as an offer of a totally different style of life and not just a different religion and system of morality. The promise of political and economic change was implicit in the missionary message, for the rejection of the Muslim Fulani domination by a Gbaya necessarily implied a decision to embark toward a new style of life. For a person unfamiliar with West Africa, the extent to which a person's religion is intimately connected with so many facets of his secular life is difficult to imagine. A man's religion is often reflected in his choice of name, of clothes, of language, of employment, of schooling, of health care, of political allegiance, as well as in other aspects, large and small, of his lifestyle. Indeed, many early Gbaya converts to Christianity interpreted the missionaries' insistence on a strict moral code in essentially political terms. As a "pil-

The Gbaya and the Sudan Mission   125

lar" of the Meiganga church explained to me, "Even the Muslim Fulani respect Protestants (by implication, more than they respect Catholics who are considered to be less strict in adhering to the moral code of their religion) because they have so many rules to follow. That is why we keep the rules strict even today."

The faith missionaries, with their "other-worldly" aims, had no particular desire or capacity to cope with this political phenomenon. Unlike French Catholic missionaries who felt able to involve themselves in the politics of a French colony, the Americans preferred to adopt the stance of "rendering unto Caesar...." Today, with Africanization of the church, Protestant Gbaya see their young church in Meiganga as a "Gbaya church"; and, as such, it should defend Gbaya interests, whether these be related to religion or not, they feel. This political orientation is accentuated by the fact that traditional Gbaya society contained no such large-scale, well-structured organizations capable of pursuing collective interests over the longer term, and the Gbaya Protestant Church has begun to assume such a role in the modern day.

Economic development and Christianity

Although the Gbaya themselves have used the Mission as a political vehicle, many of them can understand why the American missionaries declined to play an active political role. However, this is not true when it comes to the matter of economic development and opportunity. In the minds of the Gbaya, the American mission effort is inextricably linked with the more general phenomenon of the introduction of Western civilization into the Meiganga region. As the mission became better financed and the living standards of the missionaries rose, a wealth of modern technology in the form of automobiles, generators, washing machines, refrigerators, power tools, and brick homes was displayed daily in front of Gbaya eyes. Taking Christianity to represent a whole style of life which included these things, the Gbaya simply have never understood why the missionaries were unwilling to share their knowledge and wealth with them. In objective terms, of course, we can understand that no matter how open-handed or development oriented the mission had been, it could never have fully satisfied the wants created in Gbaya minds as a result of their contact with the Western economic system.

But this is not really the point. By consciously ignoring the socioeconomic side of Gbaya life, the mission threw away the opportunity to aid in the development of a Gbaya peasantry able to respond to the economic requirements and possibilities of present-day Cameroun. The Gbaya economy, even though it is now monetized to a great extent, remains today at a technological level very comparable to that of precolonial days. Gbaya incomes are low and are certainly insufficient to provide the necessary financial base for an independent African church. Moreover, up until comparatively recently, the missionaries made no real effort to create and train a group of Gbaya church leaders who would have the administrative skills, and would receive sufficiently large salaries, to deal with the economic realities confronting the church in the context of modernizing Cameroun. Such a one-sided approach to mission work, even though it conformed to the principles of the faith missionaries themselves, has left the young church in a very weak position to face the future. And the question of who will foot the bills of an independent African church is far from being solved.

The transmission of Christianity in modern Gbaya society

With Africanization of the church and the change in missionary roles from that of parish pastor and evangelist to that of administrative functionary and teacher, the missionaries have looked to Gbaya pastors to take on the main work of religious teaching in the local communities. But this strategy has not been a resounding success, and much of the blame for these difficulties must be attributed to the missionaries' inadequacy in dealing with the realities of Gbaya socioeconomic life. Having dragged their heels for many years in setting up mission schools with the full French-language primary school curriculum, it was only to be expected that the missionaries would experience difficulty in finding sufficiently well-educated Christian Gbaya to enter their theological seminary. An apt, if painful, comparison can be made between the Sudan Mission's inadequate early education policy and that of the Sudan Interior Mission and other Protestant groups working at a similar date and in similar social conditions in northern Nigeria. Today, mission-educated Protestants provide much of northern Nigeria's intellectual and political leadership, and a strong pastorate has been built on these much firmer educational foundations.

Of those relatively few Gbaya who have the qualifications to become pastors, only a small proportion are attracted to this profession because of its inadequate pay and the greater appeal of other careers. The marked disparity between mis-

The Gbaya and the Sudan Mission   127

sionary incomes and those of Gbaya pastors is also an embarrassment and source of friction, although in many missionaries' eyes, the missionaries are seen to be making financial and material sacrifices in their own lives and the same is expected of the Gbaya pastors. In other terms, the missionary argument that the independent African church cannot afford to pay more to its pastors is objectively quite true, yet it ignores the fact of the missionaries' unwillingness throughout most of their history in Cameroun to assist significantly in the economic development of Gbaya society and to establish a sound economic basis for the founding of the African church. The tangible results of these socioeconomic policies of the Sudan Mission are all too obvious and include continuing problems of recruitment at the seminary, a number of cases of unauthorized use of church funds by Gbaya pastors, pressure on catechumens awaiting baptism to work for the personal benefit of certain pastors in their gardens and fields, and grossly inadequate pastoral contact between certain Gbaya ministers and their congregations.

To a large measure, except in the largest Gbaya towns, the day-to-day work of religious teaching and pastoral care thus tends to fall on the shoulders of the village catechists, a generally enthusiastic group of lay Christians who, in some cases, manage to carry out their duties fairly effectively despite their minimal degree of education and Christian training and their often difficult economic and social circumstances. A complete analysis of the role of the catechist in Gbaya villages would require a separate chapter, and only a few of the more significant elements can be sketched out here. To begin with, most catechists, although Gbaya themselves, are not natives of the villages in which they work. Although this practice can be justified in terms of an attempt to avoid nepotic practices or latent political conflicts that might emerge in the catechist's home village, the alternative is at least as bad since it distances the catechist from the necessary support of his own kin, makes him an easy target for tensions and disputes in the village where he is located, and makes it more difficult for him to earn an adequate living. Economic constraints often significantly reduce the effectiveness of a catechist in such conditions because, without a kin group to provide economic assistance and with virtually no salary, a catechist must work doubly hard to make ends meet. The lack of anything more than a notional salary also labels the catechist as an essentially unimportant person in Gbaya eyes since, in the modern context, the Gbaya tend to associate wealth with social significance. Only catechists of exceptional personality and character can hope to overcome these handicaps.

The low level of education of Gbaya catechists, the majority of whom have attended a few years of primary school and/or a short Bible school course at best, is another factor of capital importance in relation to the transmission of Christian doctrine in village contexts. Some Gbaya catechists read even the Bible translated in Gbaya so poorly that the Sunday scripture reading cannot be adequately understood by the congregation. The catechists' Sunday sermons, although notionally related to a Biblical passage, have for their major content a general moral commentary on village events based as much on Gbaya concepts of morality as on Christian precepts. To give a concrete example of the very incomplete transmission of Christian doctrine in Gbaya villages, I was quite astonished to find Gbaya catechists who were unable to recount the Easter story accurately nor explain the implications of the Easter events for Christian teaching.

The questions at issue here, then, are the content and transmission of Christian doctrine to Gbaya villagers. Sociologically speaking, it is apparent that the church has only weak control over the doctrine it transmits and this largely because of the missionaries' neglect of the social, economic, and political factors in Gbaya life which affect this transmission. As explained earlier, the Gbaya have never had a highly integrated set of religious beliefs; Gbaya religion is quite variable from region to region and has always been a mixed set of ideas borrowed hither and yon from neighboring peoples. The early faith missionaries attempted to counteract this fluidity of belief by an unbending insistence on the practice of Christian morality as they understood it and by close personal supervision of their congregations. But they failed to institute social structures among the Gbaya that could replicate such a uniform religious system in the missionaries' absence, and so, in the end, Christian beliefs have been thrown into the melting pot along with all the rest. A favorite Gbaya oath, **Nin Sɔ, Allah, Jezu!** 'In the names of the Gbaya God, the Muslim God Allah, and Jesus!', demonstrates clearly that the Gbaya take no chances.

It is at the village level and in relation to the average Christian Gbaya's understanding and practice of Christianity that the Sudan Mission's evangelization effort must ultimately be judged. At present, Christianity in Gbaya villages is often reduced to adherence to formal behavioral conventions associated by the Gbaya with the practice of Protestantism, such as relatively lavish contributions to local church conferences, actions which, while having important meaning for the Gbaya in the political, economic, and social fields, bear only indirect relation to the goals of the American missionaries who converted them. These facts are often largely invisible to most of the modern missionaries, who live insulated on the large central mission stations surrounded by a very biased sample of the more educated and/or the most dependent of the mission converts. Ventures outside the confines of the mission grounds may occasionally bring the modern missionary face to face with the reality of Gbaya Christian life in the form of brusque comments to missionaries at a church conference or villagers' refusal to accept a certain catechist; but these unpleasant experiences are frequently interpreted by missionaries as personal ingratitude or as examples of backsliding from the missionaries' idealized model of what a Gbaya Christian should do and believe, rather than as symptoms of the much more fundamental socioeconomic problems facing the Gbaya church.

To some extent, the arrival of younger missionaries in the last fifteen years has helped the mission to become more aware of such problems, and the present volume is a remarkable symbol of this fact. But it is not possible to undo the errors of more than fifty years in this short time. And the hour is very late for the missionaries, for the independent African church has already embarked on its own path with weak finances, weak training, and weak leadership; and the missionaries find themselves less and less able to influence developments. The Gbaya church in Meiganga is no longer at the stage where the dominant question was, "What should the Gbaya believe?" The important questions now are, "What do the Gbaya believe?" and "Will the Gbaya church be able to play an effective role in the future?"

Bibliography

Philip Burnham. 1972a. "Racial Classifications and Ideology in the Meiganga Region: North Cameroon" in Race and Social Differences, ed. by P. Baxter and B. Sansom. Harmondsworth: Penguin Books.

------. 1972b. Residential Organization and Social Change among the Gbaya of Meiganga, Cameroon. Ph.D. dissertation, University of California at Los Angeles. Ann Arbor: University Microfilms.

------. 1975. "Regroupement and Mobile Societies: Two Cameroon Cases." *Journal of African History*, 16:577-94.

------. 1979a. "Permissive Ecology and Structural Conservatism in Gbaya Society." In *Social and Ecological Systems*, ed. by P. Burnham and R. Ellen. Association of Social Anthropologists Monograph 18. London: Academic Press.

------. 1979b. "Raiders and Traders in Adamawa." In *Asian and African Systems of Slavery*, ed. by Watson. Oxford: Basil Blackwell and Mott.

------. 1980. *Opportunity and Constraint in a Savanna Society: the Gbaya of Meiganga, Cameroon*. London: Academic Press.

Christiansen, R. 1956. *For the Heart of Africa*. Minneapolis: Augsburg Publishing House.

Hilberth, J. 1962. *Les Gbaya*. Studia Ethnographica Upsaliensia 19. Lund: Ohlssons Boktryckeri.

Tessmann, G. 1934. *Die Baja: Materielle une seelische Kultur*. Vol. 1 Stuttgart: Strecker und Schröder.

------. 1937. *Die Baja: Geistige Kultur*. Vol. 2 Stuttgart: Strecker und Schröder.

Vidal, P. 1976. *Garçons et Filles*. Recherches Oubanguiennes 4. Nanterre: Service de publication du laboratoire d'ethnologie et de sociologie comparative de l'Université de Paris 10.

12. An Interpretation of Gbaya Religious Practice*

by Philip Noss

Man's religion is a reflection of his questions and his needs. Although basic similarities in belief and mores occur among different culture groups, there are also differences in both general philosophy and specific practice. In order to communicate the Christian message to another people or to understand their adoption of Christianity, it is necessary to understand the basic premises of their traditional religion.[1]

I

Central to the thought and life of the Gbaya of Cameroun and the Central African Republic is the concept of sɔ̃. Günter Tessmann, a German traveler and writer of the early part of this century, begins his discussion of Gbaya religion by suggesting two categories of sɔ̃ (1937:1):

> The Gbaya call God **sô or**--in order to distinguish him from the spirits who are also called **sô--gba-sô,** that is, Great Spirit.

Jean Hilberth, a Swedish missionary writing much more recently, notes the same ambiguity in the term sɔ̃ (1962:67-68):

---

* Previously published in International Review of Missions 61:357-74 (1972).
1 I would express my gratitude to Rev. Paul Darman and Mr. Kombo Samuel for comments and examples provided during discussion of the topics dealt with in this chapter. To Rev. André Yadji and Mr. Daniel Sodea my appreciation for the information and prayers provided for the ceremonies described. All translations in the text are mine.

So is at the same time a common noun and a proper noun. As a common noun it designates the genies without other names or with proper names who inhabit the forests, savannahs, large trees, river sources and mountains.

So--or **Gbaso**--is a proper noun translated by the first Europeans who came in contact with the Gbaya as God.

Both writers recognize a division of **sɔ** into two categories, on the one hand a single God or Great Spirit, and on the other, spirits or genies.

Both writers mention a spirit called **Gbasɔ**. In early Gbaya thought, **Gbasɔ** may indeed have been the supreme God, the God of creation, the Father of Man, as both Tessmann and Hilberth write; but in current belief this is no longer true. Oral tradition today depicts **Gbasɔ** as a vicious creature of the gallery forest or the plains, which are both considered uninhabitable by man, the former because it is wet, cold, and unhealthy, the latter because plains are without water. From his dwelling place he comes to seize game that others have killed or to devour women and children who stray into his domain. He is the enemy of society in tales representing the powers that would destroy life itself (Noss 1971).

The name **Gbasɔ** also appears in riddles, sometimes referring to a godlike personage, but often merely in reference to a fictitious subject. Tessmann cites several riddles about **Gbasɔ,** among them the following (1937: 221-22):

When **Gbasɔ** goes for a walk, all know it. What is it?
Answer: A year passes and everyone knows it.

Gbasɔ's road goes everywhere. What is it?
Answer: Water.

Gbasɔ sits up there and when he shoots his gun, he doesn't kill any animal down here. What is it?
Answer: The coming of rain, i.e., thunder.

The supernatural may be implied in these riddles about **Gbasɔ**, but the riddle is essentially a form of fun and amusement. The proverb, of a more serious nature, rarely if ever includes reference to **Gbasɔ** or to **Sɔ**.

On the basis of this evidence, **Gbasɔ** may be excluded when considering Gbaya concepts of God. Instead of **Gbasɔ**, the Gbaya today speak of **Sɔ** or **Sɔ-e-wi** 'God-place-man', the great God responsible for the universe and all that is in it, the Creator God whose origin, according to Tessmann, is not known (1937:1):

Gbaya Religious Practice

Regarding the origin of God, the Gbaya can give nothing specific: he must always have been.

Popular etymology, however, links the name Sɔ with the verb sɔ 'to ooze; to smear'. The first meaning is used for something which boils or oozes out such as the secretion which an earthworm emits forming a mud ball on the ground. The image is not beautiful, but it does effectively convey the notion of a God who creates himself. As an entity or as a person, he may have had a beginning through self-creation, but the power necessary for creation was already in existence, and in that sense Tessmann is correct.

Other folk etymology associates God's name with his eternal existence. If part of the bark of a mimosa tree is sliced off, sap oozes out filling the cut. No matter how many times the sap is scraped off, it always oozes out again. In the same way, it is explained, God never ends.

Within the realm of the supernatural, there was a limited hierarchical structure with Sɔ unique and alone at the top. Below him were the other categories of sɔ, the sɔ-kao first and below them the sɔ-daa.

Sɔ-kao were the gods or spirits of nature, the spirits of the world about us, the spirits associated with outstanding and inexplicable wonders of nature, tall trees, great hills, large pools, and massive rock formations. The term itself, **kao**, is considered by the Gbaya of Cameroun to be of Mbum origin meaning 'earth, land.' It is also, however, maintained that the concept of **sɔ-kao** is very ancient, predating Gbaya association with the Mbum, and Hilberth's observation that the Gbaya-Kala around Bouar in the Central African Republic recognize **Kao** as a "spirit who rules over the savannahs, the forests and the rivers" would tend to support this claim (1962:69). **Kao** is action, he writes, reigning over and protecting fish, game, and produce, so that fisherman, hunter, and farmer alike must pay homage to him. Hilberth treats him as a single spirit while the Gbaya Yaayuwee of Cameroun consider **kao** to be many spirits, or perhaps many manifestations of one Great Spirit.

Sɔ-daa were the spirits closest to man, the spirits of the departed ancestors. Life, while man lived, was a dichotomy of ɔmi 'breath' and **dan-tɛ** 'life essence'. ɔmi was the physical aspect of breathing which ceased when a man dies, while **dan-tɛ** was the abstract quality that is life, the quality that departed at death. The etymology of **dan-tɛ** is two words, **dan**

'friend, companion' and **tɛ** 'body', or literally, 'friend-body'. Thus, **danɜtɛ** is that which accompanies a body in which there is breath.[2]

The spiritual counterpart of **dan-tɛ** was **sɔ̃-tɛ** from the words **sɔ̃** 'spirit, god' and **tɛ** 'body' or 'spirit-body'. At death **dan-tɛ** departed, but man continued to exist as **sɔ̃-tɛ**. This distinction between **dan-tɛ** and **sɔ̃-tɛ** differentiates between the essence of life before and after death, the temporal and the eternal, the <u>Lebensseele</u> and <u>Totensseele</u>, respectively (cf. Jensen 1963:281).

Joseph Ndongué, the son of a traditional Gbaya priest in Djohong, suggests, however, that the two terms were synonymous. One can say that at death either a man's **dan-tɛ** has departed or that his **sɔ̃-tɛ** has departed, with no difference in meaning, he maintains. When man dies, he simply becomes **sɔ̃**. "You will go home as spirit" was a common threat or curse that meant that the person so addressed would die before reaching home. His **sɔ̃**, his spirit, would continue on to his home alone. But this distinction is blurred by the usage of both **sɔ̃-tɛ** and **sɔ̃** to refer to man's deepest emotions:

> My **sɔ̃-tɛ** doesn't like things like that.
> My **sɔ̃-tɛ** hates that very much.
> My **sɔ̃** likes that very much.

Sɔ̃ is used in these expressions for positive emotion and **sɔ̃-tɛ** for negative emotion. But regardless of the precise definition of **sɔ̃-tɛ**, the term did signify the spiritual or divine quality of life that existed in man, perhaps before, and certainly after, death.

In addition to the three facets of life mentioned above, there were two others, **giỹɔ-tɛ** and **hɔɔ-tɛ**. **Giỹɔ-tɛ** 'shadow-body' was man's shadow, but it also embodied something of man's essence sometimes thought to be his **sɔ̃-tɛ**. "One does not fool with another's shadow" was an accepted principle. To pretend to injure or mutilate a man's shadow was to threaten his very existence, evidenced by the fact that after death there remained no shadow.

Hɔɔ-tɛ might be translated 'phantom'. It was an aspect of man that could go wandering while a person slept. It might be encountered by others some distance from the sleeping person, but when spoken to, it would not answer. If it did speak, the

---

2 See also S. Kombo's chapter "Ordinary and Extraordinary People" in this volume.

person hearing its voice would die. Those who saw it would rush back to the sleeping person₃ and beat him with certain branches; otherwise, he would die.[3]

A dead man's image was also occasionally seen, but that was said to be his **sɔ̃-tɛ**. Like the phantom, if it spoke, the person spoken to died. Normally, however, a dead man's spirit was not visible even though it was present. For at death a man was not gone, he had simply gone on a journey. Before he was buried, his wife might hold the corner of the mat on which his body lay and wish him a good journey, but his departure was only from his former physical state to a non-physical existence. He continued to live near his home and to influence the affairs and life of his family. A Gbaya mother answering a question about her family said that she had five children, two living and three dead. Of infants and very aged people it is frequently said that they have "gone back."[4] But they are not dead, they have not ceased to exist, as the well-known Senegalese poet Birago Diop writes (Reygnault 1971:86-89):

> Listen more often
> To things than to Beings.
> The Voice of Fire is heard,
> Listen to the Voice of Water.
> Listen to the Wind.
> The Thicket sobbing:
> It is the Breath of the dead Ancestors,
> Who are not gone
> Who are not in the Ground
> Who are not dead.

The fathers died, but they were not gone, they were not under the ground, they were not dead--they were the **sɔ̃-daa** who remained with their people.

3 The branches were the **ndende,** mimosa tree, and the **gana-guna,** a type of prickly bush.

4 This euphemism for death suggests the concept of a prior existence to which infants and the aged return at death. It also reflects the commonly held belief that only newborn infants and very old people die of natural causes.

II

Sɔ the Creator of Man was good. He was good, the Gbaya believed, because he was the Creator; it was through his power that life originated. But there was that in the world which would destroy life. There were the forces represented by **Gbasɔ**. There was misfortune and evil. There was sunshine and rain, for example, but too little or too much of either spelled disaster. Thus, God may be thought to be a capricious God.

Gbaya-Kaka suggests that God originally intended that man should die, be buried, and one day later rise again, but man became impatient to know his fate and sent a message to God (Tessmann 937:8-9). A certain great man summoned the chameleon, an animal that was pleasing to God, and sent it to ask whether death was the end: was it all over at death, or after a man had been in the grave a while, would medicine be placed in his eyes to bring him to life again? The chameleon set off on its journey, slowly moving along as though counting its steps. After waiting some time without receiving any answer, the great man sent the toad with the same question. It hopped along, quickly passed up the chameleon, and arrived to find God angry, first that he was being bothered with questions at all, and secondly, that such an ugly creature as the toad should be the messenger. His answer was an angry, "Yes, it is all over. When a man dies, all that remains is to weep over him and dig the grave and that's all. Tell that to the big man!" The toad returned with its message; and, even though the chameleon finally arrived, the answer remained the same. Men die and do not rise again.

The Gbaya insult, "You are ignorant like God!" reflects the same capriciousness; and occasionally a Gbaya suffering misfortune might even insult God, "If I knew you, I wouldn't go home to you!" But the Gbaya did not normally hold the Creator God responsible for the troubles and evil in the world. These difficulties were most often laid to the influence of other **sɔ**, as the foregoing phrase reflects more explicitly in its full form, "You are ignorant like an evil god!"

Forces capable of doing evil were acknowledged to exist; and in order for life to continue, they had to be appeased. The Gbaya village was situated within geographical confines, and land was considered to be the domain of **sɔ-kao**. Each year at the beginning of the dry season, the village chief would call his people together for the annual ceremony honoring the

Gbaya Religious Practice

local spirit. A formulaic question-and-answer session would be held in which the chief, reminding his people of their good fortune during the past year, would ask them when they had performed last year's ceremony. The answer was known by all--it had been at the beginning of the dry season. He would then fix a day and a time for the next ceremony. The day before the event, he would remind his people of its approach, and from among the elders, one who spoke calmly, who was not a troublemaker, and who could speak well would be selected as their leader. An out-of-the-way place beside a great rock, a large tree or hill, or beside a deep pool would have been selected beforehand, and the people bearing their gifts would follow the priest to the site. The procession would include the priest first, followed by the drummer, then the chief, and lastly all the people of the village.

When they arrived at the site, the person appointed to be priest would turn to the people and ask the men to hand him the wooden spears they had cut for the occasion. He would gather them carefully in his arms lest any fall, lay them at the shrine, and then ask the women to hand him their gifts of food. All the people would then be seated, and he would prepare a fire to cook the eggs provided by the chief on the pieces of potsherd brought by the women. He would make cassava paste with the flour they had brought and spread it together with bits of egg on large leaves that had been spread out on the ground before the shrine. Next, he would mix water with a little flour, command that all lie flat on the ground, clap his hands and pray:

> **Sɔ̃-kao,** we prayed to you last year and you gave us health, you gave us food; **kao** of the Bute and of the Mbum, give us food, help us this year again.

After the prayer he would pour the water-flour mix over the wooden spears and over the shrine to complete the ritual. As the people returned to their village, in reverse order of arrival, the women would ululate and the drums would beat in honor of the chief, confident of **sɔ̃-kao**'s help and protection during the coming year.

Similar ritual ceremonies were performed when a man went hunting or fishing or planned to camp in the bush. There were thought to be specific **sɔ̃-gun-te** 'spirit of tree base', **sɔ̃-ta** 'spirit of rock', **sɔ̃-kaya** 'spirit of hill', and **sɔ̃-dir-yi** 'spirit of pool of water', throughout the land, all of whom were **sɔ̃-kao**. In each locality there was a spirit to be propitiated if a successful and safe venture was to be assured.

A second potential source of misfortune was the dead. As in their earlier life, the departed could be pleased and displeased, and they could bestow both good and evil. Harry Sawyerr of Fourah Bay College in Sierra Leone writes (1965:350):

> In Africa the family is of supreme importance. We make a covenant with our dead and thereby maintain an active covenant relationship among the living.

When a man experienced a series of hardships or catastrophes such as death in the family, personal injury, crop failure, or hunting misfortune, those around him would either recall something specific that he had done, or would assume that he had done something for which he was being punished. It would then be his responsibility to ask the elders, if he did not know, what offence he had committed. Only when he had made expiation to calm the spirit of the injured ancestor would he be assured that no more misfortune would befall him.

But normally one did not wait until misfortune struck. The propitiatory ritual, which was the same as the expiatory ritual, was a regular part of Gbaya life. When a man died, it was the duty of his son to perform the ritual of propitiation at regular intervals. The first performance would occur about two years after the man's death, or three to four years if he had been lost and his body never found. The dead man's relatives and children would all gather to select the eldest married son to perform the ritual. A brother of the dead man, or a son of his sister if no brother was living, would set up three termite mounds to form a triangular fireplace on the right side of the house where the returning hunter normally set his spears. The eldest son would obtain a large rooster, which the one who had prepared the fireplace would receive and then hand back to him with the words,

> Your father died. Now today I give you this chicken for placating the spirit of your father.

And the son, taking the chicken, would address his departed father:

> Father, you took good care of us, you looked after us well. It is for that reason that we set down your termite

mounds today. Look after me together with all my brothers and all my uncles and all my sisters. We just ask you and the living God, buffalo bulls, elephants, wild hogs, that is to say, all animals, you will give us.

The son would then beat the head of the chicken against the termite mounds, or sometimes cut its throat, and hold it so that its blood dripped onto each of the three mounds. A fire was then lit in the fireplace prepared for the dead man, the feathers were burned off the chicken, and it was cooked. The son's wife would bring the cassava dish that she had prepared in the regular household kitchen, and the spears of all the man's sons would be brought and laid beside the fire. Then the son would take a small bit of the cassava in his fingers saying, "Just as I have already prayed to you." Then he would dip the cassava into the chicken broth and toss it onto the spears, "Father, so eat your share."[5] Then the son, his brothers, and the nephew, if he was present, would eat the ritual meal together.[6]

Following the first performance of the ceremony, it could be performed by the son whenever he felt it necessary. The same ritual was also performed, although not as frequently, to **sɔ̃-naa** 'spirit of mother' and **sɔ̃-zɔm-daa** 'spirit of grandfather'. Occasionally three fireplaces were prepared side by side, and the ritual was performed simultaneously to the departed father, mother, and grandfather. If performed for the grandmother, the mother's fireplace was used.

A standard formula in the prayer was the following:

> When I go to the bush, may I kill;
> may we be well, and my wife and my children;
> may I be prosperous.

Or more succinctly:

---

5 The second person singular pronoun is used in all the prayers cited in this paper instead of the plural pronoun normally used in addressing superiors. Rev. Darman suggests that the singular pronoun may reflect modern Christian usage where God is often addressed in the singular.

6 For other descriptions of this ritual see Hilberth (1962:69ff.) Christensen (1971:68ff.), and Vidal (1962:24ff.).

>   May I have animals,
>   may I have wealth,
>   may I have children.

In the prayers, the three main requests were for health, for prosperity in the form of food and wealth, and for offspring. In the case of specific misfortune, the request might also be made:

>   Remove evil from over me.

The requests in the prayers to **sɔ̃-daa** and **sɔ̃-kao** were very similar. In practice, the rituals also followed similar patterns. The full village prayer to the spirit of the land and the full family prayer to the spirit of the deceased ancestor were performed at specified times by men chosen for the task. However, at frequent intervals and as the need arose, individuals would offer prayers to specific **sɔ̃-kao** and to their **sɔ̃-daa**. One friend relates that his father would sacrifice to his **sɔ̃-daa** whenever there happened to be a large chicken around the house or whenever his wife had obtained money that he could claim for the purchase of a chicken. The meal that he would enjoy without the rest of his family was cause enough to remember his father as often as possible.

Offerings of thanksgiving were given after a successful hunt by ritually preparing and eating the breastbone of the animal killed in the same manner that the chicken was prepared and eaten. In the case of the harvest, the first fruits would be prepared and eaten according to the same formula. Even when eating a simple meal or when drinking beer, the first serving might be thrown or poured onto the ground as an offering to **sɔ̃-daa**. In this way the **sɔ̃-kao** and the **sɔ̃-daa** who exercised influence over the daily lives of the Gbaya were propitiated.

III

A small number of Gbaya tales, including several recorded by Tessmann, may be considered mythical explanations of origin, but by far the greater part of the Gbaya inventory of oral tradition is not etiological. Gbaya religion accepts the fact of creation; it affirms that God created man and the world man lives in, but it does not develop that affirmation into a complex grid of myth and belief. Life exists on both sides of death, but the duration of eternity need not be specified. Thus, the idea of past eternity as expressed in Psalm 43:13, "Blessed be Yahweh, the God of Israel, from all Eternity and forever" (Jerusalem Bible), is extremely difficult to render explicitly in Gbaya.

Gbaya thought also accepts the fact of death. While alive, man possesses **dan-tɛ**; at death, the eternal spark of life embodied within him departs to join his fathers who have preceded him into the world of eternity of which **Sɔ̃** 'God' is an explicit part. Man's destiny is thus clearly known. He will die and pass on to a world that is an extension of the present world and that is not really more unknown to the Gbaya than heaven is to the Christian.

It must, of course, be admitted that there was ambivalence toward death. Although death was accepted as an occurring fact, it was not welcomed. Death was not merely a step in the continuation of a mystical eternal life--it was also the end of the physical present. It was a tragic event that carried away loved ones, leaders, and providers. It was to be feared, for man did not by nature want to die.

Within the hierarchy of Gbaya religion, God was distant, but he was not inactive; he had not withdrawn and abandoned his creation. He continued to influence men's affairs on earth and men sought ways to influence him. But because he was an almighty awe-inspiring God who could not be approached directly, mediation was necessary. The departed fathers had entered the world of **sɔ̃** and were thought to be able to influence the higher powers. Thus, in the prayers to **sɔ̃-daa** it is not surprising to see invocation of the "Living God" or the "God who made the heavens." The fathers were mediators between man and God. Likewise, on the larger social plane, the **sɔ̃-kao** who dwelt in the land but who also belonged to the world of **sɔ̃** were mediators between the village unit and God.

A relationship existed between man and the various levels in the hierarchy of **Sɔ̃**, a relationship of created to the Creator, of inhabitant to Lord, and of son to Father, respectively. Rebirth, a new way of life, a new relationship was not necessary--it already existed. **Sɔ̃-kao** was there and man lived within its territorial domain; **sɔ̃-daa** were there and they were still father, mother, uncle, aunt, grandfather, or grandmother to those who lived after them.

This relationship that grew out of the natural physical relationship of parent and child should normally be good. The father should be eager to grant his children the health and prosperity needed for life; he should want to grant the offspring necessary for life to continue. But ancestors could be angered by being slighted or forgotten. The spirits of the land could be provoked by being ignored. It was therefore necessary to assure them that they had not been forgotten. If their feelings had been hurt, it was necessary to appease and calm them. This was the function of the ritual ceremony known as "fixing, placating the spirit." It was a ceremony generally referred to as sacrifice, but it was more precisely ritual killing and symbolic offering whose end was propitiation and expiation.

The dead father was calmed by the ritual killing of a chicken or the preparation of other meat according to a standard formula. But although the ritual involved killing, it was not, in Raymond Firth's terms, true sacrifice (Lessa and Vogt 1965:185-94). It neither represented a significant economic loss--for little effort or expense was wasted on the care of chickens--nor was it destroyed. Only a small portion of the cassava dish was actually given to the **sɔ̃-daa,** and none of the meat; the major portion of the meal was eaten. It was explained that the ancestor was very powerful; he was the source of all and could multiply the symbolic offering into whatever quantity he needed. The importance of the ceremony was therefore ritualistic and symbolic.

The ritual associated with **kao** was more clearly offering, because it entailed the bringing of gifts to be left at the shrine for the spirit of the land. Firth's definition of offering is perhaps applicable here because the giver acknowledges by his gift his inferiority to the spirit. But the gift is not strictly voluntary, for without it man fears that the divine will be angered and will visit misfortune upon him. The offering is, however, symbolic; for the spears are not real, the pottery is broken, and the eggs are representative.

Part of the importance of the **kao** ritual lay in the significance of the chief in the ceremony. He was the representative of the people, and according to tradition the land is his. It was he who granted land for houses and gardens, and it was he who could take land away. The ritual demonstrated and emphasized his acknowledged position and authority--namely, that his right to the land had its source in the **sɔ̃-kao,** who had been the real possessors of the land from the times of the Mbum who occupied it before the Gbaya, and the Bute before them. The ceremony supported and justified the chief's position. The immediate obvious function of the ceremony was, of course, to assure safety and prosperity during the coming year or in the venture at hand.

The function of the ritual performed to **sɔ̃-daa** was multiple. It had the practical effect of ensuring old-age care. The closer the aged came to the grave, the more they were revered, lest on dying they take out their grudges by bringing misfortune upon the living who had ill-treated them. The immediate purpose of the practice was to assure the everyday needs of life. And on the broader level, it maintained order and continuity in society. "Indeed, we regard the ancestors as coguardians of the mores of our communities," writes Sawyerr (1965:350), and Ilogu adds the following (1965:340):

> The concept of society, therefore, is a perpendicular one. The present is rooted in the past through respect and obedience to the wishes of the ancestors, and the future is assured of stability through the obedience of the present generation.

When an ancestor had been wronged, whether through neglect or through the breaking of a social norm, it was in fact God himself who had been wronged, because he was the source both of man and of the social code according to which man's life was ordered. Man's norms were in reality part of a greater order of things which had its source in the supreme God. When the code had been broken, expiation was required.

But not all offences were considered to be against **sɔ̃-daa**, not all were of the same caliber. Children who ran carelessly through someone's garden or who broke the bottom out of an old lady's cooking pot were sometimes reprimanded with the question, "Don't you fear God?" or "Don't you fear the Creator God?" The question implies the notion of divine retribution, and an adult who was cruel to children was warned that he would be punished in a place of fire.[7]

There was another category of deeds which was very serious and which required purification, but which did not relate directly to either **sɔ̃-kao** or **sɔ̃-daa**. It involved the taking of life. If a man killed another, even in war or in self-defence, he had transgressed a basic commandment and purification was obligatory. If he had killed a leopard, a dangerous and respected animal, or an eland, the world's largest antelope, purification was necessary.

The rite of purification entailed a ritual bath to remove the curse of **simbo** that fell upon the person as a result of

---

7 The reference to a place of fire or hell may be a reflection of relatively recent Islamic influence.

the killing. An old man would first lead the guilty one around any one of certain trees, most often the **sore**.[8] The function of the **sore** was to calm or to make peaceful that in the offender which had been upset, for the **sore** tree was thought to have soothing effects, whether for insect bites, for anger, or for the curse of **simbo**. If a village feared that some danger or evil was about to befall it, **sore** branches would be cut and placed across all the paths leading into the village to calm and dissuade the threatening force. In the midst of battle, if there were too many deaths, old women would place **sore** branches between the warring parties and the fighting would cease. **Sore** was a powerful force whose effect was pacification.

As the old man led the offender around the tree, he would speak of the deed and ask that the curse be removed. He would then brush his head against the tree and the guilty would do likewise. Next he would scrape bark off the tree and lead the guilty one to a nearby stream which he would dam up with **sore** leaves and branches from certain other trees. He would then direct the killer to sit down in the water and, pouring water mixed with bark crumbles over him, would say:

> The **simbo** curse for the person whom you killed, it is for that that I bathe you; may the curse depart with the water!

He would then break the dam and wash the leaves away in the stream, commanding that the flowing water carry away the curse. If the guilty one was not purified in this manner, it was believed that the death for which he was responsible would come back upon him and upon his people.[9]

It may be concluded from **simbo** that human beings and certain great animals, although they could be killed for legitimate reasons, embodied life. **Simbo** was the violation of that life, which was inherently inviolable. No mention of the divine occurs in the purification ceremony, but the concept

---

8 The **sore** is the Annona Arenaria Thonn. tree; for further discussion of the significance of **sore** see T. Christensen's "Rites of Reconciliation in Traditional Gbaya Society" in this volume.

9 Other purification rites were also practiced, such as washing a body before burial, and ritual bathing by a widow or widower following the prescribed period of mourning. The symbolic drowning of the initiation <u>rite de passage</u> might also be considered a form of purification from one life stage to another.

of life apparent in **simbo** is the same as that occurring in **sɔ̃-daa** and **sɔ̃-kao**. Thus, Gbaya religion was one of life, above all, life here and now; for even the purification from the curse of **simbo** was intended for the practical purpose of warding off death. It would perhaps not be inaccurate to conclude that Gbaya religion was life itself. Philosophies of death, eternal bliss hereafter, Nirvana, or Happy Hunting Grounds were not necessary. God's greatest gift to man was the life that he possesses now.

IV

Christian missions have been among the Gbaya for over fifty years; and under their influence, together with the pressures of Islam, colonialism, and even urbanization, traditional beliefs have been profoundly affected. **Sɔ̃-kao** is rarely remembered, and **sɔ̃-daa** is usually ignored. But the old religion continues to influence Gbaya life. J.K. Parrat and A.R.I. Doi, writing about the Yoruba of Nigeria, make the following observation (1969:109):

> It has frequently been the case that when a foreign faith has moved into an area which had hitherto a traditional or indigenous religion, some traditional practices invariably remain and are absorbed into the newer faith.

Whether the new believers realize it or not, their old faith almost inevitably influences their understanding and practice of the new. Among the Gbaya, the importance of the dead, the secular nature of traditional faith, the role of laity in worship, and the significance of ritual and symbol in sacrifice are aspects of the former faith that continue to have an influence on the life of the Christian church.

Traditional Gbaya religion was first of all a religion of society and family. It is not acceptable to use the general expression "ancestor worship" because the relationship with the departed was very personal. A man did not worship his ancestors--he remembered his father and grandfather, his mother and grandmother. He did not merely "beg" for things from them--he "talked with, greeted" them.[10] He believed that it was right to remember them; and he believed that, just as

---

10 For prayer the Christian church has adopted the expression **kofa-So** which means, literally, "begging God," The traditional term for prayer was **wora-So** from the verb "speak, greet," conveying the broader sense of conversation and communion.

in life he could make requests of them, so after their death he could continue to make requests. In life his father had taught him what was right and what was wrong; likewise, in death his father's wishes were not to be ignored. To forget one's father was to challenge the code and fabric of society without which life itself was doomed.

The Christian church opposed **sɔ̃-daa,** as did Islam. The consequences of this opposition are stated very strongly by Ram Desai (1962:20):

> By opposing ancestor worship in the early days, the church innocently raised havoc with the mores existing in African societies.

Christ came "not to abolish but to complete" (Jerusalem Bible) the Law and the Prophets. Even though Christianity brought in the Ten Commandments, did it destroy rather than fulfill? Allegiance to the fathers who represented law and moral order has been destroyed; the commandments themselves, many the same as the Old Testament Commandments, handed down through initiation rites, have become irrelevant as traditional initiations and have disappeared under church and government pressure. But the dead are not gone.

The Christian is thus left in an impossibly ambivalent position that Sawyerr deems incompatible with Christianity (1965:347-48):

> Do we feel differently toward our ancestral dead from non-Christians? Or do we live two lives--the one Christian, which has little, if any, concern for our dead; the other when we shed Christianity and become Africans again...? This is a psychological state of paranoia, of split personality.

A Gbaya Christian commenting on a recent funeral stated that had it been his grandchild, the child would have been buried beside his home according to traditional Gbaya custom. Never would he have consented to have the child removed from the family to be buried in a distant cemetery. The dead are not dead; they are not gone; they are not to be forgotten.

"If the church is to make a real impact in West Africa, its doctrine of God must be restated to stress His universal fatherhood and to provide a Christian counterpart of the pagan concept of God as our Ancestor," writes Sawyerr (1965:351). Perhaps the church has not stressed God's fatherhood enough. A further answer is suggested in the Roman Catholic observance of All Saints' Day.

"But who could deny that the church in Africa would be infinitely richer if she were allowed to commune with her own saints in ways that are familiar and meaningful?" asks William Crane, writing about indigenization in Africa (1964: 417). Above all, the church must stress the Fourth Commandment, "Honor your father and mother"; for in days of increasing social mobility and urbanization, responsibility to family is not lessened.

A second feature of Gbaya religion was that it was pragmatic. It was a secular religion in the sense of bringing the realm of spiritual reality down to the level of everyday need. Its purpose was not to concern itself with some other world or future life, but with the needs of this life in the world where we now live.

The Gbaya response to Christianity may be interpreted sometimes as viewing Christianity as another means of coping with current need. As James Fernandez writes of the Bwiti of Gabon, "Our medicines began to fail us; our ancestors no longer listened" (1964:281-82). Under the new pressures of colonialism, the old answers were no longer adequate; and the Bwiti began to search for "new traits and complexes with which to strengthen his own failing religious institutions." In much the same way, Christianity provided new options for the Gbaya, new ways to overcome illness, hunger, and even possible eternal punishment. In some cases, mission approaches to evangelization may have supported the idea that Christianity was also a secular and pragmatic religion. By providing, hand in hand with the gospel, medicine and education, both of which the Gbaya saw to be useful and even necessary to everyday life, missions may have confused and diminished the purity of their message. At least, it often seemed that the desired education could only be obtained by professing some kind of Christian faith, and medicine by sitting through a sermon. The necessities of life were seen to be tied to acceptance of the Christian message.

Since the early days of rapid church growth among the Gbaya, the church has slowed down under the pressures of urbanization, nationalism, second-generation Christianity, and even Western materialism.[11] But there is also another reason; namely, the fact that Christianity is now seen to be unnecessary in obtaining the necessities once associated with

---

11 For a discussion of the growth of the Christian church among the Gbaya and certain neighboring peoples in Cameroun, see C. Michelsen's thesis, "The Evangelical Lutheran Church of East Cameroun."

it. The gun takes much of the danger and uncertainty out of the hunt; the tractor and improved seeds and fertilizers increase crop production; medicines and medical skill heal illnesses that often brought death before; above all, the franc has the power of bringing virtually anything into one's possession. In an age of scientific knowledge and cultural change, the Christian message appears to be as irrelevant as the former faith of the fathers.

The church's response must be the pure and simple proclamation of its message. The gospel speaks both to eternity and to this world. It claims to be practical, not in the way Gbaya religion was, but because of the assurance it offers the believer that his relationship with the Creator God is indeed right, and secondly, because the Christian faith is worked out through the believer's love for his fellow man. The church has the means of providing education, agricultural assistance, literacy training, and medical service; and it provides it, not merely as a means of luring people to the gospel, but because as Christians we are our brother's keeper.

Thirdly, Gbaya religion was a religion of the laity. It was a village elder who was selected to lead the people when they prayed to **sɔ̃-kao**. He was the priest, and his son might be chosen after him, but there was no priestly class or caste; there was no high priest responsible for all Gbaya worship. When a man went on a hunt, he became a priest to propitiate the local spirit. For **sɔ̃-daa**, it was the son selected by his family who performed the ritual; but in time of need, any son could remember his father in ritual performance.

This may in part explain the early success of the Christian church among the Gbaya. The catechist was a lay leader; he was one of the people, one selected by them to be their priest. He was not one of the elite class of professional people dependent on the people for all their livelihood. Hierarchical structure was not a feature of traditional Gbaya religious practice or even of Gbaya political life until very recently. Life centered about the family and the clan; village structure was based on clan structure; and the focal point of religion was likewise the family, the clan, and the village unit.

On the basis of the lay nature of Gbaya religion, the church should place more emphasis on the layman and on the priesthood of all believers. Local family, clan, and village leaders should be the leaders of the church; and the church itself should be centered within the natural social context of family and village.

Finally, the essence of Gbaya religious practice was ritual and symbol. It was not true sacrifice, and therein lies a significant difference between the gospel of the New Testament and the religion of the Ancients. In the Christian faith, God gave his Son as a true sacrifice, not merely as ritual or symbol.

The ritualistic nature of Gbaya religion is also of significance in a more practical way. It suggests that the church should incorporate ritual into its worship services, for it was ritual that was meaningful to the Gbaya in his own worship. Liturgy might be developed using Gbaya music, rhythm, and even art and dramatic form. The content might be new, but the use of ritual and its form would be Gbaya.

The symbolic offering of traditional practice also has important implications for the Christian church. The offerings to **sɔ̃-kao** and **sɔ̃-daa** were symbolic; great gifts were never given. In the ceremony performed to **sɔ̃-kao,** artificial spears, potsherds, and symbolic offerings of eggs and food were given. To the ancestor only a bit of cassava food dipped in broth was offered. God was the source of everything; it was quite unnecessary--it would even be arrogant--for man to attempt to provide God's needs. It was rather from him that man asked for what he needed. What was important to the spirit was that he be neither ignored nor forgotten. Thus, the Old Testament practice of tithes and offerings is contrary to all Gbaya understanding of God. It would be unthinkable for a Gbaya to have a successful hunt and then offer one out of ten of his kill to the spirit as a thank offering. Giving small gifts is not lack of faith and commitment but evidence of strong faith in an almighty and omnipotent God. According to Gbaya thought, what God desires is not gifts, but gestures of assurance that he is remembered. And since there was no traditional class of priests, the idea of full support for a full-time pastor or for a complex church structure is foreign to Gbaya thought.

In conclusion, if the Christian church is to be meaningful and relevant to the Gbaya, it must take cognizance of the old. It must provide answers to Gbaya questions and needs; it must allow the Gbaya to worship according to his own forms of expression. To do this, it must first of all understand the nature and function of traditional Gbaya religion.

There is, however, a conflict in the preceding argument that is not easy to resolve. Certain people who live near the Gbaya, the Dwayo and the Mbororo, for example, have tended to remain apart, closed to outside influences and faithful to their own traditions. They are deserving of respect for their strength and their faith in what has been handed down to them by their fathers, for that is what they believe to have been given to them by God. Christensen touches on this problem when he writes (1971:113):

> We do not believe that the ... study of Gbaya values ... should be "used" by a Christian missionary as a gimmick or tool in his attempt to reinterpret the Christian message "in terms of" the Gbaya situation. Such an approach would pre-empt Gbaya freedom and Gbaya responsibility.

Yet, the way in which the gospel fulfills Gbaya needs must be proclaimed by the Christian if he takes the Great Commission seriously. On hearing the Christian message, the Gbaya must be allowed the freedom to interpret it according to his needs. This is not syncretism but, in Christian tradition, the truest sense of God fulfilling man's needs and of man responding to God's will.

Bibliography

Christensen, T. 1971. "Gbaya Value Orientations as Opportunities for Dialogue with the Christian Mission." S.T.M. thesis. Chicago: Lutheran School of Theology.

Crane, W. 1964. "Indigenization in the African Church." International Review of Missions 53(212):408-22.

Desai, R. 1962. Christianity as Seen by the Africans. Denver: Alan Mellow.

Diop, B. 1971. "Souffles." Reprinted in Trésor Africain et Malgache, ed. by C. Reygnault, pp. 86-89, Paris: Editions Seghers.

Fernandez, J. 1964. "The Idea and Symbol of the Saviour in a Gabon Syncretistic Cult." International Review of Missions 53 (211):281-89.

Firth, R. 1965. "Offering and Sacrifice: Problems in Organizations." In Reader in Comparative Religion, ed by W.A. Lessa and E.Z. Vogt, pp. 184-94. New York: Harper and Row.

Hilberth, J. 1962. Les Gbaya. Studia Ethnographica Upsaliensia 19. Lund: Ohlssons Boktryckeri.

Ilogu, E. 1965. "Christianity and Ibo Traditional Religion." International Review of Missions 54(215):335-42.

Jensen, A.E. 1963. Myth and Cult among Primitive Peoples. Chicago: University of Chicago Press.

Lessa, W.A. and E.Z. Vogt, eds. 1965. Reader in Comparative Religion. New York: Harper and Row.

Michelsen, C.M. 1969. "The Evangelical Lutheran Church of East Cameroun." M.A. thesis. Pasadena: Fuller Theological Seminary.

Noss, P.A. 1971. "Wanto--The Hero of Gbaya Tradition." Journal of the Folklore Institute 8:23-36.

Parrat, J.K. and A.R.I. Doi. 1969. "Syncretism in Yorubaland: A Religious or a Sociological Phenomenon?" Practical Anthropology 16:109-13.

Reygnault, C. ed. 1971. Trésor Africain et Malgache. Paris: Editions Seghers.

Sawyerr, H. 1965. "Christian Evangelistic Strategy in West Africa." International Review of Missions 54(215):343-52.

Tessmann, G. 1937. Die Baja: Ein Negerstamm im Mittleren Sudan. Vol. 2. Stuttgart: Strecker und Schröder.

Vidal, P. 1962. L'Initiation dans l'Education Traditionelle, Population Gbaya-Kara: Nord-Ouest de la Republique Centrafricaine. Le Havre: Bangui.

A traditional Fula ruler of northern Cameroun

A Mbororo (Fula) cattleman

13. Social Pressure for Religious Conformity in the Fulani Community

by Ronald Nelson

The bottom end of the social totem pole

In order to gain some perspective for the place in which the religious outcast finds himself in the Fulani community, it will help to get a look at the bottom end of the Fulani social totem pole. The people in this category are the person of poor lineage, the bastard, the slave, and the outcast in descending order.

The person of poor lineage is one whose family is noted for unsocial behavior such as theft, poor hospitality, and, above all, adultery. It can also be a person who has very few relatives, especially uncles, both paternal and maternal, or a person with very few brothers and sisters, or one whose family besides being small is scattered geographically. Another person in this category is the one who is habitually unkempt or dirty--who doesn't care about his appearance. Although such people are tolerated in the community, people do not normally have any more to do with them than necessary. They do not normally want to be seen engaging in conversation with such a person, but they will greet him. The other main way of maintaining such a person in his place is by refusing intermarriage. Strong pressure is put on either sons or daughters not be become interested in a person of poor lineage.

There are several similarities between slaves and bastards, but the attitude toward each is different because a slave is considered property, whereas a bastard is considered as a member of society. When a girl gives birth to an illegitimate child, she has no way to keep it as her own, so she must bring it to her parents. The grandmother is obliged to keep the child because there is no one else to care for him. From the time the child begins to grow up, he is not considered as a worthwhile member of the community even by his closest relatives. The grandmother cannot allow herself to grow affectionate towards the child, but must always treat him as a sort of hired hand who is good for running errands and not much else. She cares for him because it is her duty and she must be patient in doing her duty. He will be able to eat with the family as long as he is in need, but the only clothing that will be provided for him is leftover rags. His clothing will be a constant reminder of his status.

When the bastard grows up, his lot becomes even more difficult. No one will take seriously what he says. He will never be called as a witness in a trial even though he may have witnessed the incident in question. If he were to butcher meat, others would not eat it. Even if he becomes rich and powerful in spite of his status, people will not honor him. No one will give his daughter to him in marriage. He could go to another place where no one knows him and there find a wife. However, if his wife discovers his status, she will most likely leave him unless they have had children, in which case she will do her duty and stay on for the sake of the children. When people discover that he is a bastard, they will refuse to eat with him. In fact, even in his grandmother's home, he must eat separately. The only ones who might eat with him are children of the family who are his own age.

The slave is yet lower than the bastard because he is considered as property. Leftover clothing is given to slaves, but no food is provided for them unless something happens to be left over after the meal. Men slaves are not permitted to marry, and women slaves belong to their master. A slave must find his own food. He may be permitted to cook the husks left over from cleaning guinea corn. There is nothing wrong in talking with him to give orders, but no one would ever think of becoming friends with his property!

Such are the attitudes toward three of the lowest members of Fulani society. Lower than any of these three is, or at least has been, the apostate, the religious outcast. But before going into how the society handles this special category, let us take a brief look at the positive ways in which religious conformity is encouraged.

Fulani Social Pressure

Upbringing in the Muslim home

"Train up a child in the way he should go, and when he is old he will not depart from it" is true not only of the Christian home. Muslim upbringing of children has traditionally been consistent and thorough in Fulani society, and it has had a profound effect.

From the time a child is old enough to walk around and observe, he begins to learn what it means to be a Muslim. The most striking and consistent evidence of the Muslim presence is the daily prayers and the month of fast. Before a child is of age, he will begin to imitate his older brothers and sisters who, together with their father, say at least the morning, afternoon, and evening prayers. For these ritual prayers he will use the Fulani verb **juula**. Ritual purity also makes an early impression on a Fulani child: dogs, pigs, feces, urine, and many other things he quickly learns are not to be touched.

When the child is seven years old, the formal training begins for both girls and boys. The first thing to learn is to **juula**. This is not difficult since he has seen it since he was old enough to see, and the lessons are repeated; for each time the father goes to **juula**, he calls his children and they pray together. This includes the predawn prayer: from the age of seven years, the child acquires the habit of waking up before dawn, and his first activity of the day is to give himself the ritual washing and then begin to **juula**.

As an alternative to teaching his own children, if a father wants them to have more serious instruction, he will arrange to take them to the **mallum** 'teacher', who will normally keep them in his home for four years, during which time they are to memorize the Koran. Often the **mallum** will take the children to another town for their instruction so that they will be completely in his care. Those who have been away to school will be expected to teach younger brothers and sisters when they return home.

Another alternative, if a father does not want to send his children away from home and does not know the ritual prayers and necessary Koranic quotations well enough to be able to teach his own children, is to hire a **mallum** to tutor his children at home.

When the four years, or their equivalent, of Koranic instruction are finished, the child returns home and receives a sort of confirmation in which he is accepted as a normal member of the adult religious society. After this rite, he may return to a **moodibbo** 'learned one' for further instruction. The first four years are enough for him to learn the necessary Koranic passages and prayer formulas, but they are not enough for him to learn many of the points of Muslim law, nor to understand much of what he has been reciting, nor to be able to express himself in Arabic. So, if he shows some inclination, he will be encouraged to further Koranic studies. The **moodibbo** is more capable than the **mallum**. If the child takes some additional studies, he will be qualified to hang his shingle as a **mallum** himself, but he need not necessarily do so. He may just take additional studies in order to be a better Muslim.

After a few years as a full-fledged member of Muslim society, the young person enters the critical teenage period. Revolt is common. He may refuse to practice the Muslim ritual--the liturgical prayers that he had learned since he was a small child. He may refuse to observe the fast or to gather at the mosque on Friday. He may seek out prostitutes or start drinking and smoking. This conduct shames and embarrasses his father who tries to make the teenager come to his senses by tongue lashings or by actual beatings, if he is not too big; or he may eventually chase him from the home. Sometimes the teenager will go to another town, in which case his father, if he still cares, will follow him up. In a homogeneous Muslim society, the father will be able to get cooperation from the authorities in the new town. He may go to the chief and tell about his son; the chief sends out an order for his arrest; he is brought and is beaten or else thrown in prison. If none of this brings him to repentance, his father can ask for a formal ostracizing procedure to be brought against him. However, it is not always necessary for the father to ask for such a formal procedure. If the person is an adult, the people in his village may, by popular consensus, ask for him to be ostracized. This procedure is one of the most effective weapons for returning a person to the Muslim fold.

Ostracizing and the status of the outcast

Worse than a person of poor lineage, worse than a bastard, worse even than a slave, is the apostate--the religious outcast. In turning his back on the Prophet and on the religion revealed by the Prophet, not only is he offending society, he is offending God. **Hombugo** 'ostracizing' is the last step after a person has been counseled, beaten, imprisoned, after all of the available means have failed to return him to the faith. It is a formal act performed by the chief in consultation with and in the presence of the elders and other persons concerned.

A formal charge is brought either by the parents of the offender or by prominent members of the community. If the father is bringing the charge, he talks first with the members of the chief's court and explains the situation. They talk it over to make sure that it is really necessary to ostracize the accused. Then they finally bring it to the chief with full particulars. The accused is called and told all that he has done or failed to do; then the chief tells him that he will be ostracized. This is not done in the presence of the father. The father is then called in and told that his son is going to be ostracized. The father says that he cannot object since his son has done so and so. Then word is sent out for all the townspeople to gather. When they are gathered, the courtiers announce, "We are gathered to ostracize so and so." One of the older men in the crowd who was not present in the court may ask, "Has the chief heard about this?" and the whole story will be told to the crowd by the courtiers. The men in the crowd will reply, "Well, since his father has brought charges and since the chief agrees, who are we to disagree?" At this point the chief may get up and leave, heaping insults on the **kombaaDo** 'outcast'. These will be the last words spoken by anyone in the community directly to the outcast. Through the whole process, the outcast has no chance to reply. At this point the courtiers begin shouting and announcing to everyone, "So and so has been ostracized!"

The father, or sometimes the chief, sends courtiers to buy kola nuts which are distributed amongst all the villagers as a symbol or seal of the ostracizing. People leave, and servants or slaves of the chief take kola nuts to all remaining villagers and announce that so and so has been ostracized. Then the children are gathered at the chief's court, children under ten years of age, and are instructed that so and so has been ostracized and that they are to jeer at him wherever they see him. They chant,

Wooo, wooo, hombaama, hoombama-- balwinaama--warti bana waandu!
'Hey, hey, ostracized, ostracized--blackened--become like a monkey!'

Then sons of the courtiers, young men of the same age as the outcast, are called together and letters of announcement are prepared to be taken to all the places the outcast is likely to go. Kola nuts accompany each letter. If a letter is to be sent far away, money will be sent for local purchase of the nuts. If a Muslim holiday is near, the message will be saved until the holiday, and each one will be told when he goes to greet the chief, if he has not already heard via the grapevine.

From that time on, the outcast is no longer a member of the community. No one must talk to him under any circumstance. If anyone, including his own parents, is caught talking to him, they will be considered one with him and will have to repent publicly and pay a fine in order to be reinstated. If his mother sees him coming, she must cover her head in shame and act as if she does not know he is there. If a group of people is conversing and they see him approaching, they must disperse. If he comes upon a group of people eating, they must stop the meal and disperse. But before dispersing, they throw out the remaining food into the dirt so that the outcast cannot possibly eat any of it. If he comes into a building, all the people in it must go out. If anyone has anything to do with an outcast, he has committed a mortal sin and will go directly to hell unless he repents. If someone is walking down the road and sees an outcast coming, he must leave the road entirely and pass by at a great distance in the bush. The outcast will not have shelter, and no one can provide food for him. No one would think of giving his daughter to him in marriage. If he moves to another Muslim area, word that he has been ostracized will already have reached there so he will be treated in the same way. When he dies, he will go directly to hell.

The ostracizing is for a definite length of time--a few months. When that period is finished, the outcast is expected to report to the chief, confess and repent publicly, and pay a fine, which for cattle people will be one or two cattle. If he complies, the stigma will be declared lifted by the chief; his head will be shaved, and he will be bathed and given a fresh set of clothes. Then he can be accepted back into society. If he fails to show up or to repent and pay the fine, he will be declared ostracized for another period. By this time, he will have either left the territory, or succumbed to the pressure.

Recent developments

Since national independence in 1960 there has been a rapid change in the pressures available to the Muslim community. Informants consulted knew of no formal ostracizing for strictly religious reasons within the last eight years. Although ostracizing is still practiced from time to time, it is done almost entirely for social reasons rather then for strictly religious reasons.

The change is due to several factors. There is, first of all, the secularity of the government. Normally, no questions of religious nature will be treated by the courts. In fact, some Muslims are under the impression that a person can sue a community for ostracism for religious reasons. "Each person is free to choose his own religion," it is said. Secondly, there is the influence of the schools. Primary education is compulsory. In primary and secondary school, children are brought into contact with cultures and ideas which are not based on Muslim theology and law. They realize that some of these other cultures are advanced even though not Islamic. Thirdly, there is the secularization and modernization of contemporary society. The term for this in Fulani is **perndam** 'civilization, keeping up with the times' or 'awareness'. Young people of today want to belong to the times; and taking Islam (or any religion for that matter) seriously does not belong to the times. There is a large segment of youth in the society who seem to be much more interested in wearing bell-bottom trousers and flashy shirts and going out with girls than in a religion which they consider restrictive. This generation does not take the older people seriously and does not cooperate with the community in ostracism. At the same time, there does remain among the youth an elite who still practice ostracism. In fact, some informants feel that this group of youth have a stricter system than the adults are able to maintain. Again, however, the ostracism is practiced for social rather than for religious reasons.

Even though formal ostracism appears to be no longer practiced for religious reasons, a large part of the system still remains. The ceremony is not held, the letters are not sent, and some of the cohesiveness and effectiveness have been lost. If an apostate goes to a new location, it may take some time for the community to decide to apply pressure on him. Nevertheless, he can never become a respected member of the community, and if the Muslim influence is strong, most of the other devices of ostracism can still be applied in varying degrees.

160   Faith and Belief

   Anyone who has worked for a period of time in a Muslim
milieu has heard about rather drastic measures, but precise
information is difficult to come by. When Muslims are asked
about the kinds of pressures presently used, they avoid the
issue. In many cases, there can only be inferences. Pressure
is still applied, sometimes in extreme forms, but in a less-
organized way than formerly.

Muslims in prayer at the end of Ramadan

14. Is God Venĕb or Yaama?*

by Bouba Bernard

The Chamba people live in northern Cameroun along the frontier with Nigeria. They occupy the summits of the Alantika Mountains and the plains to the east and west. Rejecting Islam, they retained their traditional faith until the arrival of Protestant missionaries in the area about fifteen years ago. A great number have now adhered to the Christian faith, but among the old men the former religion continues.

The Chamba believe in a god called Venĕb whose dwelling is in heaven and who is too far away to be seen or heard by men. This god is believed to exist in miniature inside all that can be found on earth, in grass, rocks, and trees. All things, no matter what their nature, shelter a little Venĕb called **Venĕb-waa** 'Venĕb's child'. These **Venĕb-yĕba** 'children of God' are, however, independent of their dwellings. They can go in and out whenever they want to play or have a siesta together. Some spots, like rivers, hills, and the shade of certain large trees, are supposed to be their regular meeting places, where they entertain themselves when nature is silent--usually at noon or from midnight to dawn when all is asleep. The rest of the time each Venĕb-waa is in its dwelling, which is may use as it wishes, but which is not its own.

Each animal and human being has a personal Venĕb-waa, a light which manifests God's presence. This Venĕb-waa enables it to participate in the divine and, in fact, maintains its life. The animal or human Venĕb-waa cannot give itself to play as the other Venĕb-yĕba do, for if he did, it would stop

* Previously published in <u>Missiology</u> 1:1:109-11 (Jan. 1973).

the activities of its host. But at night, while the host is sleeping, it may set out on adventures which are reflected in the dreams and nightmares of the sleeping person. Accordingly, Chamba behavior conforms to the life of the Venĕb-waa. This behavior consists of leaving the Venĕb-waa the freedom to take its strolls. In this respect, man will not go out from his house at the time when the Venĕb-yĕba stroll together in their groups. He will not throw a stone into water lest he injure a Venĕb-waa.

There is, however, no danger in assailing nature, no matter what means man uses, as long as he is in search of food. Before beginning the activity, he must utter the words **Venĕb o yaakin me ku!** 'May Venĕb have compassion on me!' to prove that he is not destroying nature on purpose or at random. Venĕb can then send his "children" who might be injured, elsewhere, leaving man free to accomplish his task. As a token of gratitude, before man eats he must take a bit of millet, dip it in meat sauce, and throw it on the ground for the Venĕb-yĕba, pronouncing these words as a prayer: **Venĕb-bid boo ko' nĕĕn ba!** 'May the gods bless the meal!' In this way Venĕb ensures that his homeless children, whose dwellings have been cut down by man and who must now live in the open air, are not neglected, but are fed and cared for. Man must be careful neither to wound nor to kill a "child of God"; for if that happened, man is threatened with death, a very rapid death that always begins with a violent headache.

Thus, every object created by Venĕb shelters a Venĕb-waa, and every object created by Venĕb is possessed by a Venĕb-waa.

Yaama, the sun, is also an object created by Venĕb, and as such, it shelters a Venĕb-waa. But this "child of God" is Venĕb himself who lives also in the moon and the stars, but stays permanently in Yaama. The great light projected from Yaama which shines on all the earth is Venĕb's eye watching over the whole creation. The two expressions, **Venĕb be' aa** 'God has seen' and **Yaama paa-yee be' aa** 'Sun up there has seen', are used to convey the same idea, namely, "God is my witness." The fact that Yaama is the permanent dwelling, not of a Venĕb-waa but of Venĕb himself, gives him the right to be called Venĕb. When one thinks of Venĕb, one thinks at the same time of Yaama; likewise the name Yaama evokes the image of Venĕb, especially of Venĕb as Light. Thus, the Chamba initially concludes that Venĕb and Yaama are the same person, that both names refer to the Supreme Being, God the Father.

Is God Venĕb or Yaama?

When Christianity came and spoke about God the Father, the Chamba accepted the new teaching, but disagreement arose over what to call the Christian God. Some called him Venĕb, and others called him Yaama, but no one used both names.

Those who call God Venĕb believe that as a creation of God, Yaama cannot be God. They believe that both Yaama, the sun, and the moon are the same distance from the earth and that both are near to God. The fact that men have walked on the moon leads them to conclude that God cannot be in the sun, for the sun is too close to the earth for him to be in it.

Those who call God Yaama maintain that the sun is a member of God's body; it is his eye. And if I can say that my arm or my eye is myself, there is no reason not to believe that Yaama ia God. In certain Chamba localities God has always been called Yaama, rarely if ever Venĕb; and so today they continue to refer to him as Yaama.

In a certain way, traditional religion found in Yaama what the Christian today considers to be in Jesus. Through Yaama, the Chamba saw God and confessed their sins to him; through Yaama they knew whether or not God accepted their deeds. But Yaama was never an intercessor for them. Man had to work out his own salvation by trying to be innocent at all times and to do good. For the Chamba did believe that after death a person received either life or punishment according to his life and deeds on earth. Christianity, however, teaches that it is because Jesus, the Son of God, arose from death that we also shall be raised.

Yaama may be likened to the Holy Spirit who contributes to our salvation by leading us to God and sustaining our faith in him. In the same way, it is through Yaama that the Chamba knew what to do to be accepted into the kingdom of heaven, and for that reason he obeyed Yaama as we should obey the Holy Spirit. Accordingly, the idea of Yaama must not be rejected outright. It has its importance in the comprehension of the Christian faith today; for although the Chamba did not traditionally know the one we call the Holy Spirit, he can easily understand the role of the Holy Spirit by comparing it to that of Yaama.

When speaking about God the Father, it would perhaps be preferable to use Venĕb, because that name makes the Chamba Christian of today think of an Almighty Person, a Supreme Force that created all things. Yaama, on the other hand, calls to mind an extraordinary creation, but a creation nevertheless. At the same time, we say that our God is rich in goodness, rich in love, and why not rich in names? Just as in the Old Testament Yahweh and Elohim both referred to the God of Israel, so Yaama and Venēb might both be used as names for God, for as the Psalmist says, "The Lord is my light and my salvation."

A Chamba purification rite for having
killed a forbidden animal or person

15. The Chamba Rite of Vɔɔma

by Bouba Bernard

Anchored in the spirit of the Chamba people is the belief that God acts among men through the ancestors by means of what they call **Vɔɔma.** This belief is the major barrier to the penetration of Christianity among the Chamba. In fact, old people continue to accept this belief, and the fear of Vɔɔma has not entirely disappeared even among the young who have accepted the gospel.

It is said that in Chamba society long ago the women did not respect the men. It was necessary to find a means of establishing respect and of punishing evildoers. After long thought about the problem, the men of one family conceived the idea of creating Vɔɔma.

Using calabashes and a type of bamboo, the men made flutes that produced frightening sounds resembling the cries of lions, leopards, and hyenas. Then they took bones, preferably finger bones, of old people long ago and buried them at a place apart from the village where a large pot had been placed or where a hut had been built to serve as "the house of Vɔɔma." It was in the house of Vɔɔma that the flutes and the other objects that were collected were kept. Everything they found in nature that had some extraordinary aspect, such as particularly smooth or shiny stones, worn-out hoes and spears, and clay pots in which they put millet beer and water for the **vənɛb-bira** (gods) to drink, were brought to this house. The Chamba believe that after death a man exists in spirit form and can appear wherever his bones are or where any of the objects that he touched during his life are kept. In this way, by placing the bones of an ancestor or objects used by him in a particular place, one is assured of the presence of that ancestor in that place. Therefore, the bones and the used hoes and spears, which are supposed to represent the soul of Vɔɔma, are kept in the house of Vɔɔma. As to the sounds of the flutes, they are called the "voices of Vɔɔma."

There are as many Vɔɔma as there are families. By family, we mean lineage, that is to say, the group that includes all those who are able to trace their ancestry to a common ancestor who is recognized as the first of the family. We could limit ourselves to the family of a single man rather than discussing the lineage back to the first ancestor, but the latter is preferable since the Vɔɔma is something that is transmitted from generation to generation. Each lineage assures itself of the presence of the spirits of its ancestors and gives each its own name. There is **Vɔɔm-yɛla** 'Red Vɔɔma', **Vɔɔm-vaana** 'Male Vɔɔma', and **Vɔɔm-dinga** 'Black Vɔɔma'. There are others whose names are difficult to interpret because the words have several meanings, **Yɛd-n-kina, Langaa,** and **Wɔɔma,** among many others. Each Vɔɔma is associated with a symbol which is arbitrarily chosen to represent it. The symbol for Vɔɔm-yɛla is the leaf of a certain tree known as **saana,** for Vɔɔm-vaana it is a head of millet, for Vɔɔmdinga a snail shell, for Yɛd-n-kina the leaf of a certain tree called **ləəma,** for Langaa a buttertree leaf, and for Wɔɔma a cow horn. Women and children are formally prohibited from seeing Vɔɔma, which means that they may not see the buried bones, the bamboo flutes, the various objects kept at the house of Vɔɔma, or the people who gather at the house of Vɔɔma on the day of the festival of Vɔɔma.

The position of Vɔɔma chief is held by the eldest member of the lineage. It is he who looks after Vɔɔma. He takes care of the area around the house of Vɔɔma, which is considered a sacred place. It is he who, on his own authority or at the request of someone else, can make Vɔɔma come out for some specific reason; for Vɔɔma is not made to come out without a reason. The Vɔɔma chief presides over the different ceremonies that take place during the Vɔɔma festival and the purification ceremony of which we will speak in the paragraphs that follow. It is the Vɔɔma chief who organizes the boys' circumcisions. The Vɔɔma chief gives part of the first fruits of the harvest to Vɔɔma before eating of them himself. Each time, he takes a small quantity of peanuts, corn, or millet and puts it in the house of Vɔɔma. If he fails to "give Vɔɔma his share," Vɔɔma can turn against him. The Vɔɔma chief also enjoys certain rights before the village chief that the rest of the people do not. While every man who kills a leopard or a porcupine must bring the meat and the skin to the chief, it is the Vɔɔma chief who takes care of the skin and the meat of these animals. The Vɔɔma chief inspires fear and respect. No one meddles in his affairs; no one reaches into his pockets; and no one takes off his hat lest they uncover a "son of Vɔɔma," an object of Vɔɔma that he might have put away. Above all, women and children do not approach him. He is endowed with supernatural power and is even considered a sorcerer, which, in fact, he is not.

At the end of each harvest, the festival of Vɔɔma, which is called "the wine of Vɔɔma," takes place. This festival is dedicated to Vɔɔma and has its purpose "to worship Vɔɔma," as it is said in Chamba. During the entire period of time that has preceded this festival, Vɔɔma is said to have been cold. That is to say that his power is thought to have diminished. Therefore, this festival is necessary to revive him, to renew his power. On the day of the festival, all the millet beer that has been prepared for this purpose is brought to the house of Vɔɔma, where a crowd of people from the neighboring towns have gathered. The first thing that is done is to worship Vɔɔma. The Vɔɔma chief takes a little of the dregs of the beer and places it where the finger bones are buried; then he pours a large quantity of the beer there and also pours some over the flutes and the other objects in the house of Vɔɔma. He accompanies this act with the following words:

> This is the custom left to us by our grandparents. We follow the path which they followed. We worship Vɔɔma, we pray to the spirits of the ancestors to help us in everything we do.

When this ceremony has been completed, the rest of the beer is shared by all those gathered. Each person drinks to the health of Vɔɔma, who, they are certain, approves their action.

It is at the time of worshiping Vɔɔma that those who wish to be initiated into Vɔɔma are received. One must have been circumcised to present himself as a candidate. Children who have not been circumcised are not eligible. The initiation takes place in two stages. The first is called "seeing Vɔɔma" and is for those who have just been initiated. Each candidate, or several together if they belong to the same family, brings a chicken which the Vɔɔma chief can raise in his home among his own flock. This chicken belongs to Vɔɔma and is used for other Vɔɔma ceremonies, for example, the rite of purification; but the chicks which it might hatch belong, not to Vɔɔma, but to the Vɔɔma chief. The difference is that if the hen, which is called "Vɔɔma's chicken" is butchered, only the Vɔɔma chief and those who have undergone the second stage of initiation may eat of it, whereas the Vɔɔma chief may use its chicks for the needs of the family. He can sell them to anyone, or he can butcher them to eat with his wives and his children. Before seeing Vɔɔma, the candidates are made to close their eyes and lie down on their stomachs in a row. Then a shower of blows is rained upon them and when they get up, their backs are all bloody. Only after their faces have been washed with cold water are they permitted to open their eyes and look at the flutes and the various objects in the house of Vɔɔma. The blows that they received were to make them understand that they must never recount to women or to little children what they saw, and the water is to keep Vɔɔma from ever doing anything to them, because when cold water is used by the Vɔɔma chief, it annuls the action of Vɔɔma. The candidates have now "seen" Vɔɔma and henceforth they may be present at Vɔɔma's various ceremonies, but they may neither drink the millet beer of Vɔɔma nor eat the couscous of Vɔɔma.

The second stage of the initiation is for those who have passed through the first. It is called "hitting Vɔɔma," which means completely understanding Vɔɔma. This time each candidate brings a chicken or several candidates bring a goat. The chickens and goats are butchered; and after cooking the meat in a very old pot that is never washed, since it is in this way that all the meals in the house of Vɔɔma are prepared, each chicken and the meat of each goat is given back to the giver to eat up completely. This second initiation gives one the right to drink the beer of Vɔɔma prepared for the festival and to eat the meat of Vɔɔma. The candidates for the first stage of initiation provide a certain number of chickens to be raised by the Vɔɔma chief. But on each occasion he must cut the throat of these chickens at the house of Vɔɔma to let the blood drip on the various objects of Vɔɔma. It is this blood that the spirits of the ancestors will drink. Only the Vɔɔma chiefs and those who have undergone the second stage of initiation may eat these chickens and touch the flutes and all the objects of the house of Vɔɔma, for they alone know the secret of Vɔɔma, which is the **Vɔɔm-waa** "the child Vɔɔma."

When the worship and the initiation have been completed, "Vɔɔma goes dancing." Under the direction of the Vɔɔma chief, a group of dancers, some of them playing flutes, makes a tour

The Chamba Rite of Vɔɔma 169

of the village. These dancers and those who accompany them have the right to take some peanuts, some millet, and some corn from the different gardens that they find on their tour, and the owners are not to complain because it is Vɔɔma who has left his mark. They stop a few moments before the chief's compound to greet the village chief who will give them a gift, a basket of millet, before going back to the house of Vɔɔma where the dance will continue the entire day. This is the time for the new initiates to learn to play the flutes. The peanuts and corn are roasted and eaten that very day at the house of Vɔɔma, but the millet is given to the Vɔɔma chief who will keep it to make beer for the next festival of Vɔɔma.

One speaks of "erasing Vɔɔma" when it is necessary to purify a victim of Vɔɔma. The victim must bring a chicken or a goat and sometimes both, depending on the requirements of the family possessing Vɔɔma. There must also be a little bit of millet. The purification consists of placing an uncooked mixture of millet meal on the chest, back, knees, and feet of the sick person by the Vɔɔma chief. As he does this he says:

> I have said that my Vɔɔma will produce this result on every guilty person, and it will not end unless the victim comes back to see me bringing me a chicken or a goat. That is what has occurred here and it has been confirmed by the diviner that it is you (and he addresses himself to his Vɔɔma, for example, Yɛd-n-kina) that is doing this to this person. Now he has come to me as I had foreordained. Withdraw yourself, leave him in peace.

This event takes place in a corner of the concession hidden from the sight of the women and the uncircumcised children. The chicken or the goat used in this rite is the chicken or goat of Vɔɔma.

The first purpose of Vɔɔma was to make women respect men. So it is that all women, whoever they may be, have no access to the ceremonies that relate to Vɔɔma. In the same way, no uncircumcised boy can know Vɔɔma because he still is living in a setting that is more feminine than masculine. He is still a child who is likely to recount what he sees to the women. Thus, not only are women and children who do not know the secret of Vɔɔma afraid of the voice of Vɔɔma, but they are even punished if intentionally or by accident they happen to see Vɔɔma.

Such a fear must be based on a solid foundation. This foundation is the spirit of the ancestors that descends on the object of Vɔɔma and that punishes every evildoer, especially thieves. The symbol of Vɔɔma is placed on a granary or in a field of peanuts or corn or on any other object. Any person who steals from it is under the curse, "May Vɔɔma stop him." If the theft takes place, the Vɔɔma chief curses the guilty person and invokes Yaama and the gods, that is, the spirits of the ancestors, against him. Some time or even some years later misfortune will befall the guilty person that will result in his own admission of the theft. Vɔɔma has then "stopped" him.

Vɔɔma is also invoked against sorcery. A plague that is ravaging the country can be checked by placing the symbols of Vɔɔma at the entrances to the village and at the crossroads to each of the neighboring villages. Any time there is a celebration in the village, Vɔɔma is invoked against any person who would seek to do evil to his fellow on that day, because some people with evil intentions use festival days to do evil to a great number of people. Any time a woman has given birth, the symbol of Vɔɔma is placed before the compound to protect against any visitor that would seek to take the life of the newborn. The symbol of Vɔɔma is raised beside a path to keep people from passing by; it is placed over a particular location to prevent women from throwing refuse there, at the spring where the village draws water to keep people from dirtying it, and on a fruit tree to keep marauders away.

Vɔɔma acts on the victim by causing an illness whose characteristics are those of Vɔɔma. We stated above that there are many lineages and that there are many Vɔɔma, and each Vɔɔma causes a particular illness. Each lineage has assigned a certain effect to its Vɔɔma. Thus, the Vɔɔma of this lineage causes this illness, and the Vɔɔma of that lineage causes another illness. For example, **Langaa** causes eye diseases, **Yɛd-n-kina** causes abcesses, **Vɔɔm-vaana** causes difficult births, and **Vɔɔm-yɛla** causes broken legs through an accident of some kind. The victim of a certain illness knows immediately which Vɔɔma has caused it, or he asks a diviner who tells him. The Chamba believes that every illness is caused by Vɔɔma. One might be led to believe at this point that every victim is guilty, but such is not the case. In Chamba society where responsibility is collective, Vɔɔma attacks a sister, an aunt, a niece, a cousin, a brother, a nephew, the mother, and when the guilty person is of the same family as the Vɔɔma chief, even he may be one of the victims. It follows then that every guilty person may be a victim, but not necessarily that every victim is guilty; and in the majority of cases, the real guilty person is not the victim. But the guilty person is nevertheless punished through the members of his family upon whom the consequences of his guilt fall. The true guilty person must also participate in the expenses involved in the purification ceremony, and it is for these reasons that everyone fears Vɔɔma.

Therefore, through causing fear and much more by its deadly effects, Vɔɔma is a means by which the Chamba maintain order in society. However, in the eyes of nearly all the Vɔɔma chiefs, Vɔɔma has become a means of becoming wealthy because of the chickens and goats that are brought for the first stage of the initiation. Furthermore, they require more and more chickens and goats from the victims who must be purified, instead of the one chicken or even the one chick that they used to ask. In this way, this practice that once had great value is in the process of losing its importance today.

The power of Vɔɔma resides in the "children of Vɔɔma," the objects of Vɔɔma on which the spirits of the ancestors descend. In effect, the Chamba believes that after death man leaves his physical body to become a god. It is thus that there exist **vanɛb-bira** 'gods', that is to say, the spirits of the ancestors who are believed to be on earth in contact with mankind granting life and health and giving good harvests and children. These spirits protect those of their relatives who are still living on earth and punish their enemies and troublemakers by causing illness to fall upon them.

In Chamba thought there is a hierarchy of gods, at the top of which is placed the great god known as Vanɛb, who created the heavens and the earth. This Creator God sees everything that exists and that takes place on earth by means of the light of the sun which is his eye. But he is too far away to act on the earth where he is represented by the "children of God" who inhabit nature: grass, trees, rocks and water. The "children of God" may be hurt, and they are therefore a danger to people who attack nature.[1] God is also represented by the spirits of the ancestors, who listen to the complaints of people and see to it that God responds favorably to their requests. As regards the relationship between Vɔɔma and Vanɛb, a Vɔɔma chief said, "Vɔɔma is not Vanɛb, but it is Vanɛb who gave us Vɔɔma so that no one would despise us." The

---

1 See Bernard Bouba's article, "Is God Venèb or Yaama? on page 161 of this volume.

expression "Vənɛb who gave" expresses a great depth of meaning for the Chamba for whom everything that exists is the work of Vənɛb, either because he created it or because he permitted or encouraged its creation. Vənɛb, who wishes for all men to live in peace with one another, fights with them against all evil. That is why he gave Vɔɔma, or more precisely, that is why he gave them the idea of creating Vɔɔma. It is by means of Vɔɔma that he influences the lives of men through the spirits of the ancestors with whom he dialogues regarding the life of men on earth.

An old initiate of the two major Gbaya initiations

16. LaBi: A Gbaya Initiation Rite

                    by Thomas Christensen

Introduction

In June 1978, participants at the annual spiritual retreat of the Evangelical Lutheran Church of Cameroun reflected together on the meaning of the sacraments. The subject was not new for the fifty-five year old church; but one way of reflecting on sacramental themes received unprecedented attention. Church leaders representing a dozen ethnic groups, both lay and clergy, as well as many theology and secondary school students, were asked to study and respond to the following questions: Are you familiar with initiation rites which remind you of the sacraments? Does reference to such rites among our people help or hinder the proclamation of the Gospel? Can we find elements, images, practices, and symbols within these rites which actually facilitate the understanding of the Gospel among our people?

The rite most discussed by the participants was laBi, the most important Gbaya initiation rite for boys. Although laBi has not been practiced in most Gbaya areas of Cameroun and the Central African Republic since the 1960s,[1] it is still well known in Gbaya society and is indeed still practiced in some areas. Many Gbaya pastors, evangelists and catechists, as well as some Bible School and seminary students, are initiates of the rite. They are the principal teachers for those of us who are the uninitiated and who seek to understand one of the most prominent elements of traditional Gbaya society.

---

1 LaBi was forbidden by the French colonial administration because it had a negative effect on adolescent boys' attendance at school. It was also condemned by Protestant and Catholic missions.

The study of laBi reveals remarkable symbols and ceremonies which form a bridge between the Gbaya world, with its life and traditions, and the biblical and Christian world, with its life and traditions. This study poses some questions for the Church within the Gbaya milieu: Is traffic on the bridge between Gbaya tradition and the Church a one-way traffic, or can the Church accept circulation going both directions? Is Gbaya tradition a resource for the Church in Cameroun? Can the Church Universal receive something of universal Christian value from that tradition? Or does the Church in Cameroun operate only as a dispenser of other traditions, channeling their flow into the Gbaya milieu?

With those questions in mind, we look at a brief description and interpretation of laBi as explained to us by several Gbaya Christians.[2]

- - - - - - - -

LaBi was the Gbaya way for providing a comprehensive education for adolescent boys.[3] A boy who did not participate successfully in laBi could not become a genuine person. LaBi was a school because the boys received important training, but it was like religion also,[4] because the training received was not only physical and mental--it was also spiritual. LaBi taught boys how to live,[5] how to distinguish between right

---

[2] I express my thanks to Matthieu Haman, Philippe Baba, Daniel Adamou, Pierre Bagoudou, and Nathaniel Ndofe, as well as a number of Gbaya pastors and catechists who were helpful in providing information. Two written sources, Günter Tessmann (1937) and Pierre Vidal (1962), give valuable descriptions and interpretations of the laBi initiation, although the material in this paper comes almost entirely from the above-named colleagues.

[3] Here the past tense is used in reference to laBi in recognition of the fact that laBi is today practiced among the Gbaya only in a few remote areas. The description which follows is, however, given in the present tense as told by the informants.

[4] Mattieu Haman used the term **dina**, an Arabic word, by which he meant "a religious practice." We use the term "spiritual" here in the wider sense to mean the development of a person's character and spirit rather than any particular reference to worship. Worship and sacrifice were not part of the laBi known by my informants.

[5] Haman used the term **dukaa** in Gbaya meaning everyday life and way of living, as distinguished from **dante** 'life'. He specifically refused to use the word **dante** because of its association with Christian interpretations of "eternal life."

A Gbaya Initiation Rite

and wrong. LaBi changed the boys into intelligent men. How did laBi accomplish this change? Any laBi initiate will explain that the change happens when a person "goes under water."

The fathers of adolescent boys, especially those from age twelve to fifteen years,[6] meet with other old initiates at the beginning of the dry season in order to create a new initiation camp.[7] These men might come from a single large village or from several smaller, neighboring villages. They inform "the one who holds the spear" of their intentions so that he will make the necessary preparation. The **narninga** 'the one who holds the spear' is the man in charge. He represents the laws of laBi, and everything having to do with laBi depends on him. He tells some of the former initiates to go build a dam at a stream near the village in order to create a pond whose depth should be about a meter and a half. They remove all sharp rocks, tree stumps, and other obstacles which might interfere with the activities which are soon to take place in the pool.

Other initiates in the village prepare the boys for their departure, counselling them, "You are going away to die. You must take leave of your parents and be sure that all is well between you. You are going to learn how to live as a genuine person. Those who are not initiated into laBi cannot know anything about life; they are worthless!"

The novices must enter initiation completely naked. Their heads are shaved and all clothing is left behind. They are about to begin a new life, a life separated and altogether different from the life they have known, and they must not bring along anything from their previous existence.

Excitement mounts in the village as the old initiates begin to teach the novices a few notions of the initiation dance, which is to be the most demanding and exacting requirement of the entire initiation. "The one who holds the spear" prepares his spear and the other ceremonial accouterments, an enormous straw hat and an assortment of ragged clothes, which will serve to disguise and conceal his iden-

---

6 Although the minimum age was about twelve, laBi often included young men up to age twenty, some of whom had taken wives, but who left their wives during the initiation period.

7 Hunting was a very important part of laBi, and that is a particularly dry-season activity.

tity. The spear, hat, and rags will not be readmitted within the village following the ceremony in the pond because, having served as instruments of death, they will be taboo.[8] The hat and rags must afterward be hung in a **sore** tree and no one must go near them. The spear is henceforth a purely ceremonial object and will never again be used for the hunt.

When the pond is ready and the boys' heads have been shaved, the old initiates cover them with white ashes, a sign of death. Then they begin to chant:

> Tomorrow these children will be changed;
> They will no longer be in the village.
> They will suffer,
> They will no longer do what they've been doing,
> They will be real laBi!
> The leopard has already taken them;
> The lion has already taken them![9]

The chant is an invocation which signals departure for the pond. They lead the novices on a run toward the pond, followed at a distance by the women and the uninitiated. The men sing, proud that their sons will become men, whereas the women wail, fearing the death of their boys. The old initiates sing and dance to the accompaniment of drums, xylophone, and harps. They begin to beat the water furiously with branches (cf. John 5:4), singing:

> **Narninga** stabs with a poison spear;[10]
> Let **Narninga** come!
> Let us go into the water;
> **Narninga** is hiding among the trees,
> They set a trap under the water.

Refrain: Are the uninitiated coming?
> Is **Narninga** coming?
> Do you see **Narninga** coming?

---

8 The term "taboo" is used here in reference to something which incurs the curse of **simbo** (see chapter 12 of this volume, "An Interpretation of Gbaya Religious Practice" by Philip Noss and chapter 17, "Rites of Reconciliation in Traditional Gbaya Society" by myself).

9 All translations from the Gbaya and laBi languages are mine.

10 The "poison" in the song simply means "deadly," since the spear will inflict a "mortal wound."

The men continue to stir up the water of the pool, working their way toward the dam. Then they return to the far end of the pool. After the second complete round of this increasingly vigorous activity, as they begin the third round,[11] the novices are carried into the water and are submerged.[12] The boys are each held by their "godfathers" who keep the boys immersed, being careful that their noses are above water, but pretending at the same time to drown them. The godfathers make the round up and down the pool twice; and as they approach the dam for the third time, the moment for the appearance of "the one who holds the spears" has arrived. He breaks out of hiding and jumps into the water from the dam, hotly pursued by the old initiates who encircle the pond; and they go after him with branches and sticks. But he is too quick for them, and he thrashes his way toward the boys. As he approaches the boys, who are lying on their backs in the water, the godfathers wash their boys' abdomens in preparation for the operation about to be performed. He then thrusts his spear at the abdomen of each novice, and when he has thus succeeded in "killing" them all, he climbs up the dam and disappears into the bush.

During the entire drama, the uninitiated and women must remain at some distance from the pool, the women wailing over the death of their sons. "The one who holds the spear" having left, the godfathers carry their boys out of the water and lay them face down on the ground near the pool, careful that the "mortal wound" on the abdomen not be exposed to the view of the uninitiated and the women. The initiates cover the bodies of the novices with straw as if they were ready for burial. If any of the boys have the reputation of being a nuisance, stubborn and disobedient, in the village, they are severely bound up in the straw to make them believe they will indeed be buried.

The old initiates then carry the novices to the "House of Blood," still accompanied by singing and wailing:

Refrain: Bi-looo! Bi-looo! (a wailing chant expressing grief over death)
The children's dance! The children's dance!
The **laBi** children are crying for food.

11 The number three occurs repeatedly in the description of Gbaya ritual where men are involved, whereas the number four is significant whenever women are involved.
12 The Gbaya term translated here as "godfather" is **daa-kasi-zu,** which means literally "father-hold-head."

> The children's mothers! The children's mothers!
> The laBi children want to dance!

The House of Blood is built in the shape of a horseshoe or womb, a simple construction of poles and leaves, facing away from the village. The novices, still dead, are laid out in front of the house. They may now be severely whipped and beaten by the old initiates, especially the boys who are known to have a rebellious character. Such boys might even have to undergo torture by fire. This is potentially the most dangerous moment during the entire period of initiation in terms of the punishment endured by the boys.

Lying face down in front of the House of Blood, the novices must endure their suffering without murmur or complaint, for to complain would only intensify the beatings. But relief comes when the initiates bring a small leaf, which, rolled up to form a little cone, contains medicine sent by "the one who holds the spear." The boys are on the threshold of a new existence (cf. Turner 1970: 93-111 and van Gennep 1964: 65-115), for the **narninga**'s medicine is to raise them from the dead! The men pour this medicine into the nostrils of each boy, the immediate effect of which is a violent sneeze. All the old initiates shout, "To your health!" and "You are saved (resurrected)!"

The resurrection of the dead has been accomplished. But only the initiated are witnesses of the resurrection, because the uninitiated and the women must believe that the boys are dead. In the eyes of the initiated, the life which follows this event is a new life--it is life after death! The novices sing:

Refrain: We died, we died, bring us food!
               Didn't we die?
              The laBi children who died under water are saved;
              The laBi children suffered under water;
              Stubborn children cannot become laBi children.[13]

The novices enter the House of Blood one by one, and several old initiates leave for the village to bring back food for the risen boys. During the relatively brief time they will spend in the House of Blood, possibly several weeks but usually less, they will receive all their food from the village.

---

[13] The last word in this song says, literally, "The buffalo does not like laBi," and was interpreted by Matthieu Haman.

A Gbaya Initiation Rite

Now enters the **gandimba** 'the one of blood', who takes charge of the initiation as the director and chief teacher. He is a respected laBi initiate who directs the instruction of the "newborn children during the three or four years designated for the completion of their initiation training. The boys are smeared from head to foot with kaolin and are known for a time as "white laBi." The color white indicates, on the one hand, death, and on the other hand, signifies that these boys are separated from the rest of Gbaya society. They are no longer Gbaya but belong rather to their own society.[14] During this period they still remain naked. White laBi are not yet mature laBi.

"The one of blood" counsels the boys:

> Beginning today, you are laBi; you are no longer of the village, you know nothing about the village. You died and rose again. From now on you must not come into any contact whatsoever with women. They must not see you, they must never recognize you, especially pregnant women.[15] If you touch a woman, you will die!

> You must no longer go the same places village people go. You must not lie, or steal, or quarrel with one another. You must obey and submit yourselves without question to the old initiates. You must not eat eggplant, because if you eat eggplant, you will no longer be able to speak the laBi language.

> You must carry wood to the old women and to other incapacitated people in the village. You must carry wood to the **narninga** and to the other old initiates. You must leave wood back of their houses, and never be seen by anyone in the village.

> When you walk along the path, lower your head, and if someone speaks to you in Gbaya, you must never answer. If you speak Gbaya, you will be sent back to the village and you will be full of shame all your life. Never explain a word about laBi during your entire life, or you will die!

When he has finished giving the above exhortations, he makes an incision of four or five centimeters in length on

---

14 This is an aspect of liminality as explained by Turner (1970: 98ff.).

15 The prominence of a pregnant woman's stomach suggests a danger of sorcery, since a person's stomach is where the power of sorcery is located.

the lower right side of the abdomen of each boy.[16] This is the mortal wound which "the one with the spear" is supposed to have inflicted with his spear in the pool. "The one of blood" then takes a raw manioc tuber, dips it into the bloody incision, and gives it to the boy to eat, telling him,

> This is your blood. Now that you eat this blood, if you should ever reveal the secrets of laBi to anyone who is not an initiate, may your own blood kill you! May you die by the knife! May the buffalo kill you with his horns! May the spear run you through! If you reveal the secrets of laBi, may all that God has made kill you![17]

This is the solemn and fearful covenant of laBi, which all the initiated are expected to keep during their entire lifetime. The boy must eat the cassava which has been dipped in his blood. If he simply licks the blood, it is not a real covenant. Cassava and blood represent genuine food, and they must be consumed to seal a genuine covenant.

With whom does the novice make this covenant? He makes this covenant with "the one who holds the spear," who represents all the laws of laBi. One cannot simply seal a genuine covenant with oneself.

Following the covenant rite, the white laBi begin to learn the laBi language,[18] and during this time their incisions are healing. They spend at least two weeks in the House of Blood, and the Gbaya language must be completely replaced by the laBi language. They must not utter another word in Gbaya until the day they leave the initiation camp to return to the village. During this time they also receive their titles and tasks, as well as their nicknames. The titles indicate a certain hierarchy among the boys, for example:

1) **Mbele:** the "president" of the novices, chosen because of his superior leadership qualities. His name means "dance" in the laBi language.

2) **Ninga:** the "vice-president". His name means "spear."

3) **Doko: Ninga's** assistant.

---

16 The place of incision varies. Occasionally it is on the left side, and occasionally a mark was also made on the novice's back to indicate that he had been run through by the **narningna**'s spear.

17 The Gbaya expression meaning "covenant" is **nootok** 'drinking blood'.

18 Vocabulary comparison reveals numerous cognates between the laBi language and Laka languages to the north. The Gbaya also maintain that the laBi initiation originally came from the Laka peoples.

A Gbaya Initiation Rite

4) **Ndanga**: a counsellor who has the right to act as judge when there are problems among the boys. He can replace **Mbele** and **Ninga** in their absence, and he has the right to beat his comrades if they fail to obey.

5) **Betare**: also a counsellor and advisor whose task is to exhort his comrades. Only "the one of blood" can counsel him.

6) **Beloko**: the "sergeant-at-arms" who helps keep order among the boys.

The following are some laBi nicknames:

Boo-kom: the one with deep-set eyes.
Gbir-baa-see: a very short boy.
Koya-sire: an intelligent boy who acts well and adroitly.
Kpang-ɓol: the one with a big stomach.
Kpang-dom: the one with a large head.
Kpang-mbitare: the one whose ears are large and fanned out.
Kpang-mbondoro: the one with a long nose.
Kpenge-dim: the one with skinny shins.
Ndeleng-baa-see: a very tall boy.
Ndeleng-dom: the one with a long face/head.
Poro: the one who loves to sit near the fire.

The novices begin a serious study and practice of **laBi** dances during their stay in the House of Blood. The two most talented dancers are named **Ko-Mbele** and **Yelem-Mbele,** and it is their task to help the other boys learn the multitude of **laBi** dance steps.

Among the elders who assist the teacher, one is called **Sere-Ndimba** 'man of blood'. It is his task to terrify the boys at night. He is equipped with a 'bull-roarer' (cf. Eliade 1965: 21-23), which consists of two different-sized wooden plaques attached together by a cord. He swings the plaques vigorously to simulate a lion's roar and shouts at the top of his lungs, "A lion is attacking us!" The boys run off in all directions; and when they are later reassembled, they are told that the lion swallowed one of their friends. The old initiates will then require the boys' mothers to send them some well-peppered peanut butter, which is presumably given to the lion in order to induce the lion to vomit up his victim (cf. Eliade 1965:22 and Laye 1953:117-41). The elder's name, 'man of blood', indicates that he is preoccupied with drinking his victim's blood.

The study of the laBi language is not carried out on the benches of a school classroom, but as the novices work together. The white laBi are engaged in the construction of a more permanent camp where they will spend at least three years of their life. They will disassemble and abandon the House of Blood and move to the **gbang-lai,** their principal camp during the remainder of the initiation period. This change of camp marks an extremely important step in their initiation. The elders summon the **okoo-pi-gangmo,** 'the woman who throws peace', in order for her to invoke and establish peace among the novices. The boys form a circle. Their fathers and godfathers present them with simple clothing, and they are permitted to wear clothes for the first time since the initiation began. They also receive some accouterments for dance, especially dried pods from the **mbuti** vine which are attached to the boys' ankles. The old initiates again smear the boys with kaolin, but this time they are also anointed with camwood.[19] The camwood shavings are reduced to powder, and oil is added to make a paste which is rolled into a ball. It is used as a cosmetic to beautify the body.

As we have noted above, the kaolin signifies that the white laBi are separated from the rest of Gbaya society; they must not come into contact with women, and they must remain pure and undefiled. The red now introduced by the anointing with camwood indicates a change in status, an evolution as the boys begin to mature. The red shows that the boys have passed through a veil of blood. They have left their past life in order to be liberated through participation in the laBi rites (cf. Turner 1970:94ff).[20]

As the boys dance, the men offer them gifts. The first money given is placed in the clay water pot of "the woman who throws peace," a pot which serves for her ritual libations and which contains the leaves of several plants, especially **sore.** Money placed in the pot signifies an invocation of peace for all that takes place during the initiation. The pot will be carefully looked after in the Initiation House, especially by **Mbele,** the president of the novices. The water in this pot must never be allowed to completely evaporate, for

---

19 For further discussion of "the woman who throws peace" and of the importance of **kui** 'camwood', in Gbaya ritual, see the following chapter, "Rites of Reconciliation in Traditional Gbaya Society."

20 Of the three phases in the initiation rite, separation, liminality, or margin, and reincorporation or aggregation, each is accompanied by appropriate ritual gestures, objects, and colors. Here white is still displayed, but the introduction of red signifies a progression in the novice's status.

A Gbaya Initiation Rite

that would bring an end to the blessing of peace which has been established (cf. Leviticus 24:1-4 and Exodus 27:20-21). The woman sprinkles the novices, using water from her pot and a branch from the **sore** tree, the tree which always symbolizes peace and reconciliation. This rite is the exclusive province of "the woman who throws peace."

The novices move to their new quarters. As we mentioned regarding the House of Blood, the Initiation House is also horseshoe or womb shaped, protected by an enclosure and facing away from the village. The time consecrated to the most serious of the disciplinary beatings is past, and the boys apply themselves to the various lessons involved in the laBi initiation. This is not to say that discipline and punishment are henceforth abolished by any means. But the beatings already endured have had their effect, and the continuation of the initiation takes place in a more relaxed atmosphere. "The one of blood" spent virtually twenty-four hours per day with the boys during the weeks at the House of Blood, but he does not usually spend his nights at the Initiation House. He goes to the village in the evening and returns to the camp each morning.

The boys are all equipped for the hunt--spear, bow and arrows, knives, and poisons--and for fishing. They each carry a stick with which they may defend themselves, for example, if an old initiate is drunk and unduly threatens them. And if they do not receive enough food from their families, they are permitted to invade their village and make off with whatever food they can grab. For such a raid, they disguise themselves by rubbing their bodies with blackened tree bark, which shows their distress and anger at having been neglected. They hide behind a large shield painted white, black, and red, and always carry their stick, which is referred to in the laBi language as the 'food stick'. The shield is not a weapon, but simply a device to discourage recognition by the uninitiated and the women. The boys often go in search of food thus armed. They crouch back of the village and whistle, waiting behind their shields for their family to bring the life-sustaining couscous (cassava balls).

The boys receive training in a number of subjects during their time spent in the second camp. They continue to learn and perfect their knowledge and use of the laBi language. But it is especially the laBi dances and songs that take precedence over all laBi activities. The real worth of each boy is measured first and foremost by his ability to execute the dance steps. He might be excused if he is not particularly agile in other matters, but it is inexcusable not to be able to perform the dances as required by the teacher. If he fails to achieve competence in the dances, he fails the laBi initiation altogether; and if beatings and harassment do not succeed in producing the desired results, the boy might be sent back to his village in shame.

Why is dance so important? It is especially in dance that a Gbaya shows his or her joy. The essential thing in dance is a person's well-being in relation to his or her fellows. Dance as it should be shows **mboo-zu** 'obedience' in the full sense of being at one heart and one mind with each other. Dance is not just a matter of jumping and leaping around. A person cannot know how to dance unless he has worked hard to achieve competence in all the intricate steps of each particular dance. Success in executing these steps brings great joy!

LaBi dances reveal all the secrets of the bush. As each animal has its own way of walking and running and talking and singing, the laBi dance steps reveal all these details. The dance is both drama and pantomime. Genuine dancing is "bursting forth" in dance. If there is no dancing in a Gbaya village, that village is simply not healthy. If there is no dancing, it is a clear sign that there is sickness and hunger in the village.

Second in importance after the dance is the hunt.[21] Hunting is not as significant as dancing because one cannot exhibit one's prowess as a hunter among people as effectively as one can show one's competence as a dancer.[22] The time spent in the Initiation House is a great time if there is plenty to eat. The novices learn the art of making and setting a variety of animal traps, and also the art of making and setting fish nets and traps. They become expert in the art of avoiding danger. Evasive and cunning action is more highly valued in the hunt or in fighting than is straightforward locking of horns. The boys must learn to be highly attentive and discreet. If a boy is excessively timid when he enters laBi, he should leave having acquired courage; if he

---

[21] The disappearance of laBi in recent years is not unrelated to the increasing scarcity of animals in the Gbaya area.

[22] Dancing is a particularly common theme in Gbaya folktales where the hero Wanto can never resist a dance, whether it is the sound of a swaying tree, a creaking bridge, or a cackling hen that reminds him of a rhythm. Whatever he was going to do, whether to perform a rite or to hunt wild game, is immediately abandoned while he dances to the sound of the new rhythm.

A Gbaya Initiation Rite

enters with a rebellious and cantankerous character, he should go home having acquired humility and the ability to work with others.

The boys learn to know and to understand the nature that surrounds them. They learn the names, in the laBi language, of all significant plants and trees, as well as their usefulness and their danger. They learn the names of Gbaya clans and the names and character of other ethnic groups in the area. Although the night is especially for dancing, they also tell tales and learn the wisdom of the fathers as transmitted by oral tradition. They learn also the Gbaya taboos and omens.

The elders insist that the novices must learn self-control. They are to shed tears upon command and stop the flow of tears as quickly as asked. If they do not succeed, they will receive a piece of charcoal to eat with their cassava rather than meat sauce.

All oaths are forbidden, with the exception of "God is witness!" Sorcery is strictly forbidden; and if it appears, it is severely punished. The boy who utters a curse or uses the sorcerer's medicine is shown no mercy. He is beaten and expelled immediately.

Why is sorcery so firmly opposed? The work and fruit of sorcery is death, and laBi is for life. There are no secrets among the novices; they must learn to live in harmony. They eat together, and people cannot share a meal with each other unless there is mutual love and respect. Sorcery shows hatred, and hatred has no place whatsoever in the laBi initiation.[23]

After having spent at least two months in the Initiation House, the novices arrive at another very important step in their initiation, the ceremony called "cut the stick to call

---

23 No pretense of perfection is being made here, for that would be to remove laBi and its practice from reality altogether. Certainly laBi was no more immune to vengeance and jealousy than is the Church. But as sorcery and hatred have no place in the Church, we must also be fair in stating what laBi tried to achieve in terms of an ethic to live by. All of God's grace and all of God's laws did not keep the people of Israel from slaughtering one another. And as the Old Testament scriptures are surprisingly candid in revealing those unpleasant details, our description of laBi would possibly be closer to the whole truth also if we made an effort to elicit the excesses in its practice. We take as our guide and purpose here, however, Philippians 4:8, "...whatever is true, whatever is honorable... think about these things."

the name." All the old initiates assemble in the Initiation House and even "the one who holds the spear" is present. We note the **narninga**'s presence to emphasize again his considerable ritual and symbolic importance, an importance not shared by "the one in blood." The death under the water was the real death, whereas the incision made by "the one of blood" is only a sign of an already accomplished fact.

The presence of another person is also required at this ceremony, that of "the woman who clicks rocks." She is a young virgin who will henceforth live with the novices in the Initiation House, where she will learn the laBi language and prepare food for the boys. She is a kind of little mother to the boys,[24] and she will have a very solemn task to perform right at the end of the initiation period.

The "cut the stick to call the name" ceremony is an examination, and the boys' godfathers are the principal witnesses. A single stick cut from the **sore** tree serves as the blackboard where the secrets of laBi are recorded. Notches are cut in the stick, and each successive notch represents one of the secret lessons which is to be recited perfectly by the novices. The middle of the stick is "the way of the **narninga**," which leads to the Initiation House. The right side of the stick is "the way of laBi," the left side is "the way of death." Although a single stick is sufficient for the ceremony, each novice has his own notched stick which he carries with him in the bush. When he takes a certain path, he leaves his stick in the middle of the path. This is a barrier warning all uninitiated and all women not to follow that particular path.

The ceremony begins when "the one of blood" says, "Today the novices will show us that they are mature. We will therefore give them their true laBi names today." He calls each boy and places the notched stick on the ground before the boy, and the recitation begins:

Gandimba: Labi, speak!
Novice: I'll tell all.
Gandimba: Speak!
Novice: Tell everything. (As he speaks, he indicates successive notches on the stick.) Tell about laBi. Look at the people. Look at the man with the spear. Look at **Narninga,** look only at **Narninga.**

---

24 Iessman had the audacity to suggest a comparison between this young virgin and the Virgin Mary (1937:61).

A Gbaya Initiation Rite

The novice then recites a series of one-line parables, or proverbs, each of which gives us an insight into the values held dear by laBi. Following is a rough translation and brief interpretation of each proverb:

1) One cannot know laBi from outside; one can only know laBi under the water.

   Only a person who has been killed under water during the laBi initiation can really know the secrets of laBi and understand what laBi is all about. Herein lies the fundamental myth about laBi.

2) The insects join their hands in order to cross the river together.

   It is necessary to help one another in order to overcome difficulties and obstacles. Once a person knows the secrets of laBi, he will not suffer as he did, because knowledge of the laBi way changes everything. Mutual help rendered by initiation brothers forms a bridge that enables one to pass from death to life.

3) Look at the color of the genet and the color of the partridge, and these colors will show you something about laBi.

   LaBi helps one to distinguish between right and wrong, between good and bad. The genet is a taboo animal, an animal associated with sorcery. Its white coloring is a sign of death. The partridge has good colorings, which indicate that one's steadiness and obedience will not go unrewarded. The genet's colors change, whereas the partridge's colors remain constant.

4) The one who drinks his brother's blood drinks what is very bitter.

   This proverb is directed against the sorcerer, who is the most destructive element in society. Sorcery is anathema to laBi.

5) The virgin girl knows laBi, but she will never breathe a word of it to anyone else or she will die.

   This parable refers to the little mother of the novices who knows the laBi secrets, but cannot reveal them to another person. In a more general sense, this is a law forbidding a person to reveal the secrets of another person. If someone has told you the secrets of his life, it remains between the two of you, and if you reveal those secrets, you will die. Even if those secrets involve someone's serious sins, you must forgive and end the affair rather than tell others about it.

6) If someone tries to kill you, you must survive/escape.

One must avoid death and not seek revenge. Evasive action and avoidance of danger is highly valued, whereas anyone who looks for trouble will surely find it.

7) What happens when you show off your strength? You'll find a battle.

This proverb in the form of a riddle again counsels against imprudent and proud display of strength. The strongest person is the one who avoids death, not the one who shows off his muscles. Quarreling leads to death.

8) The one who begins his work knows how to finish it.

This word is meant especially to praise "the man of blood" who has begun teaching the novices and who knows how to bring the laBi initiation to a successful conclusion. It can also mean, "You've made your own bed; now you can lie in it."

9) What medicine do you take when you're cold? Fire.

This is another riddle, and it suggests, as interpreted by a laBi initiate, that doing good is what keeps a person from doing evil.

10) The axe that cuts the wood will not remain next to the fire.

If you do evil to someone, you'll never achieve a good result. This proverb sees the axe as an object bearing the curse of death, because it is here understood as an instrument of death. If you sow evil, you will reap evil.

11) The knife that cuts up the meat will never eat the meat.

The hatred that has caused a person to kill his brother must cease; it must not push him even further to eat him! The lips that have pronounced evil words against a brother can never help anyone.

When the above proverbs have been satisfactorily recited by the novice, the teacher responds, "Now this laBi knows what is necessary." The novice receives his real initiation name, and when all have passed the examination, their success is celebrated by dance and a festive meal.

Another important event in the laBi initiation is the ceremony called **danga-lingi** (cf. Eliade 1963:265-300 and 1965:77-78).[25] The novices must first be considered mature before this ceremony can take place; in other words, it cannot precede the examination described above.

The novices are told to dig a hole in the initiation encampment, after which all the boys meet with the old initiates in the gallery forest. They take the water pot of "the woman who throws peace" and place it at the foot of a **kutu** tree, a tall straight tree known in laBi as the "dance tree." This tree will be the focal point for countless laBi dances. They fell the tree and remove the bark so that it is quite smooth, but they do not remove the leaves at the very tip of the tree. They tie a little package of medicine right at the tip of the tree with a **yɔyɔngɔ** vine. Then they all carry the tree on one shoulder back to the encampment, singing all the way. Even if there are fifty or a hundred boys, they carry the tree together. They plant the tree in the middle of the encampment so that it stands tall and firm. They again place the water pot at the foot of the tree and break forth with increasing joy in singing and dancing.

One of the leaders among the boys, for example **Ndanga**, is designated to climb the tree. **Ndanga** shinnies up the tree, right up to the top. When he makes it to the top, he peeks into the little package of medicine. This is the laBi medicine, having nothing whatsoever to do with sorcerer's medicine. In the package, which looks like a little bird's nest, there might be goat and chicken dung, fingernails and clippings of hair. The matter of **Ndanga**'s looking into this secret package is extremely important--his act gives strength and encouragement to all his brother novices, for he represents them all. He is sealing a covenant on their behalf.

The fact that **Ndanga** has succeeded in shinnying up the tree and has now looked into the secret medicine is a sign that well-being and harmony reigns in the initiation camp. If quarreling and hatred had dominated among the novices, **Ndanga** could not have succeeded in performing this act. His success is a sign of blessing on all the brothers and is again an

---

25 Some informants use the term **danga-lingi** only for the women's initiation rite **zaabolo**, and refer to **danga-yanga** for the laBi rite. Cf. Eliade's comments on sacred poles and the cosmic tree (1965:77-78, 118 and 1963:265-300).

occasion for all the boys to manifest their joy in wild dancing at the foot of the tree. The old initiates embrace the boys and each other.

Ndanga must come down head first. When he is halfway down the tree, he stops in order to give a recitation, similar to the recitation of the "cut the stick to call the name" ceremony. **Ndanga** explains the songs of the robin chat, which is the bird of laBi.[26] No bird can compete with the robin chat's songs. He sings the secrets of laBi; he tells you the good things you should do and the bad things you should avoid doing. Any genuine laBi initiate is able to interpret the robin chat's songs. He tells about the arrival of the moon and also the year; in other words, he is a kind of prophet or seer who helps you look into the future. He explains about "lying on your back at night with your eyes open," reflecting on what has happened today and thinking about what will happen tomorrow.[27] **Ndanga**'s recitation is the robin chat's song, which tells the secrets of laBi:

> I climbed up the tree in order to reach heaven, but I found death in the basket. I went up and found death, and now I am coming back to tell you. We must be careful lest we die from telling the secrets of laBi, because what I found in that basket was death and what I learned was that death is a dangerous thing and that heaven is far away. Only through dying can a person go to heaven. As initiates into laBi, we must be obedient to what we have seen in the basket. I went and saw it on your behalf, because it was not possible for all of us to go, and now we must all be obedient. I did not go without a reason; I went because you sent me to look at it in your place. Now let us be careful because of death. Death is not something to play with, death is something dangerous.

Ndanga then completes his descent and is welcomed back to earth by his brothers. "The woman who throws peace" might be

---

26 Cossypha caffra: the most melodious and spectacular whistler of West African birds. I was not familiar with him until I worked at putting these notes on laBi together, during which time he made a point of singing every day in the garden outside my office window. To be fair, he should be listed first among my informants!

27 My informants complain that this quality is no longer evident in today's younger generation. They describe today's youth as "doing everything with no consciousness of why they're doing it or where it will lead." The recitation of the robin chat's song quoted here was given by Haman Matthieu.

present that day to again sprinkle the boys in an act of benediction, and her water pot remains at the foot of the tree throughout the remainder of the initiation. When the Initiation House is disassembled, this important tree will also be pulled out of the ground.

Before we describe the final ceremonies, another of the laBi games might be noted. As mentioned above in regard to the lion of laBi, the old initiates take delight in tricking and frightening the novices. Reference to the "laBi spirit" entails a game whereby the elders obtain a bit of forced labor from the boys. During the rainy season it becomes increasingly difficult to find good dry wood. The men warn the boys that the laBi spirit is displeased with their laziness, and that he will soon be upon them because they are not carrying wood as they should. In the middle of the night they encircle the encampment and raise a terrible noise. The novices, believing that the spirit of laBi has indeed come to carry them off, disperse in all directions and remain in the bush until encouraged by the old initiates to return. It is hoped that they will henceforth take more seriously their responsibility to provide wood.

We proceed, then, to the final ceremonies. The day arrives when "the one of blood" and the old initiates decide that the boys are ready for graduation. They are told to disassemble the Initiation House, and very early in the morning they meet next to a stream with "the one who holds the spear" and with "the one of blood." They are led into the stream where **Gandimba** washes each one, telling them in the Gbaya language, "We wash you in order to take away laBi, because you are now a new person." **Narninga** also washes each boy. If they are not washed, they will not be able to speak Gbaya again. After the boys have also washed themselves, they return to the banks of the stream.

The old initiates then prepare a little fire of grass. The boys jump over the fire one by one; and the last one extinguishes it, stamping it out with his bare feet, thereby putting an end to the trials and the suffering of laBi. A branch of the **sore** tree is also laid on the ground, and each boy must jump over the branch. LaBi is a thing of death, and the **sore** calms the taboo so that the boys can re-enter their village purified of any pollution.

Another purification rite is that involving a goat. Although the connection is not clear, in the Gbaya language the word for "goat" and for "sorcery" is the same: **dua,** in addition to the rites of washing and of jumping over fire and a **sore** branch, the boys also stamp a goat to death. They jump on the victim one by one until it succumbs. Unlike the scapegoat of Hebrew tradition, however, the laBi scapegoat is eaten by the old initiates (cf. Leviticus 16:6-28).[28]

If the initiation does not last its full term, for example, if it lasts less than one year, the above rites precede the triumphal re-entry into the village. But if the initiation goes its full several-year term, the genuine graduation ceremony is that which follows.

The little mother takes two white stones and dips them in oil.[29] The boys all lie down in a row before her. **Narninga** 'the one who holds the spear' takes **Mbele**'s right hand; **Gandimba** 'the one of blood' takes his left hand; and little mother says, "Here are the laBi stones, which I touch over you." When she touches the stones together, they must give a firm click as a sign that the boy has succeeded well during the initiation. The oil from the stones runs down the neck of the first candidate as a sign of blessing (cf. Psalm 133), and little mother continues her work on down the line. These boys are now "laBi over whom the stones have been touched." They have received their diplomas with honors.

If the initiation does not last its full term, the old initiates put a medicine in the boys' ears to enable them to again understand the Gbaya language. But if it goes its full term, the above ceremony replaces the medicine.

Narninga washes his hands in front of the old initiates and the boys' fathers, signifying again that the dangers of laBi pollution have been effectively washed away and that the boys can now be freely reincorporated into normal Gbaya society.

The moment of the joyful re-entry into the village has at last arrived. Known as "climbing up (of) laBi" and as "pulling out (of) laBi," it is an event of general celebration and rejoicing for the graduates and for the entire community. The old initiates, especially the godfathers and the fathers, adorn the boys with all the accouterments of dance, and their bodies are anointed with camwood and oil. This time it is no longer a question of kaolin, the sign of death! However, when

---

28 In some areas the novices do not actually kill a goat, but stamp on the leaves of the **gbor** plant. It is nevertheless called **dua-ndu-yi** 'goat by the water'.

29 Stones also play an important role in folktales and myth. For another instance where two stones were important, see "Karnu: Witchdoctor or Prophet?" in this volume.

A Gbaya Initiation Rite

the boys return to the village, they are first hidden under newly woven grass mats and are not immediately identified by their families. These mats again recall the death-resurrection theme, because the Gbaya wrap their dead in new mats for burial. The procession is accompanied by this song:

> All you laBi, hide under your mats, come quickly!
> Oh you mothers of laBi,
> your children have come to dance!

When the boys are all assembled before the villagers, all crouching under their mats, **Narninga** appears again on the scene with his spear and disguise and repeats the same performance which marked the death of the boys under water. As he approaches the boys for the third time, they throw off their mats, resurrected from the dead. And the resurrection dance breaks forth, the entire population consumed by the frenzy of joy that indeed bears witness to the raising of the dead!

If the boys have not succeeded in learning well the teacher's lessons, especially if they show no competence in dancing, their godfathers are quite unhappy and the boys themselves are mocked by everyone. On the other hand, success is generously rewarded by gifts of money and clothes.

The boys have emerged from their status as novices to become initiates. Their character and behavior should henceforth witness to this fundamental change. They must conduct themselves wisely and judiciously as sensible men who contribute to the well-being of Gbaya society. Those who have suffered the trials of laBi together and who have honorably succeeded have a special fraternal relationship for the remainder of their days. They should respect and help one another and never deceive each other.

As mentioned above, in order for a Gbaya boy to achieve genuine adulthood, he must follow the path indicated by "the one of blood" and the old initiates. But what about someone who, for a valid reason, has never been able to participate in the laBi initiation? Compassion is occasionally shown to such men when the initiates take them to the House of Blood and, without making the laBi incision, reveal the secrets of laBi to them. They have not actually been killed under water and cannot be considered genuine laBi initiates, but the shame of total exclusion has nevertheless been removed.

If a boy dies in the bush during laBi initiation, it is strictly forbidden to speak of his death to his mother. All the boys are, in any case, to be considered officially dead until they appear openly in the village during the final celebrations. On that day, the old initiates place a **sore** branch over the doorway of the boy's mother. By this sign she knows that her son is indeed dead, and she mourns death in solitude.

- - - - - - - -

Conclusion

Participants at the spiritual retreat mentioned in the introduction to this discussion responded positively to the questions regarding initiation rites. There are indeed images, practices, and symbols within these rites which facilitate the understanding of the Christian message among African peoples. They noted especially the themes of death and resurrection, purification, communion, reconciliation, covenant, obedience, contrast between old and new, blessing, and celebration in the laBi rite which, from a Christian perspective, appear as foreshadowings that prepare for the understanding and reception of the gospel. These themes provide the Gbaya, for example, with redemptive analogues through which the gospel can come to new and unprecedented expression for them (Richardson 1976:10).

LaBi is not part of history as recorded in the Hebrew scriptures, nor can Gbaya traditions replace Old Testament traditions. But "whatever is true, whatever is honorable, whatever is just, whatever is pure, whatever is lovely, whatever is gracious, if there is any excellence, if there is anything worthy of praise" (Philippians 4:8; see Koyama 1974:43-45) in laBi, the Gbaya can think about those things as belonging to a larger salvation history in which God has been active in order to bring the Gbaya to faith in Jesus Christ.

Such an understanding is in no way diluting or drowning the gospel. It is rather discovering anew how "God so loved the world," and that "God sent the Son into the world, not to condemn the world, but that the world might be saved through him" (John 3:16-17). His messengers have been going into all the world preaching the gospel to the whole creation; and ever since the Apostle Paul, wherever this preaching has found a genuine hearing, the body of Christ has grown. Christ has drawn countless peoples to himself, and the Church has

A Gbaya Initiation Rite   195

received into herself countless traditions. That is one way God continually enriches the Church. Reflection on the laBi initiation rites among Gbaya Christians today will certainly not result in a revival of the initiation, but it can prepare and help the Gbaya into a deeper appreciation and appropriation of the gospel.

The laBi covenant is a fearful covenant. It strictly forbids the revelation of the laBi secrets revealed in the foregoing pages, and in some Gbaya milieux today the laBi initiates would be furious with those who have provided us with this information. The Jews were furious with Jesus when he broke with their traditions in order to bring those traditions to fulfillment--to their full meaning. The laBi initiates who have entered into the new covenant with Christ do not fear breaking their old covenant, and they have witnessed to their freedom in Christ by telling us the laBi secrets. By so doing, they are certainly not despising their old covenant; they are not looking with contempt on laBi and what they learned there. They are recognizing that God did not leave himself without a witness in traditional Gbaya society, and that whatever is honorable within their tradition has been given by God for their fulfillment as his people. So they can freely share their secret with those of other traditions, because in the new family created by God in Christ, "there is nothing hid, except to be made manifest; nor is anything secret, except to come to light" (Mark 4:22).

Bibliography

Eliade, M. 1963. Patterns in Comparative Religion. Cleveland: The World Publishing Company.

------. 1965. Rites and Symbols of Initiation. New York: Harper and Row.

Koyama, K. 1974. Waterbuffalo Theology. New York: Orbis Books, Maryknoll.

Laye, C. 1953. L'Enfant Noir. Paris: Librairie Plon.

Richardson, D. 1976. Peace Child. Glendale, California: G/L Publications.

Tessmann, G. 1937. Die Baja: Ein Negerstamm im Mittleren Sudan. Vol. 2. Stuttgart: Strecker und Schröder.

Turner, V. 1970. The Forest of Symbols: Aspects of Ndembu Ritual. Ithaca: Cornell University Press.

van Gennep, A. 1964. The Rites of Passage. Chicago: University Press.

Vidal, P. 1962. L'Initiation dans l'Education Traditionnelle, Population Gbaya-Kara: Nord-Ouest de la République Centrafricaine. Le Havre: Bangui.

17. Rites of Reconciliation in Traditional Gbaya Society

by Thomas Christensen

Introduction

The Gbaya are conscious of three basic levels of relationship which must be maintained in order to assure a peaceful and harmonious existence. At one level is the relationship to be maintained between man and God, between man and the spirits. At another closely related level is the relationship to be maintained between man and the ancestors. The Gbaya have within their tradition very specific ways, that is, rites, the practice of which is believed to keep these relationships intact. Referred to as "fixing" the spirits and "fixing" the ancestors, traditional Gbaya rites at these two levels of relationship have especially conciliation in view.[1]

The third basic level of relationship to be kept intact is also the most urgent from the Gbaya point of view--everyday interpersonal relationships. When things go wrong between the Gbaya, there are many ways to repair the broken or damaged human relationships, specific ways which are taken according to the particular circumstances. Some are more or less informal; others attain the status of ritual where ritual objects, procedures, and gestures occur. When the Gbaya perform their rites to conciliate the spirits and the ancestors, they are seeking a blessing of peace, harmony, and continued orderly existence. When they respond to the need for reconciliation among themselves by means of special ceremonies and rites, they are actively seeking the same blessing. In the following

---

[1] See chapter 12, "An Interpretation of Gbaya Religious Practice" by Philip Noss, for a description and interpretation of these two types of Gbaya ritual.

paragraphs, we will describe some examples from Gbaya tradition which show us the "Gbaya way" for effecting reconciliation in day-to-day living relationships.

Informal ways of repairing broken relationships

We will first describe the basic way of reconciliation between two Gbaya who have fallen out with each other. How do the Gbaya patch up a serious quarrel? What is the traditional way of solving heavy words between two individuals?

When words which involve accusations of wrongdoing break out between two men in a village and those words threaten to disrupt peace between the two families involved, the village counselor goes to counsel the two men. This counselor is self-appointed. That is to say, he and all the villagers believe that God has given him his task. He is somehow naturally equipped for it, and everyone in the village respects his position and relies on his work. He goes first to the one person, then to the other, and when they have both calmed down, they meet to greet each other. They address each other in words something like these:

> Brother, the words which upset us are finished. I don't hold any words in my heart against you. What you said (or did) to me made me angry, and we quarreled, but now it's finished!

Ideally, they then embrace, forget the matter, and resume a normal relationship. We note here especially the role of the counselor in the work of reconciliation.

Many Gbaya maintain that it is not in their tradition to say in so many words, "Forgive me," or "Pardon my sin against you." One way of understanding what is sin in Gbaya thought is in terms of whatever breaks the peace and disrupts harmonious relationships. This may involve, for example, the breach of certain societal interdictions (Evans-Pritchard 1970:17). Reconciliation can then be effected when the quarreling parties freely say to each other, "I no longer hold those words in my heart (literally, 'liver')."

If a person has offended someone, but the offense was accidental, the offender goes to the offended and says,

> Father, I beat hand to you; what happened was not my intention. I did not prepare this thing!

"Beating hand" is a traditional Gbaya gesture of supplication and request for forgiveness.[2] The offended person responds to the gesture by saying that he does not hold the offense in his heart, and the two greet each other to signify that peace is restored between them. The offended person will not accept that the offender be brought before the village court, because the offender has "beaten hand" to him, a gesture which is recognized as having effected reconciliation.

Another basic method of reconciliation among individuals is for the offended person to send a counselor, an elder, to the offender. If Garba has damaged Adamou's garden, Adamou will send an elder to Garba in order to "close thing" or "pay thing," that is, to "fix" the affair. Garba kneels before the elder and beats hand to him, asking him to go to Adamou and beg for mercy on his behalf. Garba does not speak harsh words or deny his fault, because that would urge Adamou to bring him before the court. Adamou accepts the request for mercy transmitted by the elder, and Garba must then go to thank Adamou for his compassion.

If two men quarrel as they are hunting together in the bush, their words must not return to the village. They must "fix" the words prior to their return. If there are words between men concerning the kill on a hunt, it would be shameful for such words to reach women's ears. If there are words between women, the men must take the initiative in patching them up, because, claim male members of Gbaya society, "Women don't kill words between themselves very quickly!"

Reconciliation of the simbo curse

From informal ways of repairing broken relationships, we turn to one of the most significant of Gbaya rituals, that performed to purify a person of the curse of **simbo**. The curse of **simbo** falls upon anyone who kills his fellow man, or who kills any one of several especially revered animals. That person's relationship with all his fellows has been broken and cannot be restored until he has undergone the purification rite. To be purified of the curse of **simbo** is to be reconciled with the higher forces which have been offended, and at the same time to be reconciled with fellow members of society whose existence has been threatened by the offense.

---

2 See Psalm 143. The Jerusalem Bible entitles this psalm, "A humble entreaty," and verse six reads, "I stretch out my hands, like thirsty ground I yearn for you."

This ritual is perhaps the most important and representative of Gbaya reconciliation rites because, as Noss explains, "**Simbo** was the violation of that life which was inherently inviolable."[3] Here the danger of broken relationships is at its utmost; here the need for reconciliation is most urgent. The **simbo** rite effects reconciliation both vertically and horizontally, between the offender and God, and between the offender and his fellow man.

If a person has killed an animal with which the **simbo** curse is associated, for example, a leopard, when that person returns to his village, he must carefully deposit all his hunting equipment and all the articles which accompanied him on the hunt in a single designated spot. When he enters his village, he must not speak to another person. He must not associate with any member of his family. The only person who may speak with him is someone who has previously killed the same **simbo** animal and who has undergone the rite of "washing **simbo**." His hunting companions must remain on the path outside until the "person-do-**simbo**," the lay priest, has prepared the scrapings from the **sore** tree in a pot or gourd. He puts water in the gourd over the scrapings and then goes to all those who participated on the hunt and applies his preparation, first to their shins, and then to all their weapons in order to calm or neutralize the curse. The hunters may then go on home without further ceremony, except for the men who actually killed the animal. The man who initiated the kill and his companion who finished off the kill must go and sit under the little shelter at the center of the village. Food is brought to them in pots and gourds. The person permitted to bring them food is someone who has himself gone through the **simbo** ritual, probably the lay priest himself. They must remain in this shelter for three days, during which time their children and wives, as well as all the villagers, must keep their distance from them.

When this period has elapsed, the lay priest goes to them very early in the morning in order to lead them out to the place where they will be washed. Everything that accompanied the men during the hunt must be brought along: clothes, weapons, and also the eating utensils used during their three days in the shelter. If anything is omitted, the curse of **simbo** will come upon them again. The lay priest strips the men of all clothing and all their personal belongings; then

---

3 Quoted from "An Interpretation of Gbaya Religious Practice" in this volume.

he leads them into the gallery forest where they will descend to the stream for the washing ceremony. As they leave town, the lay priest gives them loincloths to wear. He leads them first to a **sore** tree. The three men join hands and walk around the tree, after which the priest takes some scrapings from the tree. They go to a **kiri** tree and do the same thing. The priest again takes along some scrapings. The same procedure is followed with the **gbalamgba** tree. Then the priest takes leaves from the **zee** tree and a piece of the **yoyongo** vine, after which he proceeds to dam up the stream. The priest has also gathered several other leaves on the way to the stream, and now he places all the leaves on the water which has been dammed up, and the three men enter the water together. The priest invokes the blessing. He calls the name of the person who washed him of the **simbo** curse and who entrusted to him the task of washing others; then he washes the two men. As he washes them, he places all the tree scrapings under water. When the washing is completed, the priest opens up the dam so the water can run freely again. As the water carries away the **simbo** curse, the ceremony is over and the men come up out of the water.

The priest gives to each of the men a new cloth to wear. He takes a piece of **yoyongo** vine as a belt for each of the men, and another piece of this same vine in order to tie leaves of the **zee** tree to their right hand. Then he leads the men home to the village. As they return home, the priest picks some leaves of the **zobo** tree. He leads the men to a house where they will get ready to be presented to the villagers. To make themselves presentable and as a sign that **simbo** has been washed away, they must "invoke **tobo**."* This is symbolized by red and white spots that are painted on the men's faces. Then they can leave the house, and the great dance and festivities may begin. They each carry a special shield, and they engage in mock warfare with the villagers. After having made the round of this mock warfare three times, the villagers come to honor the two men. They present small gifts to them. There is great excitement and much fun as everyone pushes close to see the two men. For this event a special drum called the **kanga** drum is brought into service.

---

* **Tobo** is a test and proof of innocence or guilt. In this case it is a test to prove that the curse of **simbo** is gone. A person accused of the death of someone may be required to "drink **tobo**," that is, to drink water that the dead person's feet have been washed with, or to eat food that has been placed in the corpse's mouth. If he is guilty, he will die. --Ed.

Among the Gbaya, whenever men hear this drum, they stop and reflect on their deeds of bravery and times of personal danger encountered in the past.

In the evening, the priest prepares a meal of the **zobo** leaves. He calls the two men who killed the leopard, and he calls their families and some of the villagers. The priest places food in the mouths of the two men and in the mouths of all those present. Then the men are free to return to their homes and eat again with their families as before. They can now visit with each other again and resume normal relationships, because the washing of **simbo** has been completed. The curse has been neutralized; the danger is past.

We noted above that the **simbo** rite effects reconciliation both vertically and horizontally, between the offender and higher powers, and between the offender and his fellow men. Certainly the effectiveness of virtually all Gbaya ritual embraces both dimensions at once, and where one level of relationship is explicit in a particular rite, the other levels are implicit. The three levels of relationship are not mutually exclusive, but are simply parts of a whole. The focus of particular Gbaya rites makes explicit and helps to distinguish those specific relationships which are deemed important in Gbaya society.

Gbaya rites are all straightforward acts with a very clear goal in mind. Objects, procedures, and gestures in the rites are symbols from Gbaya tradition; they are special vehicles of Gbaya thought and myth that are dramatized in the rites.

We now proceed to the description of various rites which focus on particular relationships in the Gbaya community. The relationships alluded to in each case have developed problems, and the rites of reconciliation serve as practical ways of handling and solving the specific family or community problem.

Some problems arise as the result of tragic occurrences, others because of disputes. Sometimes a general malaise hangs over the community, as if some inexplicable dry rot has set in and brought everyone's physical and mental health into jeopardy. The Gbaya refuse to observe all these things fatalistically, they refuse to leave things to chance; instead, they seek practical solutions. This might entail the reconciliation of differences between people, or the reconciliation of forces which affect human relationships. But if the Gbaya are not fatalists, neither are they cold pragmatists. They are reverently utilitarian in solving their problems!

Their rites indicate that they are a people who feel deeply, a people who have a reverence for life and for the stuff of life.

Reconciliation necessitated by a hunting accident

If a buffalo has killed a person within a certain territory which had been burned for the hunt, when the time has come to hunt in that territory again, an elder of the family whose blood was shed on that ground will assemble the village in order to **tok yongo** 'invoke judgment'. More specifically, the elder will **tok de yongo** 'invoke God's blessing' upon the ground and upon all who walk there, both man and beast.[4] The elder explains to the people assembled how the blood of his relative was shed on this land, that the man's blood "paid for this place." He explains that all will be well here now. There is no longer reason to fear danger when hunting in this particular territory, because a man's blood has been shed here and God has blessed the area.

The same procedure is observed when a man has drowned. All subsequent fishing in that part of the river must await the blessing to be invoked by the family of the deceased. Families not related to the deceased must ask special permission to hunt or fish in such areas. The ground where a man was killed on the hunt, the area of a river where a man was drowned while fishing--these territories have been purchased by the blood of the deceased and, upon request by his family, blessed by God. God has put peace on that land or on that water.

This rite is an example from Gbaya tradition that expresses the need felt for divine intervention in human relationships. The rite constitutes a simple appeal to God for him to exercise his justice, and especially that he bless the community by restoring order to the hunt. As in the previous example, blood has been spilt, a life has been taken, and

---

4 The opposite invocation, **toka dang yongo,** would be to call for God's judgment in the form of a curse. As regards the relationship between blessing and curse, see Evans-Pritchard (1970: 172):

...as with curses, blessings are thought to be effective only because God makes them so. Just as a curse is an imprecatory prayer (for if God is not formally addressed, it is understood that it is his affair), so a prayer is implied in a blessing. It is a benedictory prayer.

Note that **tok** means 'to pierce' or 'to spear' (**toka sadi** 'spearing animal': **toka laa** 'piercing cloth, i.e., 'knitting').

that is not to be taken lightly. The spilling of blood has changed the order of things and has necessitated an act of reconciliation.

We now turn to several types of Gbaya ritual in which special objects are used to symbolize peace and well-being. In all our examples of Gbaya rites which focus on reconciliation between persons and on peace within the community, we should note that the prayer for blessing is either explicit or implicit. Rites are performed in order for God to "bless us."

"Throwing sore"

We have already encountered **sore** as something that placates **simbo**. It is a tree of the savanna which produces edible fruit early in the rainy season.[5] According to Gbaya tradition, the **sore** is a very special symbol of peace and reconciliation, as the following examples illustrate.

If you wish to fight with someone but that person has no desire to fight you, he may "throw **sore**" to you, either by taking a branch of the tree and placing it between you and him, or by saying, "I throw **sore** to you!" which is to say that he will not fight you. If you respect this gesture of reconciliation, the fight is finished. But if you cross over the **sore**, people will say to one another, "Did you see that behavior which merits a curse?" You have sinned, you have breached an interdiction of Gbaya society. If you do not respect **sore**, you can expect trouble, and your trouble can be interpreted as God's will for you.

The Gbaya gave the title "**sore**-conciliate-thing" to certain elders who were especially adept at calming fights and reconciling differences. If a fight is raging between two persons, a neutral person may cut a **sore** branch and throw it between the fighters. Whoever crosses over the branch and continues to fight is subject to dire consequences. On the other hand, if you have words with someone and a third party wants to interfere in the affair, you can say to him, "I throw **sore** to you," in which case, he must keep his nose out of your business.

If an adolescent boy dies during **laBi**, the initiation rite of passage, no words about the boy's death are reported to his mother. The men in charge of the initiation will, how-

---

5 The **sore** is the Annona arenaria Thonn. tree.

ever, place a **sore** branch over the entry of the mother's house during the night. In the morning everyone will know what has happened, but there will be neither discussion nor mourning of the death in the village until the other boys have completed the initiation. The **sore** is to "put peace" on the boy's mother.

Someone who has killed another person may leave town by the nearest path. If he throws a **sore** branch behind him in the path, those wanting to follow him see it as a barrier thrown up in front of them. They must give up the chase and return to the village. In this case, **sore** has throttled plans for vengeance and has at least temporarily freed the murderer.

Let us suppose there is a big quarrel between two villages. A person living in either one of these villages who is related to one village through his father and to the other village through his mother is qualified to act as reconciler between the two, provided that he himself has no personal quarrel with an individual living in the other village. He may then "throw **sore**" between the two villages and thereby effect reconciliation.

Is **sore**, then, a medicine with magical properties? Is the **sore** tree sacred in Gbaya tradition? However the Gbaya conceive the values and even the power associated with **sore**, its importance for the Gbaya is that it shows or symbolizes peace, reconciliation, and wholeness. The Gbaya have no interest in analyzing **sore**, "root and all, and all in all," as would the curious Westerner.[6] Their interest is in what **sore** effects for them.

The above examples illustrate the Gbaya belief in **sore** as one of the ways available to them for effecting reconciliation among themselves. The **sore** tree is looked upon them as an eminently good tree. But it is also an eminently common tree whose fruit is enjoyed by all. It is a common thing set apart in particular circumstances to do something good and useful, but around which there is no aura of magic or sacredness. The same can be said for all the other objects we meet in the following examples.

---

6 Quotation from Alfred Lord Tennyson's poem, "Flower in the crannied wall" (Strange 1974:274).

"Anointing kui"

Kui is camwood, a tree of the savanna. Shavings of the **kui** tree are pounded and water is added to make a kind of mash or pulp to be rubbed on a person. Oil is rubbed over the red pulp to make it glisten. Red symbolizes celebration, fulfillment, and well-being; red is the color of life.

If a hunter accidentally kills another hunter with his arrow, the family of the deceased will seek vengeance.[7] The family responsible for the death will therefore "anoint **kui**" on a young virgin and take her to the offended family. Their acceptance of the young girl signifies that peace has been restored. She is not kept as a slave, but is taken as a wife. Her first child will bear the deceased hunter's name.

When a married person dies, his parents or his brothers may anoint the widow or widower with camwood to witness that the marriage had been successful. In other words, the survivor, who is their daughter or son-in-law, had not committed adultery and had been faithful in looking after the needs of the deceased. In this case, camwood symbolizes fulfillment and well-being in the marriage relationship.

If a woman has left her husband in order to marry another man, she will bear no children in the new union until the first husband has been appeased. She and her new husband take some gifts and go to spend the night with the first husband. The gifts represent their desire that the offended husband invoke a blessing on them so that the woman will bear children in the new marriage. The offended husband will rise early in the morning and anoint his estranged wife with **kui** as a sign that all is forgiven. The woman has received the blessing, peace has been re-established, and she will certainly bear children by her new husband.

When one person owes another a large sum of money and sees no way of repaying his creditor, he may anoint one of his young daughters with camwood and give her as a wife to repay the creditor, saying to him, "I'm giving you a wife to repay my debt to you. Let this be a covenant between us!" In this case, camwood symbolizes fulfillment of a promise and restoration of order between the two families.

---

7 The following expressions reflect the importance Gbaya culture attaches to vengeance:
> "You'd better believe that I'll get even with that guy!"
> "A real man won't be wounded on the back of his head!"

"Washing mouth"

When a person has been enraged by false witness against him within his own family, he may be moved to curse those responsible for the slander. Once he has calmed down and begins to reflect on the consequences of his curse, someone in the family approaches him to suggest that he "wash his mouth." Unless he does this, both he and his family might suffer because of what he said in anger. When he decides that he no longer wishes to hold words against those who wronged him, he tells his family to gather in front of the house early the next morning. When they all arrive, water is poured on a spot next to the man's house, the leaves of the **bun** tree are thrown where the water was poured, and all present gather around the spot and grasp a single pestle.

As they all pound with the pestle, the person whose rage had overpowered him will repeat all the oaths and curses that were uttered during his wrath; he will continue by saying that these words were not good and have separated him from his family and he desires to reestablish a good relationship. Each person is then anointed with a bit of mud from the pestle, and the person who uttered the curse spits "toufē!" in the direction of the company as a sign of blessing. The spitting is more a ritual gesture than actually sending spittle onto the persons being blessed. This is simply another Gbaya way of blessing.

The offender then makes the gesture of washing his mouth. Then all the participants grasp the gourd from which water was poured onto the ground and pour the remaining water over the same spot to signify that the ritual is finished. The blessing has been received; peace has been restored in the family.

"Freeing up the village"

If there has been a series of troubles within the residential quarter of a village, and the feeling of well-being has been threatened or lost, an experienced elder who may or may not be related to the residential group will be summoned to perform the "freeing-village" ceremony. All fires in the quarter must first be extinguished. The elder digs a trench which leads from the troubled area out into the bush. He then pours water into the trench, and the water runs out of town. The elder goes into the bush and returns with a bundle of new grass. He proceeds to each house in the quarter and pulls one of old grass from each roof, immediately replacing it with new grass. And finally he lights a new fire. All the women in the quarter receive fire from his hand, and as the new fires light up throughout the quarter, the sense of peace and well-being returns.

"Proclaiming new orders"

A **genga** is a practical rule issued to guide or to encourage new behavior, whereas the verb **gai** usually refers to the "quieting down" of people or a situation. The rite known to the Gbaya as **gaia-genga** has the same general purpose as the rite described above, except that it is not reserved for the troubles of a single residential quarter.

If an entire village has suffered from sickness, arguments, and other problems over a period of time, early one morning the elders arise and begin to howl, "Hooooo! Hooooo!" They might also blow a little whistle that is otherwise used in the annual rite to placate the spirits. These special noises are at once a signal for everyone to stop quarreling and a supplication to God to drive out the problems and re-establish peace and good health in the village.

"Throwing peace"

An elderly woman who has acquired knowledge of the usefulness of many leaves may keep a gourd hidden in her house in which various leaves have been placed in water. This is a gourd out of which no food has ever been eaten. One of the leaves in the gourd is sure to be from the **sore** tree. All the people in the village know that this woman is a "woman-throw-peace" and that she is always going about her work so that peace may reign in the village.

If a man is having hard words with someone, he may go to this woman at night. The woman takes her gourd and washes the face of her visitor using the prepared water, and she says, "Let there be peace in our village!" or she might say, "May our village be great!"

In the case where a member of the family has left the village and has been gone for a very long time and no one knows where he now lives, the help of this woman may be sought. She takes her gourd and accompanies the person seeking her help. They proceed together out of town on the path originally taken by the missing person. The woman says, "Be still. I'm going to call him and listen for his voice." She calls out the missing person's name in a very loud voice until the answer is heard, "Yeeeee!" The woman asks, "Did you hear that? He's not dead!" She will then "change that person's heart," and he will know that he must return to his own people. His heart will not be at rest until he returns.

Village hunters may also call upon this woman in preparation for a hunt. She sprinkles water on them from her gourd by taking a leafy branch of the **sore** tree and shaking it over the men. The hunters are consequently at peace and are confident that they will not be harmed in the forthcoming hunt.

These examples indicate at least three purposes of the "throwing peace" rite: 1) that peace might be restored between quarreling individuals; 2) that peace might be restored to a family by the return of a prodigal son; and 3) that men might be at peace as they go out to follow their major calling, which in Gbaya tradition has been the hunt.

Conclusion

We can speak of three levels of relationship that are meaningful for the Gbaya, and our examples have focused especially on horizontal relationships. Another way of describing these relationships would be in terms of the dimensions of participation and belonging experienced by the Gbaya which contribute most to their understanding of human existence. The rites described above are expressions of major Gbaya concerns about life. They express what the Gbaya sense as a need for peace, harmony, order, and wholeness within family and community; and they show specifically Gbaya ways for attaining and preserving those qualities of life.

Today many Gbaya have a relationship with the Christian church. What do these rites have to do with Gbaya who would also be Christian? Gbaya Christians are answering that question in their own preaching and teaching by calling upon certain elements of their tradition to help give a Gbaya expression of the Christian message. They are discovering that the Christian message can come to clearer expression within Gbaya culture when they let their own tradition dialogue with biblical expression than when they treat their own heritage as a vacuum. In their opinion, God's new covenant in Christ encounters the Gbaya in a way that is analogous to Christ's encounter with Israel. Gbaya tradition, their old covenant, is judged in Christ, not by way of condemnation, but in terms of fulfillment and transformation whereby "the old passes" because in Christ "all things become new." For as Kenneth

Cragg has said, "If the old is taken away, to whom is the new given?" (1968:57).

We believe that the Christian message, that is, Christian proclamation, ministry, and fellowship, has universal implications and imperatives by virtue of its orientation around God's redemptive action in Jesus the Christ. That message has infinite possibilities for evaluative and aesthetic fulfillment in and through the medium of symbolic systems of human morality, religion, and culture. For example, the Gbaya who decide to reorient their lives and values around the Christian message receive at that moment the freedom to evaluate and to express the "new being" in the symbolic terms of the lifestyle and customs meaningful to them. The bearer of the message has no authority to withhold that freedom, although he does have the responsibility to interpret it (cf. Acts 8:26-40). He does not have, however, the sole or even the primary responsibility of interpretation, but rather a co-responsibility.

As the Christian message meets Gbaya values, the encounter is in the first instance interpersonal and conversational. The messenger represents a vast tradition--that of the church out of which his own interpretation inevitably comes. If the Gbaya accepts and receives the message, he must be free to take it into his own tradition, in the course of which it is inevitably reinterpreted in terms meaningful to him. At the same time, his own tradition is open for re-evaluation and reinterpretation. The old is free to become new.

The rites of reconciliation described above are evidence that the Gbaya Christian theologian has special resources upon which to draw for illustration and interpretation in his work as counselor, liturgist, preacher, and teacher. These resources are not only a matter of interest and curiosity, but, from our perspective, a matter of substance. The **simbo** rite, for example, lets us know that the Gbaya have symbolic means from their own tradition for understanding Christian baptism.[8] And many of the other rites described are rich in symbols which Gbaya preachers are using to help interpret for their people what it means that God was in Christ reconciling the world to himself (II Corinthians 5:19).

---

8 The **labi** initiation ceremony, for which see the preceding chapter, is also full of symbols which are points of contact with the symbols of Christian baptism.

Bibliography

Cragg, K. 1968. *Christianity in World Perspective*. New York: Oxford University Press.

Evans-Pritchard, E. E. 1970. *Nuer Religion*. Oxford: Clarendon Press.

Strange, G. R., ed. 1974. *The Poetical Works of Tennyson*. Boston: Houghton Mifflin.

18. Wanto and Crocodile: The Story of Joseph*

by Philip Noss

The literature of the Gbaya is oral, passed on from generation to generation. It is made up of several literary forms, but the lines of distinction between them are not always clear.

The **to** 'tale' is a narrative of from less than a hundred words up to six thousand words, relating one episode or a series of episodes about human characters and birds, animals, and water creatures. A **lizang** 'parable' is an object lesson drawn from nature or a short narration of human experience from which a lesson is drawn. The only distinguishing feature between the tale and parable may be a song. Almost invariably there is one song in a tale, and in a long tale there may be up to ten or more, but in a parable there are no songs.

A **tua wen** is quite simply a proverb, but if it is longer than a sentence it may be considered a **lizang,** a term which is broadly used to cover both parable and proverb. Unlike the others, the **sumgba** 'riddle' is never didactic and thus stands by itself, except that the plot of a tale or the theme of a parable may center about a series of riddles. There are **gima** 'songs' for every occasion: hunting songs, work songs, death songs, play songs, drinking songs, initiation songs, sorcery songs, etc., and they are usually accompanied by dance. But the song cannot be separated from the tale in which it plays a major role. Furthermore, in a tale a phrase representing direct discourse that is repeated several times becomes a chant and this is **gima.**

* Previously published in Practical Anthropology 14:222-27 (1967).

Of the above forms of literature, the tale shows the greatest development of plot and character, neither of which is needed in the other forms. This plot is frequently humorous and always entertaining, but it must also have meaning. The tale is often didactic; otherwise, as one narrator said, it would not be worth repeating. Since it has been passed down from their ancestors, to the Gbaya it represents the experience and wisdom of the ancients.

Both the tale and the parable comment on life and society and are timeless because they depict human character and relationships. The human characters are portrayed in their associations with each other and with wild animals, who themselves have many human characteristics. Many of the tales explain how certain practices within the society originated, how food and water were first obtained by mankind, or why certain animals live and act as they do.

The main character in Gbaya **to** is Wanto, a person whose name means "Master of the Tale." Through this character the listener sees himself because Wanto is understood by everyone to represent mankind. Though often displaying an intelligence and capability that sets him apart from the animals, Wanto is never a hero; he is never noble. Most of the time he is selfish, cowardly, vain, lazy, greedy, and he is always hungry. His four children are named after types of food or utensils used in preparing food, which is indicative of Wanto's nature. He has an intense curiosity which frequently leads him into trouble. He can never walk away from excitement. His foolishness and stupidity are sometimes rewarded with death, but more often with a beating from his conscientious wife.

Wanto's antagonist, though not appearing in the tale to follow, is Gbaso, a name which means "Great God." Although he has certain powers which seem superhuman, he is not a god. Like Wanto, he is a person, but he is separated from society. In the beginning it was he who possessed water and seeds, but he kept them from mankind, thus keeping man in servitude. Wanto tricked him, however, stole some seeds and let the water out of the hidden dam, making man no longer dependent on Gbaso. He is often shown trying to kill and eat people, and this desire to eat his victim may be compared to the sorcerer, who is said to "eat" his victim in killing him. Gbaso, therefore, represents the destructive element in a community which must be destroyed if society is to continue. But Gbaso also represents justice. Those in the community who out of jealousy do not respect others and who will not accept advice, frequently blunder into Gbaso and are killed.

Wanto and Crocodile

The following tale, which explains the origin of the enmity between men and crocodiles, shows Wanto in one of his better moments as he outwits the crocodile. The tale has a further interest in that the African pastor who tells it interprets it as an Old Testament story which he says the ancients knew in part and told as this tale. This Gbaya pastor and other Gbaya Christians believe that their fathers once knew about the true God and that they had at least part of God's word, but that it was confused and then forgotten. Whether this is true or not, the tale and its interpretation by Pastor André Yadji shows how Gbaya Christians believe the wisdom of their fathers relates to their Christian life today.

Wanto and Crocodile

The tale that we will hear now is the tale of Wanto and Crocodile. It takes place during a time of famine. Everyone was trying to find food. As Wanto was out looking for food he happened upon the home of Crocodile, who at that time lived on dry ground like all the other animals.

It had rained a little that afternoon, and when the rain ended there was only a little sunlight left. In the dim light a guinea fowl[1] climbed up into a tree and called, "**To fea! To fea! To fea!**"

Wanto, hearing the bird, said, "Oh, is that so! I'm the one who puts the speckled markings on your feathers and now you say that I'm dead! Okay, it doesn't matter."

Crocodile overheard Wanto and said, "You're a big liar! How can you make the markings on the guinea fowl's feathers?"

"The reason you doubt me is because the medicine for doing it is expensive and very difficult to get. If I had my medicine here, whatever happened, I'd make the markings for you to see."

Crocodile answered, "No matter how difficult it is to obtain the medicine, I will get it for you to make those markings on my children."

"Well, this is the medicine. You will set out from here on a three-day trip. On the fourth day you will look for my special kind of wood; you will sleep there one night and then

---

1 "**To fea!**" represents the call of the guinea fowl, but here it is also a pun meaning, "Wanto is dead!"

spend three days on the way back. When you get back here you will go to peel the bark of a tree, which you will twist into rope for fastening the door. That's the medicine."

Saying, "I will go," Crocodile set off with all his people, even the women and children. When Wanto saw that they had left, he began making cord to use for snares to catch guinea fowl. He caught two full-grown birds, a male and female, and two young ones, male and female. These he put inside the house where Crocodile's eggs were kept.

When Crocodile returned, Wanto went into Crocodile's house and the door was closed. Only a window was left open so they could give food to Wanto inside. Then Wanto started eating the crocodile eggs. He would put an egg on the fire, and when it exploded **kpuf!** He would pick up a guinea fowl and hold it up by the window. "Uncle, look at this one that just hatched! You heard the sound of it a minute ago."[2]

When they saw the guinea fowl in Wanto's hand, thinking that it was a little crocodile, all the young crocodiles outside said, "Father, make marks for me, too!"

Wanto ate all the eggs this way and then said, "Now you will build a bridge for crossing the water." There was a hot spring there. If a person put his foot in it, his skin would peel. "Then, when I have crossed, you will chop it down before you open the door to your house so that when the little crocodiles try to find my scent and follow me, they will be unable to." Crocodile obeyed.

Wanto crossed the bridge and called, "Crocodile, cut the bridge!" From both sides they chopped the bridge; and when they had cut it Wanto said, "Look at you, you stupid idiot! I tricked you and ate all your eggs!"

Crocodile didn't know what to do. Then he decided, "Okay, what I'll do is this--I'll announce a dance. I will give a great dance and I will command that everyone must come to the dance with his own dance drum. And everyone who comes to the edge of the town will have to sing his song and beat his drum, and then when his voice has been heard he will be allowed to come into town." Crocodile was scheming in order to capture Wanto.

When Wanto heard that the command for the dance had been given, he set to work chiseling his marimba. He chiseled his

---

2 Ideophones that were used in the original have been retained in the translation.

Wanto and Crocodile 217

marimba, tuned it all up, and then on the day before the dance he gathered dry leaves into a big pile **dendeng** on the ground. He cut a rubber tree, spread the sap over the leaves, and then rolled himself in them **yamayumuu.** He took honeycomb the size of an egg and put it on one side of his nose and then on the other side of his nose. He dropped his name Wanto and called himself "Honeycomb Nose."[3]

Everybody had already come to the dance and they were waiting for Wanto, who was late. When Wanto came to the edge of the town clearing, he tried out his marimba. When they heard the sound of his marimba with its very loud beating, everyone came into town to meet Wanto and see what he would do. This is the song that he sang:[4]

    Ileng, ileng,
Honeycomb Nose, Wanto he ate Crocodile's eggs,
  indeng, indeng
  ate Crocodile's eggs, indeng
  Wanto you ate Crocodile's eggs,
  indeng, indeng
Honeycomb Nose, Wanto you ate Crocodile's eggs,
  indeng, indeng
  ate Crocodile's eggs, indeng
  Wanto you ate Crocodile's eggs,
  indeng, indeng
  ate Crocodile's eggs, indeng
  Wanto you ate Crocodile's eggs,
  I am geze geze
Honeycomb Nose, Wanto he ate Crocodile's eggs
  ate Crocodile's eggs
  ate Crocodile's eggs, indeng
  Wanto you ate Crocodile's eggs,
  indeng, indeng
  Indeng, indeng, indeng, indeng, indeng
   indeng, indeng, indeng
  Indeng, indeng, indeng, indeng, indeng
   indeng, indeng, indeng
Honeycomb Nose, Wanto you ate Crocodile's eggs,
  indeng, indeng

3 Wanto's assumed name is **Zoo ne ndia,** which translated literally means "Nose is honeycomb."

4 **Ileng, ileng** and **indeng, indeng** represent the sound of the marimba, which is occasionally changed to **geze geze** indicating different notes. This change in the sound of the instrument and the phrase, "I am **geze geze,**" is understood by the listener to represent Wanto himself and the way he assumes different roles.

>   Honeycomb Nose, Wanto he ate Crocodile's eggs,
>   indeng, indeng
>   ate Crocodile's eggs, indeng
>   Wanto you ate Crocodile's eggs,
>   indeng, indeng
>   Honeycomb Nose, Wanto he ate Crocodile's eggs,
>   I am geze geze
>   Honeycomb Nose, Wanto he ate Crocodile's eggs,
>   indeng, indeng
>   Honeycomb Nose, indeng
>   Wanto you ate Crocodile's eggs,
>   indeng, indeng
>   ate Crocodile's eggs, indeng
>   Wanto you ate Crocodile's eggs.

When Crocodile heard the song he said, "That's really a beautiful song! This is the one for whom I prepared my dance. I have found him!"[5] And he gave this order: "For my part, I arranged the dance, I gathered the people; but now the dance leader is no longer myself, the Crocodile. The dance leader is Honeycomb Nose. Everything that you would have given honoring me in this dance you will give to Honeycomb Nose; you won't give it to me. Everything that you would have given --the beautiful clothing, all the pretty things--you won't give to me, you will give to Honeycomb Nose. And to show my own pleasure I will pick one of my daughters, a very pretty one, to give to Honeycomb Nose." And he picked the prettiest of all his daughters and gave her to Honeycomb Nose. In this way all the people gathered and gave gifts to Wanto.

Then Crocodile said, "Now you will go to the entrance of the king's palace and sing your song again," and it was there that the dance was held. Everyone danced for a long time. When the dance was finished, they gave Wanto gifts of cattle, goats, sheep, all different kinds of things that I would be unable to count--even great treasures of money that they had been keeping hidden in their houses.

"Thank you! I am very happy with the way you have honored me. Now, Crocodile," Wanto said, "on my way home my path crosses the hot springs, so when I am going to cross I beg you to build a bridge for me lest I step in the hot water and be burned. Then when I have crossed the water you will chop down the bridge, because if the bridge is there all these animals will come back to your place."

---

5 Crocodile does not realize the truth of this statement. Hearing the beautiful song he has forgotten the original purpose of the dance.

Wanto and Crocodile

He crossed the water with all his animals, his cattle, sheep, pigs, donkeys, and camels, and they chopped the bridge down. When the bridge was down, Wanto pushed on the honeycomb and it popped off his nose **kpong;** he tore off the leaves that had covered him **yamayumuu** all over; and there he was--Wanto himself. He shouted, "I, Wanto himself, the husband of Laiso, it is I who tricked you this way! I ate all your eggs. You called a dance and I came back and took what you had here! See, here is your daughter that I took. No matter what you think or try to do, you will be unable to cross the water to come to me!"

What a predicament! Crocodile didn't know what to do. Wanto had destroyed all his eggs. He had then come again, and the daughter that Crocodile should have taken care of he had given to Wanto. Wanto had also taken all the good things that had been in his town. Finally Crocodile decided, "I'm going to the water. I will not live on dry land any longer. We will live by the water, and when Wanto wants to cross we will catch him. Even if we don't catch Wanto, when someone else tries to cross we will catch him in the water. That's all right, too. And when I kill someone, the blame isn't on me; it's on Wanto. It is because of him that I am going to live in the water." He took everything--his people, animals, and possessions--and went to the water. That is what happened to cause the Crocodile to go and live in the water.

The story of Joseph

Now, it was the same way in the Old Testament, because, before, when our fathers did not know God's word, they took the story of Joseph and told it this way. Wanto who went to look for food during the time of famine was Joseph when his brothers sold him. After being sold, Joseph went from one prison to another. A prisoner will not eat good food; a prisoner does not have a good place to sleep. When they had put him in prison, he explained the meanings of the dreams of two men that Pharaoh had sent to prison. So, regarding the search for the medicine that Wanto ordered: "If you get this medicine for me I will make the markings," that medicine and the markings were the dream of Pharaoh and its explanation: "For seven years things will be good, and for seven years there will be famine. If you wish, choose a good man to gather your seeds." The seven years were the seven days required to obtain the medicine. They selected Joseph and made him ruler.

The eggs of the crocodile that Wanto ate represent Joseph's appointment as a ruler. The Egyptians gave the rule to him. That is to say, it is as though they gave all Crocodile's eggs to him. The first thing that he received was the authority to rule.

When Joseph was ruler the Egyptians saw how the people of Israel were becoming more and more numerous, and they said, "No, we must chase them away!" And when the Israelites were about to leave, everything good that the Egyptians had--beautiful gold--they gave to the people of Israel to take. But when the Israelites went out, the Egyptians said, "No, we will not let them get away for no reason at all! We've let our workmen and our slaves go! We must chase them to catch our slaves who have gone."

The bridge built across the hot spring was the Red Sea which divided when Moses raised his rod over it. When it divided it was like a bridge, and the statement of Crocodile, "I won't live outside," was when the Egyptians saw that the people of Israel had gone and chased after them. When they had gone onto the bridge--that is, when the Egyptians had entered the valley of water--it closed together over them.

So it was, since the ancients did not know God's word, they took a good word which was all mixed up for them, and they made tales out of it. Therefore, we see that it is good for us Christians today to know God's word well, to learn it carefully and hold it tightly. See, the good word which the ancients told, Wanto hunting for food was Joseph who was sold, but they didn't know that it was Joseph's brothers who sold him. What is written they didn't know. So it is good for us to hold it carefully; then if something happens, if we lose our eyesight, if we are unable to talk, we will have what will help us. Let us look at John 8:31 and Psalm 119:105 which say, "If you abide in my word, you are truly my disciples," and "Thy word is a lamp unto my feet and a light unto my path."

19. A Meeting of Biblical Wisdom with Gbaya Wisdom

by Thomas Christensen

We can be happy to have the Bible for many different reasons, not least because it has made Hebrew wit and wisdom accessible to us. Scripture is notably rich in didactic expression, much of it pungent and salty. Proverbial and epigrammatic sayings, transmitted orally as homely vehicles of moral norms for Hebrew society, were "sanctified" in the pages of Holy Writ. Common ethnic wisdom became sacred materials in the hands of God's chosen kings and prophets.

Gbaya proverbs (**tuawen**) correspond to what was probably the first stage in the development of Hebrew proverbial expression (**mashal**). They are virtually all one-liners; for example, **wormo sur zang na:** "Many words will not fill one's belly."[1]

Gbaya proverbial wit specializes in the "you'll get yours" domain:

> "The fool's spittle falls right back in his own face."

> "Where the pig has had his fun is where the pig will be undone."

The foregoing example illustrates a simple parallelism that is as common to Gbaya proverbs as it is to Hebrew verse. Both traditions appeal to common sense passed on by those who should know what they are talking about, the fathers who can attest to the truth of the sayings by virtue of their own experience:

---

1 **Wormo** is also the usual Gbaya greeting; thus, mere greetings are not enough to keep a man happy.

> Like a dog that returns to his vomit is a fool that repeats his folly. (Proverbs 26:11)[2]
>
> "The fellow dressed in rags has learned quite well how to wear his rags."[3]

Whatever learning occurs in the oral transmission of Gbaya proverbial wisdom, whatever contribution toward the development of acceptable character might result from the exercise of verbal wit is usually a by-product of humor. The celebration of wit and laughter is an uncommonly effective way to learn what is often well worth remembering.

Gbaya proverbs, and the same can be said for Gbaya tales, remind the listener of Everyman's common foibles, or worse. A collection of Gbaya proverbs is a collection of pocket-size mirrors. Mirrors have a certain reputation, but that is not the fault of the mirrors, but rather of those who use mirrors injudiciously. One can overdo the use of a mirror and one can overdo the use of a proverb:

> Like a lame man's legs, which hang useless, is a proverb in the mouth of fools. (Proverbs 26:7)

The overdone proverb becomes a cliché, for instance, "a stitch in time saves nine." But both mirrors and proverbs are potentially useful if you take just a little time to let the image sink in. James has some words on this subject:

> For if any one is a hearer of the word and not a doer, he is like a man who observes his natural face in a mirror; for he observes himself and goes away and at once forgets what he was like. (James 1:23-24)

To which the Gbaya might remark,

> "There you sit next to the water, yet you are sure to die in your own dirt!"[4]

Proverbs, whether Hebrew or Gbaya, are not so remarkable for their profundity as for their ready logic and practicality. Any effort to elaborate on a proverbial expression is certainly no compliment to the listener, as it implies that he has missed the point. The effect of the proverb is in its

---

2 All Scripture translations, unless otherwise noted, are from the Revised Standard Version of the Bible.
3 Throughout this article Gbaya proverbs are enclosed in quotation marks, distinguishing them from Biblical proverbs.
4 This proverb is the name applied to a creature that lives in the mud beside streams and is always dirty.

Biblical and Gbaya Wisdom   223

conciseness and in its initial impact. Its power is lost in translation. The best response to a proverb is another proverb--"It takes more than a day for a mushroom to rot!" Yes, indeed, but "a mushroom grows to rot!" It is "born to die." The successful proverb is keen on the economy of words. It is often well wrapped in linguistic and cultural subtleties, the meanings of which are not readily apparent to the outsider.

Hebrew and Gbaya proverbs emerge from cultural and religious milieux preeminently concerned with successful everyday existence rather than preoccupation with heavenly rewards. This interest in earthly rewards is frank and undisguised:

> A slack hand causes poverty, but the hand of the diligent makes rich. (Proverbs 10:4)
>
> The hand of the diligent will rule, while the slothful will be put to forced labor. (Proverbs 12:24)

The Gbaya would say:

> "When you are looking for money, you are careful not to pick a fight!"
>
> "You will never get fat by refusing food!"
>
> "The little tadpole is thrilled to death when he happens upon a pool of soaking cassava roots!"
>
> "Everything that enters the fish trap is a fish."

Gbaya proverbial tradition is thus consistent with Gbaya religious tradition, practical, secular, frankly interested in anything and everything that works.[5]

- - - - -

The most natural place in the New Testament for Gbaya wisdom to meet Biblical wisdom is probably in the little sermon of James. James was a Jewish-Christian teacher-preacher who had a keen grasp of Hebrew wit and wisdom, including that which he had learned from the Jewish rabbi he served, Jesus. James preaches a faith that works. Some people may question his sense of humor, and others have questioned his understanding of the Good News, but most would agree that he was very alert to both issues.

5 See "An Interpretation of Gbaya Religious Practice" by P.A. Noss in this volume.

In the meeting of Biblical and Gbaya wisdom that is proposed here, there is no need to dramatize theological issues or the consequences of the encounter between Jewish-Christian and traditional African value orientations. It is just a pleasant and worthwhile meeting, mutually beneficial and enriching. It is clear that James's sermon can find ready response today in an African-Christian society, both in terms of content and style. William A. Smalley supports this view when he notes that "in one church in West Africa a study of several thousand sermon texts revealed that proportionately the largest number came from Ecclesiastes and James!"[6]

James's expression and images can be met with comparable expression and images from Gbaya oral tradition. His practical insights can be complemented and localized by the Gbaya well versed in his own tradition. On the other hand, Gbaya wisdom can be fulfilled, "get a full meaning," from the Christian point of view and within the Christian context. As the Gbaya says,

> "The right hand washes the left hand while the left hand is washing the right hand."

James's sermon may be divided into four subjects or themes: 1) rich man and poor man; 2) the tongue; 3) faith and works; 4) patience, prayer, and perseverance. He treats these themes in shotgun fashion rather than in the above order. With one exception,[7] his sermon does not quote Hebrew proverbs, but it is replete with succinct observations that relate closely to proverbial expression. The verses chosen from James and the Gbaya proverbs chosen to meet them are not confined to single meanings, but are open to many dimensions of meaning. Proverbs are eminently flexible. A single witty phrase can take off in any number of directions and still find its way home.

Rich man and poor man

> For the sun rises with its scorching heat and withers the grass; its flower falls, and its beauty perishes. So will the rich man fade away in the midst of his pursuits. (James 1:11)

---

6 William A. Smalley, "Suggestions for an Order of Translation" in The Bible Translator 20:3-29.

7 Cf. Prov. 3:34 and James 4:6. See also Prov. 10:19, 16:32, and James 1:19; Prov. 2:6, 8:22-31, and James 3:15; Prov. 15:1-4, 7, 23, 26, 28 and James 3:2; and Prov. 10:12 and James 5:19-20.

Biblical and Gbaya Wisdom   225

"The fish will be cooked in his own water."

"**naa-dɔk-ini** collects the wood that will fry him."

Quite familiar to the Gbaya, **naa-dɔk-ini** is a caterpillar-type worm that builds a cocoon of sticks around its body, which it drags along evidently unaware that its portable house is a superb fire-trap!

James strikes at the rich man in language reminiscent of the prophets:

> Come now, you rich, weep and howl for the miseries that are coming upon you. (James 5:1)

The Gbaya preacher might follow with,

"To sit on the end of a limb is to sit over a trap."

The limb in question is the heavy log triggered to drop on an unsuspecting animal as it passes or enters below, and the meaning is that you have gotten yourself into the kind of dilemma that can only be resolved by the loss of your head!

> Your riches have rotted and your garments are moth-eaten. (James 5:2)

"Your wealth is not made of rock."

Only materials of rock-like quality can resist the termites of central Africa, and termites show no favors to the wealthy. James continues:

> Your gold and silver have rusted, and their rust will be evidence against you and will eat your flesh like fire. You have laid up treasure for the last days. Behold, the wages of the laborers who mowed your fields, which you kept back by fraud, cry out.... (James 5:3-4)

> "The fellow with a full belly has no idea where the famished old wretch makes his home."

The rich pile up their wealth with no thought for those who have served them, says James, and the Gbaya might recall that "the tortoise promenading happily in the bush ignores the troubles of his brother turtle under water!" But serious trouble is already upon the rich:

> You have lived on the earth in luxury and in pleasure; you have fattened your hearts in a day of slaughter. (James 5:5)

The following proverbial tale refers to the kind of self-induced slaughter that James evidently had in mind:

> Fly married Lizard. Their relatives prepared a feast of peanut butter for them. After they had polished it off, a gob of peanut butter was left at the side of Fly's mouth, so Lizard said, "Hey Fly, lick the peanut butter off your cheek!" As Fly tried to lick the peanut butter from its cheek, its neck broke **beẙek!** Lizard called out, "Hey, laugh it up, gang! Look what happened to Fly!" And then Lizard's belly burst **tup!**

James's castigation of the rich nonetheless has a salutary note:

> Be wretched and mourn and weep. Let your laughter be turned to mourning and your joy to dejection. Humble yourselves before the Lord and he will exalt you. (James 4:9-10)

The Gbaya knows well that "the wood will burn away but will leave the **kusi** intact." The **kusi** are the three rocks or termite mounds which support the cooking pot. Fire will burn away what ought to be burned away as tears will help cleanse the heart, and the fireplace, or the heart, will be left more humble, yet nobler. Thus purged, it is well to remember that "the fly that sticks to the corpse will be buried with the corpse!" In other words, it is the better part of caution to nurture a just life. James continues:

> Come now, you who say, "Today or tomorrow we will go into such and such a town and spend a year there and trade and get gain." (James 4:13)

The Gbaya, coming as he does from a seminomadic tradition, is likely to agree with those who say it's no good sitting out one's life in a single spot. In the Gbaya idiom,

> "The little antelope who sticks to the same old clump of trees will never get herself pregnant."

For those with grand projects, our preacher has a sobering thought:

> You do not know about tomorrow. What is your life? For you are a mist that appears for a little time and then vanishes. (James 4:14)

Gbaya wisdom concurs that we do not always have the chance to live up to our expectations.

> "Little chicken got in a rush, and her teeth failed to grow!"

And again,

> "When the house catches fire, the roaches no longer stop to greet one another!"

We do not always have the luxury of pursuing our favored projects.

James's advice often runs counter to Everyman's creaturely habits:

> My brethren, show no partiality as you hold the faith of our Lord Jesus Christ, the Lord of glory. (James 2:1)

This comes as "news" to the Gbaya as to all other peoples and is thus an occasion to distinguish the "good-new-word," the gospel, from former words and ways. According to Gbaya tradition, people are to be treated in different ways. Social relationships and positions are determinative of social acceptance, interaction, and behavior.

> **Gɛnɛ duk nɛ be-duk na**
> "A stranger is just not part of the family."

There is a word play here on **duk** and **be-duk: duk** is the verb "to be, to sit," but it is also the name for mortar; **be-duk** is "a member of the clan," but it is also the name for pestle. Thus the proverb may also be translated, "The stranger doesn't sit on the pestle." Another proverb states,

> "If you let your neighbor put his hand into the pot before you, you will go to bed hungry."

On the other hand,

> "If it's your brother who is at the beehive, you will not have to eat wax!"

The tongue

> So the tongue is a little member and boasts of great things. How great a forest is set ablaze by a small fire! And the tongue is a fire. The tongue is an unrighteous world among our members, staining the whole body, setting on fire the cycle of nature, and set on fire by hell. For every kind of beast and bird, of reptile and sea creature, can be tamed and has been tamed by humankind, but no human being can tame the tongue--a restless evil, full of deadly poison. (James 3:5-8)

This is a superlative attack on the tongue which anyone would be hard put to match. Perhaps the closest the Gbaya can come is,

> "Your big mouth will eat you all up!"

The Gbaya agrees that the tongue can boast of great things:

> "If you have no tongue, your mouth will say nothing!"

And,

> "The tongue is a soft thing and is therefore placed between a strong set of teeth."

In other words, because it is soft and pliable, it can survive in a dangerous position. But again, there is good reason to discipline the tongue, keeping in mind that "what binds a man does not kill a man." That is, just as you are sometimes obliged to bite your own tongue, you often have to sit on someone in order to induce reasonable behavior.

Faith and works

> Know this, my beloved brethren. Let every man be quick to hear, slow to speak, slow to anger. (James 1:19)

Gbaya wisdom asserts that "thinking beats talking," and that "the place of words is the place of death." The latter reference is not just to any kind of words, but the kind of words produced when "the buffalo fails to hear the thunder of his own pounding hoofs!" Listening is not without a good purpose, nor is careful speech, for "if the battle drum does not speak clearly, who will prepare for battle?"

James's listeners are a contentious lot:

> You desire and do not have; so you kill. And you covet and cannot obtain; so you fight and wage war. (James 4:2a)

To these folk the Gbaya might say,

> "The fellow with an open wound will not pour salt water on it (if he has any sense)."

The covetous person should also be reminded that "the excrements under water got the best of the fly!" In the fly's haste to get at its delight, it failed to note that its delight was under water and consequently drowned itself.

James continues:

Biblical and Gbaya Wisdom   229

> For the anger of man does not work the righteousness of God. (James 1:20)

It should also be clear that "the tears of self-pity will not raise the dead."

> Therefore put away all filthiness and rank growth of wickedness and receive with meekness the implanted word, which is able to save your souls. (James 1:21)

> "When you bury a corpse, you do not leave one of its feet sticking out of the hole!"

In other words, leave your old sins behind you, and remember that "you will not find a mouse sharing with the same hole with a snake." Wicked conduct does not mix with God's word any better than snakes mix with mice.

> What does it profit, my brethren, if a man says he has faith but has not works? Can his faith save him? (James 2:14)

In the same vein, the Gbaya says, "The fellow who hides his fruit seeds will never get the chance to plant them." James's point is that a man's actions witness to the quality of his faith and that no amount of words can substitute for the genuine act of faith. The Gbaya proverb expresses the good sense that a person's efforts should be actively committed to the realization of his potentialities. What good is faith, or a fruit seed, if you do not let it grow and actually bear fruit?

> So faith by itself, if it has no works, is dead. (James 2:17)

> "If you have no broom, your dried cassava will be swept away by the rain."

The Gbaya spread their cassava in the sun to dry. When rain comes, neither strong thoughts nor strong talk will save the cassava--the work of the broom is essential! The Gbaya can be confident in a "faith that works" because, as he says,

> "The handle of your hoe will not wear out in vain."

Patience, prayer, and perseverance

> Count it all joy, my brethren, when you meet various trials, for you know that the testing of your faith produces steadfastness. (James 1:2-3)

We noted above that termites are very busy in Africa. They can be compared, both in number and style, with the relentless attackers of the Christian faith. But let it be known, says the Gbaya preacher, that "termites can do precious little to a rock!" James encourages the nurture of a rock-like faith:

> Be sure that your endurance carries you all the way, without failing....(James 1:4 TEV)

Without failing, for example, as did the little rat who said,

> "Just give me a chance to grow up and I'll get big and strong!"

Alas, he never grew up.

> But let him ask in faith, with no doubting, for he who doubts is like a wave of the sea that is driven and tossed by the wind. For that person must not suppose that a double-minded man, unstable in all his ways, will receive anything from the Lord. (James 1:6-8)

When you engage in the adventure of faith, you can be sure and confident about where you are headed: "The elephant climbing a hill does not stop to look behind him." And you can be confident in the means you have to get you there: "Once you have mounted a horse, it would be silly to go back to riding an ass!" If there are troubles on the way, that is only normal; just remember that "a crooked stream will not break a fish's neck!" James declares,

> Blessed is the man who endures trial, for when he has stood the test he will receive the crown of life which God has promised to those who love him. (James 1:12)

And James concludes,

> Be patient, therefore, brethren, until the coming of the Lord. (James 5:7)

> "The fellow in a big rush will have no part in the king's couscous."

The Gbaya preacher is thereby affirming that the person who does persevere will indeed enjoy the King's banquet!

- - - - -

The Hebrew sages collected wisdom of their people which was eventually joined to other holy writings and canonized. Drawing from these sacred writings, from the sayings of

Biblical and Gbaya Wisdom

Jesus, and from his own experience and live imagination. James fashioned an enduringly popular and instructive Christian message which preachers in diverse cultures are still retelling.

The Christian message keeps renewing itself in the words of new preachers for new times and new places. Gbaya wisdom can be just words, but words always have the potential for becoming "good-new-words" when brought into the service of the Word of God, Christ Jesus.

20. Karnu: Witchdoctor or Prophet?*

by Thomas Christensen

Introduction

Karnu is certainly the most famous person in recent Gbaya history. His name is especially well known among those who are familiar with French colonial history as the leader of an unsuccessful revolt against white administration and against Fulani power. His name is increasingly revered among Gbaya of the area where Karnu once lived as a prophet who announced a new religious orientation and commitment, and who foretold the coming of a new social and economic order.

The description of the events in which Karnu participated has two versions, the one told by European researchers,[1] the other told by Gbaya researchers. The two versions diverge at crucial points, as do the interpretations and conclusions reached by the respective researchers. It would be simplistic to describe the European perspective as objective on the one hand, and the Gbaya perspective as subjective on the other hand. This could suggest that we ought to consider the objective account as true and the subjective account as exaggerated, if not false. Distinctions of this kind would not help us to hear what is today being said by the Gbaya about Karnu.

By the same token, it would be unfair to characterize the Gbaya version as the inside story, thereby suggesting that the European account is unfavorably biased and unsympathetic. Distinctions of that kind would preclude the possibility of anyone but the Gbaya really understanding what happened--and

---
* Previously published in Missiology 6:197-211 (1978)
1 We use the term European as employed by francophone Africans to designate all whites.

what is happening--in regard to the Karnu event. It would be more useful to hear both versions of the event for what they are, and from both accounts attempt to learn something more about the Gbaya people, their culture, and their tradition.

The European account[2]

A peasant revolt against French colonial administration in the Ubangi-Shari broke out in 1928 and continued for several years.[3] The revolt centered among the Gbaya people, who had furnished a large number of laborers for the administration's construction projects, and whose interests were primarily at stake. The administrators identified an individual named Karnu, who lived in the bush about fifty kilometers from Bouar, as instigator of the revolt. Karnu was described as a Gbaya chief and witchdoctor (diviner) who wished to rid the Gbaya territory of all whites and of all Fulani. He claimed that his mission had been revealed to him by a sign from heaven, a star which plunged into the Lobaye River.

Karnu refused to use any objects or wear any clothes that were imported and sold by whites. He announced that the whites' departure was imminent and that their departure could be hastened and encouraged by the application of a medicine he provided. The Gbaya would be freed from white domination, he said, if they bore the sign of **kôngô-wara** 'handle of the hoe' on their bodies. This is said to have consisted of a mixture of honey and ashes rubbed into an incision made in the skin. The revolt became known as **kôngô-wara** among the Gbaya. To the French administration it was "the Gbaya war."

Karnu is said to have decreed a nonviolent resistance to the whites. He wanted the Gbaya to refuse to pay taxes, to discontinue any work in the whites' service, and to avoid any

---

2 The summary of the European account given here is abstracted from the following works: (1) Pierre Kalck (1974:235-238, 273-278) was a French colonial administrator in an area near Karnu's home during the period 1953-1956. (2) Philip Chester Burnham (1972:80-87). Both Kalck and Burnham quote Marc Michel who researched the French colonial archives at Brazzaville for information on Karnu. (3) Miss Ruth Christiansen (1956:39-41) was an American Lutheran missionary who began working among the Gbaya in 1932, several years after Karnu's death.

3 Known as the Ubangi-Shari under French colonial administration, from independence it was the Central African Republic until December 1976, when it was renamed the Central African Empire by Emperor Bokassa I. [In September 1979, Emperor Bokassa I was overthrown. Since then this country is again known as the Central African Republic.]

commerce whatsoever with them. Karnu expressed a desire to visit the Roman Catholic priests in Berberati, two hundred kilometers south of his village. He said, "I'll pray; I'll discuss matters with the men of the whites' God. They will go home and leave this land for the blacks. If they threaten me with their guns, I'll tell them to go ahead and kill me if they so wish! I will not defend myself. No blood must be shed" (Kalck 1974:237, all translations are mine).

In June 1928, violence erupted between Gbaya villagers and Fulani herders in the Bouar area. The Gbaya accused the French administrators of giving their land to the Fulani, whose further immigration into Gbaya territories of the Ubangi-Shari had been discouraged during a conflict in 1896. Village after village joined in what soon became a major insurrection throughout western Ubangi-Shari and east-central Cameroun. Some reports claim that Karnu intended to drive out both the French and the Fulani, and then proceed to divide up the region under the rule of several Gbaya chiefs.

Whatever Karnu's intentions had been, they were frustrated by the French decision to send more troops from Bangui. The administration's forces in the Bouar area were increased in October 1928. On December 11, 1928, Karnu himself was discovered. Reports from colonial archives indicated that he offered no resistance to the soldiers and let himself be killed as he had said he would do. But Karnu's death only inspired the Gbaya to more active rebellion against French authority, and this rebellion continued for several years. The French also continued for a number of years to pursue and arrest any Gbaya they identified as a disciple of Karnu.

European interpreters of these events have described the entire phenomenon as a nativistic or messianic movement, terms which underline its antiwhite character (Fernandez 1969:384-404). Because of Karnu's success as a witchdoctor and miracle worker, his authority among the Gbaya can be explained from a traditional and magical perspective. Philip Burnham emphasizes especially the political character of these events, but also notes what he calls the "mystical aspect" of Karnu's leadership and his charismatic ability to exercise leadership above and beyond clan ties (1972:85-86).

The above description of Karnu and the events surrounding him is the version put together by European social scientists whose special concerns are reflected in their account: they have sought to record accurately the history of Karnu. Their attempt to faithfully uncover what actually happened and to interpret those events includes material which Gbaya informants say Karnu said and did. We noted that this description diverges at some points, even at crucial points, from the version now being recounted in the Gbaya community. We will now consider what the Gbaya tell about Karnu, an attempt to capture and recount a small piece of their contemporary oral tradition.

The Gbaya account[4]

This is the story of Karnu about what happened during his last years. It began with his wife, Naayargunu, who was Chief Naahii's daughter. She had dreams in which she heard a voice speaking to her, and she understood it to be the voice of God. She was struck with fear, being a woman; and of course women cannot be expected to understand such things, so she began to say to God, "Show these things to my husband. He'll know what to do about it, won't he?"

Thereafter, Karnu himself began having dreams and hearing God's voice. Now Karnu's name at that time was Barka.[5] He came from the village of Sērē-Boyaa, and had come to take a wife in Bodoi. The events we want to tell about began as Barka was working in his gardens where God began speaking to him. Barka was hoeing his garden; and he was troubled by a huge **ndende** tree, a tree of the mimosa family, a tree so large that it was impossible to think of a mere man cutting it down. Barka began pleading in these words, "Who will cut down this tree for me? What will I do? This tree is just too much for my field! Who will cut it down for me?"

The next morning when Barka went out to the field, the **ndende** tree had been pulled up by the roots and thrown out of the field, roots and all, into the grass! Barka thanked the one who had done this for him, whom he understood to be God himself. When Barka returned to the village, he told everyone in Naahii about the great thing which God had done for him

---

[4] The Gbaya account as given here was researched by Etienne Yongoro, a student at the Lutheran seminary in Baboua, who comes from the same town where the events described took place. Yongoro worked with several eyewitnesses to the events, including Joseph Saaré and Abraham Naahii. The latter is today a chief in the Bingué commune in the subprefecture of Baboua in the Central African Republic.

[5] His first given name, Barka (both syllables in high tones) is not to be confused with the Fulani word **barka** 'blessing' (both syllables low tone). Among the Gbaya, the name Barka meant that its bearer was to some day receive something great; he would be as a prince among men.

Karnu: Witchdoctor or Prophet?

out there in the field. He said, "It was God who did this for me; God worked for me in my garden!"

After he had cleared the field and hoed it, Barka was ready to plant his cassava sticks. He went to cut cassava sticks in his old field, and brought a bundle of new sticks to the new field for planting. Then he said, "Who will plant this cassava for me in my new field?" The next morning when Barka went out to the field, all the cassava was planted! He was very grateful and again thanked God for his help, after which he returned to the village and explained this new event to everyone.

At this time no one outside the immediate Bodoi area yet knew what was happening. Barka continued to work in his gardens, and he continued to set his fish traps. God spoke to him while he went about his work, and Barka never failed to explain these revelations to everyone in the village.

One day Barka went to check his fish trap. He worked with the trap the Gbaya call **ndalang.** Barka struggled with that trap, pulling on it with all his strength and finally managed to get it up out of the water. There was a fish in the trap; it was a catfish. However, this fish had no head and no tail. This catfish had feet like a human being. In fact, the fish was even wearing shoes! There were three things in that fish trap: one fish and two white stones. Those three things were in a single fish trap, and the fish spoke to Barka, saying, "Your name shall no longer be called Barka. From now on your name is Karnu [**kar** 'roll up', **nu** 'earth']. You will roll up this earth one day like a sleeping mat and take it away to heaven. Take these two stones along home with you, and put them carefully into your box. They will show you everything; they will tell you what is going to happen." Karnu happily agreed to do as he was told.

So he took those stones home to the village, put them in his box, and things began to happen. It was at this time during these events that many other people began to hear about Karnu. The stones spoke to Karnu when he was alone in his house, when no one else was present with him. And he began to explain many things that were going to happen, miraculous things, things which seemed like a dream. Now all these revelations took place in his own house. So he wanted to build a new house, and he suggested to the villagers that they help him. He made a very large house, ten meters by ten meters square, and many people from the Bodoi area brought him grass for the roof.

When the house was completed,[6] word about Karnu spread quite rapidly as far as Bouar, Carnot, Gbayanga-didi, Baboua, and Berberati. The white administrators began to circulate in the area in order to find out what Karnu was up to. Karnu warned everyone, "When you see war coming, do not go to battle with those who bring it. My only weapon is this pestle. My soldiers are the bees of the forest. When my bees chase away those who bring war, you may whip those men; but you must not cut them with sword or knife, you must not shed blood! Do not refuse to work for them. Work for them happily, because you will get many things when you work for them."

Karnu baptized four people: Déndéng and his wife, his own wife, and himself. It happened this way. One morning these four people rose very early and went together into the bush. They found the hole of a giant rat and sat down around the hole. They called to Giant Rat and Giant Rat came up out of his hole. They called to Giant Rat by singing this song:

> Giant Rat, Giant Rat, come quickly,
> O Giant Rat, O Giant Rat, come with your child.
> O Giant Rat, O Giant Rat, come quickly,
> O Giant Rat, O Giant Rat, come with your child.

So they took the giant rat, and Karnu cut open its stomach with his knife. He took out the liver and put it into a pot where he squeezed it in the water, and it changed to blood. He took a piece of cassava root and dipped it in the blood, then gave it to his three companions to eat.[7] Karnu told them, "Do not worship false gods any longer. There is but one God in heaven! Get rid of all those things next to your house that you keep for the ancestors. I don't want to see them again!" When they returned to the village, they got rid of all those things next to the house that they kept for the ancestors, and they told everyone, "There is but one God in heaven!"

Karnu now left his fish-trapping and his gardening. He spent all his time telling people about the one God in heaven, and he also performed many different miracles which

---

6 Gbaya houses were traditionally round. Karnu's square construction here represents an architectural innovation, interpreted by the Gbaya as a sign of things to come. Those who have recently measured the foundation of Karnu's house marvel at its perfect symmetry, accomplished without the aid of a tape measure.

7 Cf. G.M. Haliburton (1974:500). Prophet Harris's son, Aké, is said to have been baptized in pig's blood. The Gbaya refer to Karnu's rite as baptism, although it has the character of a sacred meal.

Karnu: Witchdoctor or Prophet?

people had never before seen. Sometimes he would call all the Bodoi people together, then sit on top of a mortar, a mortar which is normally used for pounding cassava. He drove that mortar around just like it was a truck. Sometimes he sat on top of a large rock, and he would drive that rock all over town in front of everyone. Now that was a great miracle the likes of which no one has seen before or since!

At that time cattle had not yet been brought into the area, nor had the locust appeared. When Karnu entered the bush in back of his house and came walking out again in view of all the villagers, he was covered with cow manure up to his knees. He showed everyone and said, "Look at this. An animal will come among us that we'll all be able to eat. You won't have to look all over for meat; there will be enough for everyone." He went back into the grass, and when he emerged again, his hands were full of locust wings. He showed them to the villagers, saying, "Let me tell you, you will receive many, many good things. Just remember to live in harmony with one another."

So these are the things used by Karnu in his work. The large rock and the mortar were his trucks. The pestle was his weapon. The two rocks he had found in the fish trap were his telephones. The bees were his soldiers. He baptized four people, including himself. He blessed many people who participated with him in **ăka-kongi**. This was a simple rite in which Karnu stood with a circle of men and held out to them small sticks. Everyone who received a stick from Karnu's hand also received Karnu's blessing and power; they received strength to do battle.[8]

Many people came from the entire region in order to see Karnu and to witness his miracles. They always brought him gifts. They even brought him young girls who were given to him as wives, but Karnu refused to marry them. He simply kept the girls as servants.

Karnu often spoke to the Bodoi people, saying, "Never shed the blood of the white men and their soldiers with your spears and knives. Just let the bees chase them away!" But

---

8 **Aka-kongi** means literally "ripping, splitting hook." A **kongi** is a hooked stick that is used to pick fruit or to pull something toward oneself. Splitting or ripping the hook apart at the joint is a symbol of peace, for the hook is in two pieces and can no longer function. The **kŏngŏ-wara** 'hoe handle' mentioned earlier has the same angular shape and when split apart has the same significance. The hook and the handle were therefore symbols of Karnu's pacifism.

they did not listen to him. They said, "We have his power, now we'll show those whites a thing or two! Let's not be afraid; Karnu is behind us." Karnu spoke to them in vain about going to war. When the administrators sent their soldiers, Karnu took his pestle and held it out toward them; and they fell to the ground as dead men. Their guns fell useless to the ground, their bullets turned to water! Those guns couldn't do a thing against Karnu. Then Karnu's friends started beating the soldiers, some of whom they killed. The bees chased away the rest so far that there could be no thought of return. This encouraged the Gbaya to pursue the battle, and they increasingly looked to Karnu as their chief.

Karnu continued for a time to do his miracles among the Bodoi people. But when they heard that the soldiers were coming back, they hid in the bush waiting to ambush them and kill them. Karnu insisted that they not shed the blood of anyone, because his pestle was stronger than the soldiers' guns. The third time the soldiers attacked, things went badly for the Bodoi forces because Karnu refused to help them. He wanted no killing. Karnu told all those who looked to him for strength. "Do not stay with me any longer. Take your wives and your children and escape into the bush, because there is no longer hope for us to win this battle. My power over the soldiers is finished, because blood has been shed! The one God will no longer bless me, so don't put your trust in me any longer. As for me, if they kill me, even if they burn me with fire and drown my ashes under water, I will go home to heaven. But you will suffer for a long time. Everyone now living will die; then I will return to roll up this land like a sleeping mat and take it away with me, and in that day your children will receive good things. But I will not die, I will go home to heaven. On the day of my return, then these things will take place."

On his last day, Karnu saw the soldiers coming and said, "The time has come! Flee!" Karnu stood up, he took his goatskin and entered his house. A Catholic priest, a white man who had accompanied the soldiers, entered the house after Karnu. Before any shots were fired, the house caught fire! The house burned to the ground, then they started shooting. Karnu's brother was killed. When the soldiers entered the house, they did not find Karnu's body, nor the priest's body. They found Karnu's son Yolai still alive and took him away with the body of Karnu's brother.

When the Bodoi people heard that Karnu had been killed by the soldiers, they all fled into the bush. In those days there were no roads, just bush. The fighting continued. Wherever the administrators and their soldiers went, they found people ready to do battle with them. The Gbaya filled the bush for war, and that is what they call "The War of Karnu."

In the abandoned village where Karnu used to live, even today strange things are still happening. And those things which he foretold have happened just as he said they would. Karnu talked about "Naazi-Krist,"[9] and it was only a short time later that "Naazi-Krist's" people arrived among us. He talked about baptism and even baptized some people himself, and today aren't we all baptized? Karnu preached about "choosing wormy nuts,"[10] and haven't we learned to follow his advice today? It hasn't even been one hundred years since he was here, and look how all these things have taken place! We should really think and reflect about this. After all, Karnu did not lie; he spoke the truth!

Karnu himself did not want war with the whites. But his words and his power attracted Gbaya from all directions; they all went to get his power so they could chase out the French. When Karnu blessed all those Gbaya in the hook-splitting rite, it was not witchdoctor's medicine he used--absolutely not! Sorcery had nothing to do with Karnu's power! He simply wanted to bless them so they would be protected from danger. Karnu himself was just a little runt; he was a fisherman who had no pretensions about leading the Gbaya.[11] His strength came from God so he could help the Gbaya to distinguish right from wrong, so they wouldn't "choose wormy nuts." Maybe the French called Karnu a witchdoctor, but that's not what the Gbaya say.

Remember that Boganda visited Bingué-Bodoi around 1950 or 1951 (Kalck 1974:278).[12] Didn't Karnu say he'd return? And

---

9 Eyewitnesses report that Karnu used this term to designate Jesus Christ, and they insist that Karnu could have had no access to anyone who might have told him about Christ. The name is believed to have been revealed to him by God.

10 The Gbaya expression **hŏka-dok-zawa** 'choosing wormy nuts' refers to the matter of distinguishing between right and wrong.

11 Both descriptions are disparaging remarks which indicate that Karnu had no natural leadership qualities.

12 Barthelémy Boganda is considered to be the father of the Central African Republic and was a charismatic leader of the drive towards independence until his tragic death in a plane accident near the Lobaye River on March 29, 1959.

wasn't that Boganda? And doesn't Karnu continue to send the whites out here to see where he lived and worked? If it's not Karnu, then why do these whites keep on coming from Bangui and from France to see his house? Didn't they carry that log out of here with them?[13]

Remember what happened around 1956-1957. The French soldiers standing in Bouar were looking with their binoculars right towards Karnu's old village.[14] And you know that they saw a huge city with great tall buildings! For two weeks those Frenchmen tore around here in their trucks looking for that city. For two weeks they kept flying over this area in their planes. And they didn't find one single thing. Just the old house where Karnu had lived! Well, we know the miracles that our people keep right on seeing out there by Karnu's house. It's really something to think about.

Comparing the two accounts

The social scientists describe and evaluate the Karnu events as important historical phenomena which are at once significant for an understanding of the French colonial presence in West Africa, and for an understanding of African attitudes towards that presence. Their account gives us the Karnu of history through the medium of written documents.

The Gbaya are today describing the Karnu events through their traditional oral medium. They are telling each other about Karnu, and in the process of telling and retelling the Karnu events. Some extraordinary assertions about Karnu are being made, many of which are without parallel in Gbaya tradition. The Gbaya account prompts us to suggest that in it we are given the "Karnu of faith" which is believed and accepted by the Gbaya Christian community. The Gbaya version is not a history of Karnu, at least not from the Western or European understanding of history. And yet, in this account the Gbaya seek to tell accurately what, from their perspective, actually happened. The Gbaya version narrates what the Gbaya Christian community today considers to be true and essential as regards Karnu and the events surrounding him.[15] Since the

---

13 Gbaya who live in the Bingué and Naahii area report that whites and government people visited the site of Karnu's house in 1975 and carried off a large beam from the remnants of its foundation.

14 It is indeed possible to stand on the hills in Bouar and see, fifty kilometers away, the Bingué-Naahii area.

15 For an account of a similar religious phenomenon in Uganda, see Middleton's discussion of the Yakan cult and its prophet Rembe (1960:258-64).

Karnu: Witchdoctor or Prophet?   243

Gbaya version is no less plausible in their ears than is the historical account to European ears, it commands a hearing that is to be taken just as seriously as the European version.

The accounts diverge at two crucial points.

1. Whereas the European version describes Karnu as an antiwhite, anti-Fulani witchdoctor, the Gbaya version describes him as a prophet who encourages the Gbaya to accept both the whites and the Fulani. The European version notes that Karnu encouraged the Gbaya to reject whatever good the whites imported, whereas the Gbaya version encourages the acceptance of all these new things.

Both versions agree that Karnu himself preached nonviolence. The accounts also agree that Karnu's disciples failed to keep his principles on the matter of no bloodshed. From this common ground of understanding Karnu's message, the Gbaya today insist that Karnu himself was not antiwhite. Why? Did he in fact preach cooperation with the whites, or has Gbaya association with whites in recent years, especially since independence, engendered a reinterpretation in the retelling of the events? As white and Fulani presence has changed from threat to something noticeably useful, something from which the Gbaya can benefit, has the description of Karnu also changed?[16] Or have the Europeans identified the substance of Karnu's preaching with the results of the activity which surrounded him? Further research into the matter might help us to answer those questions.

We note that the Gbaya account is almost prowhite and suggests an orientation towards Western civilization akin to what has been described as a cargo cult in other cultures. And we also note that a continual Gbaya reinterpretation of the events would not be uncharacteristic for the Gbaya capacity for adaptation (cf. Strayer 1976).

There is a profound ambivalence among the Gbaya for things, values, and even people, which are not their own; and the Gbaya narration of Karnu is an example of how this ambivalence finds contemporary expression. Their ambivalence expresses itself at three levels within this narrative: at the cognitive level, that is, with regard to ideas of the ulti-

---

16 White presence has been no threat ever since independence in 1960: Fulani presence is today economically important for the Gbaya. The two ethnic groups coexist in a symbiotic relationship that is not without ambivalence, but is in many ways mutually beneficial.

mate; at the evaluative level, for it touches on morality; and at the aesthetic or expressive level of existence, for the truths about Karnu are taught and transmitted in story form, and Karnu himself assumes the proportions of a culture hero comparable to Wanto, the hero of Gbaya tales.

2. When the Gbaya refuse to accept the European assertion that Karnu was a **wan-gbana** 'witchdoctor' we encounter the second major difference between the two accounts. Gbaya Christians state flatly that Karnu's power and message came from God and are not to be associated in any way with one who has **dua** 'sorcery', who in Gbaya tradition may be either a witchdoctor or sorcerer. Gbaya Christians identify **dua** as an evil power that is associated with evil purposes. Karnu, they say, was certainly no sorcerer because his work and message were dedicated to helping the Gbaya community. And he was no witchdoctor or seer, because such a person will do nothing useful or good unless he is first paid for his services. Karnu solicited no payment; he did nothing for personal gain or enrichment.

It is therefore far more appropriate to speak of Karnu, from the Gbaya perspective, as a genuine prophet who had a message from God to prepare the Gbaya community for the reception of the Christian message. He is looked upon by some Gbaya interpreters as a kind of Gbaya John the Baptist, and they see no reason why God could not or would not approach them in that way.

Their association of Karnu with Bogando, who is recognized as the Central African liberator, would also contribute to the Gbaya Christian understanding of Karnu as an essentially religious figure. Before entering politics, Boganda studied for the priesthood and remained close to the Roman Catholic church throughout his career (Kalck 1974:273ff.). For the Gbaya, the consideration of Karnu as a religious figure would not preclude his importance at the same time as a political figure; nor would Boganda's significance as a political hero be separated from his role as a religious leader. The Gbaya hesitate to identify Karnu and Boganda as precisely the same person, but their questions indicate that they believe it is certainly something to think about.

Conclusion

We have examined two different descriptions of Karnu and the events surrounding him. The European account can properly be called the history of Karnu, of which we have given only a

Karnu: Witchdoctor or Prophet?   245

brief outline. The Gbaya account is here presented in narrative style much as it is told in the Gbaya Christian community today. Can the Gbaya account of Karnu be included with the large body of Gbaya narratives called tò 'tales'? To this question, the Gbaya themselves give an emphatic no. Why? Because, they say, eyewitnesses saw all these things that Karnu did; they heard what he said. In other words, the Karnu narrative has a firm historical basis, whereas the tales of Wanto have no historical basis. Wanto narratives "came from the dark"; that is, they come out of the past and no one ever actually saw their hero Wanto.

The Gbaya Christian account of Karnu, then, is not an ancient tale. It can, however, qualify as myth in the sense of that term as employed by the theologian Langdon Gilkey:

> Myths to us, then, are not just ancient and untrue fables; rather, they signify a certain perennial mode of language, whose elements are multivalent symbols, whose referent is in some strange way the transcendent or the sacred, and whose meanings concern the ultimate or existential issues of actual life and the questions of human and historical destiny (1970:66).

The Gbaya Christian narrative of Karnu is a contemporary embodiment of "multivalent symbols" whose referent is God and whose meanings concern both ultimate and existential issues of actual Gbaya life, as well as the questions of their own human and historical destiny.

A fascinating myth about Karnu has been born and continues to live in the Gbaya Christian community. One of its most significant messages is that Karnu was a prophet used by God to announce to the Gbaya people a new religious orientation and commitment, and in so doing he also foretold the coming of a new social and economic order. Gbaya society today is a transitional society. Transitional societies employ a mixture of symbols to validate participation in an increasingly differentiated society.[17]

From the Gbaya Christian perspective, their interpretation of Karnu as a genuine prophet to whom God revealed a message and to whom he gave special power and authority would not conflict with an orthodox, Western, Lutheran interpretation of how God chooses and ordains his prophets. For example, the

---

17 Cf. de Waal Malefijt (1968:172-187). Compare also a discussion of ritual symbolism as reflector of change and transition in Swantz (1970:41-57).

Gbaya insist that when the first American Lutheran missionaries heard how Karnu's wife had already been baptized, they did not deem it necessary for her to be rebaptized. Let the missionaries tell their own version of that story! But at the same time, we listen to the Gbaya telling their own story, a story they believe is worth retelling and worth reflecting about.[18]

18 Cf. Berger (1976:xiii): "Every human being knows his own world better than any outsider (including the expert who makes policy)."

Bibliography

Berger, Peter. 1976. Pyramids of Sacrifice: Political Ethics and Social Change. Garden City, New York: Anchor Press, Doubleday.

Burnham, Philip C. 1972. Residential Organization and Social change among the Gbaya of Meiganga, Cameroun. Ph.D. dissertation, UCLA. Ann Arbor: University Microfilms.

Christiansen, Ruth. 1956. For the Heart of Africa. Minneapolis: Augsburg Publishing House.

de Waal Malefijt, Annemarie. 1968. Religion and Culture: An Introduction to Anthropology of Religion. New York: Macmillan.

Fernandez, J.W. 1969. "African Religious Movements." In Sociology of Religion: Selected Readings. Roland Robertson, ed. Baltimore: Penguin Books.

Gilkey, Langdon. 1970. Religion and the Scientific Future: Reflections on Myth, Science and Theology. New York: Harper and Row.

Haliburton, G.M. 1974. "The Development of Harrisism." International Review of Missions 68(252):499-5⁻6.

Kalck, P. 1974. Histoire de la République Centrafricaine des origines préhistoriques à nos jours. Paris: Editions Berger-Levrault.

Middleton, J. 1960. Lugbara Religion. London: Oxford University Press for the International African Institute.

Strayer, Robert. 1976. "Mission History in Africa: New Perspectives on an Encounter." African Studies Review 19:1-15 (1976).

Swantz, Marja-Liisa. 1970. Ritual and Symbol in Transitional Zaramo Society. Uppsala: Almquist and Wiksells.

Contributors

Badomo André is a free lance poet, playwright, and comedian. He is a Gbaya who lives and works in Meiganga.

Bouba Bernard is a Chamba from Balkossa who is the principal of the government secondary school in Tibati.

Lee Bohnhoff is a missionary pastor who has worked for over fifteen years among the Duru in translation and literacy work. He holds a Ph.D. in linguistics.

Philip Burnham has a Ph.D. in anthropology. He has conducted research among the Gbaya and Fulani in Cameroun and is a lecturer at University College London.

Thomas Christensen is a Bible school and seminary professor who has served in Cameroun and the Central African Republic since 1966. He has a Master of Sacred Theology degree.

Alice Eastwold has a B.A. degree in education. She and her husband spent more than twenty-five years as missionaries in Cameroun, and are now living in St.Paul, Minnesota.

Wendell Frerichs has a Ph.D. in Old Testament Studies and is Chairman of the Old Testament Department at Luther Seminary in St. Paul, Minnesota.

Dala Marcel is a Gbaya professor of physical education at the government lycée in Bertoua.

Kadia Matthieu is a Duru pastor and translator who has worked at the Duru Literature Center in Mbé.

Ronald Nelson has been a missionary pastor in Cameroun for twenty years, much of that time serving as director of the recording studio Sawtu Linjiila in Ngaoundéré.

Cecelia Noss has a B.A. degree in creative writing. She is the director of the Gbaya adult literacy program in Cameroun.

Haldor Noss is a young American poet who has lived most of his thirteen years in Cameroun.

Philip Noss has a Ph.D. in African languages and literature and is literature coordinator for the Evangelical Lutheran Church of Cameroun.

Kombo Samuel is the director of the Gbaya Translations Center. He has studied anthropology and linguistics at University College London.

Publications of the
INTERNATIONAL MUSEUM OF CULTURES

1. SARAYACU QUICHUA POTTERY by Patricia Kelley and Carolyn Orr, 1976. (Also available in Spanish as CERAMICA QUICHUA DE SARAYACU) .... $ 3.00

2. A LOOK AT LATIN AMERICAN LIFESTYLES by Marvin Mayers, 1976 .... $ 6.45

3. COGNITIVE STUDIES OF SOUTHERN MESOAMERICA by Helen Neuenswander and Dean Arnold, eds., 1977. (Also available in Spanish as ESTUDIOS COGNITIVOS DEL SUR DE MESOAMERICA.) $10.95

4. THE DRAMA OF LIFE: GUAMBIANO LIFE CYCLE CUSTOMS by Judith Branks and Juan Bautista Sánchez, 1978. .... $ 5.00

5. THE USARUFAS AND THEIR MUSIC by Vida Chenoweth, 1979 .... $14.90

6. NOTES FROM INDOCHINA: ON ETHNIC MINORITY CULTURES by Marilyn Gregerson and Dorothy Thomas, eds., 1980 .... $ 9.45

7. THE DENI OF WESTERN BRAZIL: A STUDY OF SOCIOPOLITICAL ORGANIZATION AND COMMUNITY DEVELOPMENT by Gordon Koop and Sherwood G. Lingenfelter, 1980. (Also available in Portuguese as OS DENI DO BRASIL OCIDENTAL--UM ESTUDO DE ORGANIZACAO SOCIO-POLITICA E DESENVOLVIMENTO COMUNITARIO.) .... $ 5.95

8. A LOOK AT FILIPINO LIFESTYLES by Marvin Mayers, 1980. .... $ 8.45

9. NUEVO DESTINO: THE LIFE STORY OF A SHIPIBO BILINGUAL EDUCATOR by Lucille Eakin, 1980. .... $ 2.95

10. A MIXTEC LIME OVEN by Kenneth L. Pike, 1980. .... $ 1.25

11. PROTO OTOMANGUEAN KINSHIP by William R. Merrifield, 1981. (Also available in Spanish as PARENTESCO PROTO OTOMANGUE.) $12.50

12. PEOPLE OF UCAYALI: THE SHIPIBO AND CONIBO OF PERU by Lucille Eakin, Erwin Lauriault, and Harry Boonstra, in preparation. .... $---.--

13. STICKS AND STRAW: COMPARATIVE HOUSE FORMS IN SOUTHERN SUDAN AND NORTHERN KENYA by Jonathan E. Arensen, in preparation. .... $---.--

14. GRAFTING OLD ROOTSTOCK ed. by Philip A. Noss, in preparation. .... $---.--

15. A VIEW FROM THE ISLANDS: THE SAMAL OF TAWI-TAWI by Karen J. Allison, in preparation. .... $---.--

These titles are available at

The International Museum of Cultures
7500 W. Camp Wisdom Road
Dallas, Texas 75236

Residents of Texas add 5% sales tax.

www.ingramcontent.com/pod-product-compliance
Lightning Source LLC
Chambersburg PA
CBHW071817300426
44116CB00009B/1353